THE BAHRUPIAN CHALLENGE

THE BAHRUPIAN CHALLENGE

Inventing the New HR

Editors

K.K. Sinha | S.V. Nathan

BLOOMSBURY
NEW DELHI • LONDON • OXFORD • NEW YORK • SYDNEY

BLOOMSBURY INDIA
Bloomsbury Publishing India Pvt. Ltd
Second Floor, LSC Building No. 4, DDA Complex, Pocket C – 6 & 7,
Vasant Kunj, New Delhi 110070

BLOOMSBURY, BLOOMSBURY PRIME and the Diana logo are
trademarks of Bloomsbury Publishing Plc

First published in India 2021
This edition published 2021

ISBN: 978-93-54350-11-5
2 4 6 8 10 9 7 5 3 1

Printed and bound in India by Thomson Press India Ltd.

MIX
Paper
FSC FSC® C010615

To our inspirations,

our wives,

Chitra Sinha and Chitra Nathan

&

my best reverse mentor and daughter

Suvira Shyamlee

'Nothing is more real than the masks we make to show each other who we are.'

– Christopher Barzak

CONTENTS

CHAPTER 3 – ORGANIZATION OF THE FUTURE: THE NEXT YUGA

CHAPTER 5 – THE NEO HR: THE BAHRUPIAN CHALLENGE

CHAPTER 6 – CONCLUSION: THE NEXT MANU

Forewords

Two of the most predominant themes that organizations must and are constantly seeking to deal with are organizational culture and purpose. Both are inherently deep-seated subjects that necessitate discussion and debate before they can be properly harnessed. It is also becoming increasingly evident that many organizations fail to effectively actualize the symbiotic relationship with society that they must practice. As a result, there is a fair amount of imbalance between the long-term vision of the enterprise and that of its people and society in general.

In light of this, it becomes very important to start where it is most logical to do so—in our cultural roots. We are amongst the very few nations in the world to have an ancient, cultural, academic and spiritual foundation that has thrived for over 3,000 years. As with most civilizations, our linkages with ancient teachings and wisdom have become diluted and compounded with Western thought and modern ways of life. At a time when the West itself is looking at the East to adopt and discover the potential of its ancient practices, we must re-establish our touch with the ethos derived from our culture.

The Bahrupian Challenge by K.K. Sinha and S.V. Nathan is an earnest attempt to rekindle that association and to align modern HR thoughts with the best of what our culture teaches us. With a wealth of experience behind them and a robust understanding of history, ancient Indian philosophy, Vedic teachings, and mythology, they have presented a captivating and potentially far-reaching set of ideas that can find effective use in the HR arena.

All organizations, whether commercial or social, Indian or global, will find the insights useful, particularly when they address the complex subject of 'organizational purpose'. Purpose is being redefined by most large, successful organizations. The task is multilayered and requires a deep assessment of what people in the organization aspire for—both for themselves and for society. Through their work, Sinha and Nathan have put forward bold new concepts that will challenge present-day HR practices and nudge them towards a deeper dialogue and introspection by HR professionals.

With organizations becoming far more liberal, trusting and transparent, the time is ripe to transcend to a higher level of HR evolution that concerns itself with inner well-being and knowledge of the self in addition to its modern concepts.

Harsh Goenka
Chairman, RPG Group

My association with Nathan goes back nearly 40 years to our XLRI days, and I have now seen him emerge as one of the real thought leaders in HR practice.

This book is a culmination of the vast experience of Professor Sinha and Nathan and would provide great insights to anyone in HR, in both their professional and personal lives. It makes its way to my list because it's an excellent primer for HR, and also shows how it can be used to influence and improve organizational capabilities.

This book reminds us that despite the digital age we live in, we cannot forget about the values in real, human connections. Nathan shares a unique model that takes you through the entire employee life cycle and focuses on building an original company strategy. With helpful real-life examples and an easy guide for creating added value for your personal and professional life, it is a must-read for everyone.

Sandeep Bakhshi
Managing Director & CEO, ICICI Bank

As you read the latest literature on organizations and speak to people, one detects a sense of dissatisfaction, maybe disenchantment, with today's organizations. The key questions that crop up are about the role of the organization in creating social impact or being socially conscious, and the bureaucracy or the cookie-cutter approach that is inevitable in large companies. A lot of young people are joining the workforce and if you ask them what they would be looking for, you would hear things like flexibility, purpose, social and environmental impact, autonomy—all things to do with the culture of an organization.

So clearly, the culture of an organization is going to become more critical in the future. And on the whole, the general workforce feels the current culture in organizations could be different to extract the best from each of them. So why is this such an issue? What have we missed in the process of ensuring that we can create the appropriate culture in organizations?

If you are looking for some clues to the above questions, you can find some answers in this book by K.K. Sinha and S.V. Nathan. Culture is such an all-encompassing concept and so deeply linked with who we are and where we are from that it has a greater impact than we normally think about. Moreover, we need the right lens to look at culture. Certain Western concepts, though popular globally, may not be appropriate for the Indian context. And that's where *Bahrupian* comes in.

This book will help us look at culture from an Indian lens and understand its implications better. This understanding will also help us answer some key questions that have dogged us for long. How do we build organizations that are enduring in purpose and character? What can we do to ensure that people working in organizations feel that they are making a purposeful impact? How can organizations have symbiotic relations with society and nurture people's hopes and aspirations? K.K. Sinha and S.V. Nathan bring their unique insights from our tradition and culture to give us some ideas that will help us build the right HR practices for tomorrow's organizations. I am sure we will all gain from this passionate endeavour.

Krish Shankar
Group Head, HR, Infosys

Praise for the Book

I feel very happy that Professor K.K. Sinha and Mr S.V. Nathan have written a book called *The Bahrupian Challenge: Inventing the New HR*, based on the inputs articulated by more than 60 top who's who amongst the HR professionals in the country. As high-speed changes have been taking place in the business world, HR is constantly bringing about changes in their role.

I am also happy that they have described the multifaceted, changing role of the HR as a conscience keeper of the business, bringing in the value and ethics taught through Upanishadic Vedanta. The book is a sincere effort to keep HR aligned with a human touch in the organization today and in the coming times. I wish Professor K.K. Sinha and Mr S.V. Nathan and their book the very best.

– **Naveen Jindal**
Chairman, Jindal Steel and Power Limited,
Chancellor, O.P. Jindal Global University,
President, Flag Foundation of India

Congratulations on the publication of *The Bahrupian Challenge: Inventing the New HR*. You have pursued an ambitious challenge to integrate the left-brain analytic capabilities of science-based HR with the right-brain moral compass and values taught in the Vedanta. Balance is central to a happy and productive life. Your book promises wisdom and teaching in how to achieve a harmonious balance between an individual's role in the workplace and the individual himself/herself, the family and the community. I hope your important message is understood, practised and appreciated.

– **Robert S. Kaplan**
Senior Fellow and Marvin Bower Professor of
Leadership Development, Emeritus,
Harvard Business School

The two most important corporate functions are finance and HR. While finance has become more strategic since the new corporate governance laws were enacted, HR is still more compliance-driven, reflecting its past in labour laws. To make it more strategic, HR must shift from compliance to talent development and become a talent champion.

The Bahrupian Challenge: Inventing The New HR offers excellent essays from the leading forward-thinking scholars and practitioners on how HR can contribute to making a company's ordinary employees and contractors extraordinary.

– **Professor Jagdish N. Sheth**
Charles H. Kellstadt Professor of Business,
Goizueta Business School, Emory University

It is my joy to compliment BIMTECH for bringing out one more valuable book on HRM. I had the pleasure of releasing an earlier book of BIMTECH, on leadership, a few years ago. On behalf of the potential readers and users of this book, my deep appreciation for the two editors Professor K.K. Sinha and Mr S.V. Nathan. It gives me *aananda* (happiness) to note that the core theme of the book is to explore the links between Vedanta and HRM. My mind goes back about four decades, to the 1980s, when I began talking about a possible 'Indian Management', similar to Japanese and American Management. There was understandable surprise and scepticism. We have come a long way. Indian management is now confidently blending the best in our heritage with contemporary global ideas and practices. This book is another big step in that direction. It contains articles written by professional managers, who participated in 15 countrywide workshops of about 80 participants each. The writers and editors are comfortable using Sanskrit terms, along with English, such as *Bahrupi*, *Valli*, Yuga, etc. They are also citing role models from our Indian *virasat* (heritage), such as Saptarishi, Manu, Nachiketa, Gargi, Ashtavakra, etc. The book's one valuable contribution is to blend our eternal values with modern HR. They mention, for comparison, the recent Japanese idea of Ikigai, meaning 'creating value in life'. The Indian equivalent could be the goal of a 'dharmic life'. In the context of HR, that term means the dharma of the organization, through HR, to the employee and her/his dharma to HR and the organization.

– **Dr. Mrityunjay B. Athreya**
Padma Bhushan, Management Mentor

The Bahrupian Challenge: Reinventing the New HR by K.K. Sinha and S.V. Nathan, two of our stalwarts in the HR field who combine academic excellence with practitioner insights, have brought out this collection of papers by all great HR leaders and who's who in India and Asia. India's HR is a value-driven philosophy and a way of life.

The authors have done a great job of making available this collection by leaders who are products of the Indian civilization, which itself is based on Vedas and Upanishads that are focused on the spiritual world and integrate it with the material world and to help people attain the ultimate goal of happiness through self-realization.

While most essays are business relevant, the underpinnings deal with 'being human', the most neglected part of HR, which the Vedas and Upanishads in India teach.

This book combines the most recent experiences and thought leadership in HR and business with underpinnings of the wisdom of the East and Vedic emphasis on culture and self-realization for happiness. A must-read and a valuable possession by all leaders of all professions and especially, HR and business.

I congratulate K.K. Sinha who keeps inspiring all of us with his books that combine practical wisdom with academic rigour.

I wish all success and great impact through this book.

– Dr. T.V. Rao
Chairman, TVRLS, Former Professor, IIMA

Human Resources (HR) is the most important asset for achieving organizational objectives, not only in the corporate or social sector but also in the management of diverse activities of the government. The role of HR management is pivotal also in developing the appropriate quality of the workforce and workplace with a culture for higher efficiency, productivity and health of the organization. It has a social significance as well because manpower constituting this asset is drawn from society.

Management of HR is linked to the environment and, therefore, influenced by changes in the world order, like the evolution of a global village. Technology and globalization have led to a strategic shift in building an innovative culture. Emphasis on human rights is yet another but no less important ingredient for creating a mindset with the ability to generate greater positive energy.

Against these environmental changes in society, authors have remarkably attempted to connect the present-day science of people's management with the profound knowledge and timeless wisdom that reside in the Vedanta. This was vitally important and timely because they were drifting away from each other.

The Bahrupian Challenge: Inventing the New HR is no ordinary book, compiled and edited by K.K. Sinha and S.V. Nathan from the learnings and articulations of the panellists on several HR Round Tables held during recent years. It will, I am sure, serve as a useful guide, both to academia and practising managers, and even benefit society at large.

I have great pleasure in offering my greetings to the authors and best wishes for a successful launch of this extraordinary omnibus of knowledge.

– Dr. D.V. Kapur
Founder & CMD, NTPC, Ex-Secretary to GoI Ministries of Power, Heavy Industry and Chemicals & Petrochemicals

Management of HR has always been a challenge, irrespective of the phase of development of any country or a corporate. Therefore, multifaceted (Bahrupian as K.K. Sinha calls it) character and dynamic nature are integral features of HR management. In the 21st century, this dynamism has not only received speed and momentum but also an unprecedented acceleration due to the fastest, ever-changing, disruptive technologies, exponential growth of digital outreach and, above all, equally dynamic aspirations of younger generations and also of younger societies. All these have placed incredibly high demands on those who have anything to do with management and development of human resources, and more particularly on those who are HR professionals. Sinha has contributed significantly to the literature of management in general, and HR in particular, through his several books. This valuable work, I am sure, has brought out many unexplored areas of these challenges with possible approaches to deal with them. Therefore, this book is a 'must-read' for all who are associated with management.

– R.V. Shahi
Former Power Secretary, GoI

When two veterans in any field come together, their work is likely to create a lot of heat, dust and light. K.K. Sinha and S.V. Nathan are two such HR protagonists who have done an exceptional job ff furthering the state of our thinking in HR through their Editorial work in Compiling *The Bahrupian Challenge: Inventing the New HR*.

John Locke, the 17th Century Philosopher once wrote, 'The improvement of understanding is for two ends, first, our own increase of knowledge, second, to enable us to deliver that knowledge to others.' Locke argued that knowledge originated through experience and that the two were not just interdependent, but that experience was a necessary condition for knowledge. If that is the case, one may argue that by leveraging on the experiences of others one may by proxy grow one's own experience and subsequently knowledge base exponentially. I think Sinha and Nathan have been inspired by this line of thinking to bring together the ideas and experience of so many practitioners and academic leaders within the covers of this compilation.

The benefit of this diversity of experience is accentuated given that today, we find ourselves challenged by a disruptive context more than ever before. In a world where established norms are being washed clean by the waves of change, nothing could be more inspiring than to cause beneficial change. At the same time, nothing could be more self-destructive than resisting the inevitable forces of change. We must accept the world we live in as the reality – borne from that acceptance will arise an epistemological understanding of the very same world. Then, and only then, armed with this comprehension, may be, we can venture forth to thrive in the new world.

Sinha and Nathan have curated the very latest thinking covering a diverse range of topics such as continuous growth, disruption, workforce transformation, and mentoring to name just a few. In one stroke, they have brought together reflective thinking, distilled experience, nuanced challenge and an evocative action agenda for practitioners and thinkers alike. The diversity of perspective of people from varied experience profile adds to the attractiveness of its thematic relevance. Of course, the fusion of the ideas with a Vedantic treatment is another novelty of the Book.

I'm certain any reader, whether an HR professional or not, will gain insights to competently navigate through the dynamic human capital landscape of today.

– **Dr. Santrupt Misra**
CEO, Carbon Black Business & Director, Group H.R.
Aditya Birla Management Corporation Pvt. Ltd.

When a seasoned professor joins hands with highly credible CHRO to answer the question, 'How can HR deliver impact?', the result can only be insightful! Mythology shows Vishnu take ten forms and Durga show up nine different forms—adapting and amplifying different facets of their inherent power to restore cosmic order. The *Bahrupian* is the modern-day take on the multiple forms that the HR function needs to embrace, to reinvest itself to truly power growth and unlock potential in the volatile 'new normal'. Presented in a simple way, the book captures perspectives curated from conversations with practitioners across industries. A riveting read—most relevant in today's times!

– **Mahalakshmi R.**
Head HR India, Mondelez International (Erstwhile Cadbury's)

The editors have done a great job in putting together this rich tapestry of contributions from some of the country's leading HR-PR actioners and thought leaders.

The idea is to create a framework for tomorrow's HR, which explores the application of India's profound philosophical and spiritual heritage to the problem of creating sustainable outperformance in the context of exponential change, fear and uncertainty as the perennial gale of creative destruction sweeps through the world. What emerges is the 'Bahrupian HR' framework which is a rich, holistic, multidisciplinary and whole-brain approach combining strategy, structure, processes, metrics, tools and techniques on the one hand, with wisdom, courage, focus, determination and other elements of the self on the other hand.

Highly recommended for serious practitioners and academics seeking to expand the frontiers of thought and action.

—Rajeev Dubey

Principal Advisor, Mahindra & Mahindra Ltd, Chairman, Mahindra Insurance Brokers Ltd, Member of the Governing Body, International Labour Organization (ILO), Geneva

Every day there will be new HR challenges at the workplace which will be further accentuated by geopolitical issues, climate change and disruptive technologies. In the coming decades, optimization of HR by only the application of algorithm and engineering will not help corporates much to deal with HR challenges. The book, edited by Professor K.K. Sinha and Mr S.V. Nathan, presents a new perspective of inventing HR by synthesizing Western theories with the ancient Indian wisdom distilled from our Vedantic tradition and the Upanishads. Based on the HR Round Tables organized by BIMTECH in partnership with the NHRDN and Deloitte India during the last three years, and the thoughts of more than 50 speakers who spoke on various topics of our HR Round Tables, this edited volume will definitely give a fresh perspective on *The Bahrupian Challenge: Inventing the New HR*. I hope it will be a useful reference book for HR leaders, B-Schools and researchers.

– Dr. H. Chaturvedi

Director, Birla Institute of Management Technology

'Gaining knowledge is the first step to wisdom. Sharing it is the first step to humanity.'

As a fellow professional & friend for decades, I have had the good fortune of working closely with both the authors and hold great regard for their commitment towards continuous learning for themselves and others around them. This wonderful compilation of thought-provoking articulations from HR professionals & academicians on the ever-changing role of HR is a step further in that direction. I congratulate the authors for this tremendous & timely effort. I feel this book could not have come at a better time than now, when we, as a collective, struggle to find meaning in our lives and work. What is interesting is that the role of the HR function is set to become more pronounced in this new reality. I am certain that this HR development odyssey, co-authored by two of the most eminent industry experts, will only serve as a beacon of light for the readers, guiding them towards a definite future as they learn from a past rooted in ancient wisdom.

Best wishes to K.K. & S.V. for yet another feather in their caps!

– Ajay Soni
Chief Learning and Leadership Development Officer,
Aditya Birla Group

The Vedas, the Vedanta and the Upanishads have been guiding the values in societies and moulding their way of life for thousands of years. However, the present HR and the Vedanta teachings have been drifting away from each other and the values that Vedanta afforded to human society are getting lost gradually. We are losing a very valuable asset of our knowledge base in the process.

The attempt, in this book, to reconnect the values of Vedanta, its culture and civilization with modern-day HR is, in my view, a very valiant attempt as also a very difficult one. The authors seem to have really burnt a huge amount of midnight oil in understanding the Vedanta philosophy and then in suggesting effective ways to link these to present-day HR understanding. It is to their credit that they have been considerably successful in achieving their goal and giving out a treatise which convincingly appeals to readers' mind. Undoubtedly, this book is going to create a landmark in this direction.

I wish an all-round success to their endeavour.

– Dr. Anupam Varma
Deputy Director, Dean (Academics),
Birla Institute of Management Technology

I would consider it to be a privilege to be able to express my views in any publication of BIMTECH, especially an initiative of Professor K.K. Sinha, who is an old associate of mine from the Public Sector days. I also find that Mr Nathan, Chief Talent Officer at Deloitte India, is partnering in this initiative.

To get 80 HR professionals at a round table is a humongous task, which only Mr Sinha and Mr Nathan could have been successful at due to their huge creditability. Putting the knowledge base of 80 such professionals in one document would be such a priceless collection for those practising managers in this field.

HR, which I always like to expand as Human Relationship, is the mother of all subjects, especially in our country where our old Vedic culture, the sanatana dharma, and the way of life along the Indus Valley, which the world called Hinduism, are all about the relationship of human beings.

In the modern era, HR professionals have derived new ways of educating people and I must admit here that courtesy of Professor K.K. Sinha, I was introduced to the 'Design Thinking Process'. Although I consider myself a student of strategic change management and I also got some opportunity to teach this subject at premier management schools, I can see from here how the Design Thinking Process is helping towards understanding change management. This is the skill of HR managers.

In conclusion, I would like to say that Human Relationship Management starts from the time when you are a toddler and you instinctively learn to make relationships with people who surround you, who are important for your survival, till the time when you would be carried on a stretcher to the final burning ghat/burial place; it is the human relationship that you built in your lifetime that stands in good stead.

– Dr. Arup Roy Choudhury
Former CMD, NTPC & NBCC,
Principal Advisor (Infrastructure) to Government of West Bengal

HR Round Tables organized over the years have been a great chance for HR thought leaders, practitioners and business leaders to come together and share the changing landscape of HR practices around the world. I am glad these powerful deliberations have been meticulously documented and put together in this book. It provides a kaleidoscopic and priceless view of all aspects of HR and how it needs to reinvent itself to meet the demands of the rapidly changing business context as well as aspirations of people.

– Dr. Arvind N. Agrawal
Accredited Executive Coach and HR Consultant,
Former President and Chief Executive of Corporate,
Development and Group Human Resources,
Member of Management Board of RPG Enterprises

The idea of bringing together ancient wisdom and modern HR is indeed a very valuable one. The effort to map out the wisdom contained in India's philosophical heritage and bring it to bear on current human issues and problems at the workplace is indeed laudable. I have no doubt that the book will be useful to all HR professionals. My congratulations to the editors.

– **Dr. Asha Bhandarker**
Distinguished Professor of Organization Behaviour and Human Resources, IMI, New Delhi

Heartiest congratulations to Professor K.K. Sinha and his team for bringing back the old values, ethics and beliefs from an Indian treasure of Vedas and Upanishads and aligning it with the modern HR practices in a very simple way. In the current crises, there is a strong need for effective leadership. HR can play an important role to carve and shape future leadership by establishing the right culture, values, ethos. HR needs to drive and engage individuals to give their best and internalize their happiness, which is within.... The book helps to define how to lead/live a meaningful life. Kudos....

– **Deepak Bharara**
Director, People A2Z

Bahrupian self has many dimensions, seen as well as unseen. The grand endeavour by Professor K.K. Sinha and Mr S.V. Nathan is unique. A serious and genuine attempt to bring Vedanta and HR close to each other. This book is a must-read for any professional who believes in the power of human capital. My compliments to the authors and wish you happy reading!

– **Dhananjay Singh**
Director-General, National HRD Network

In times where HR is challenged to step up to a new dimension of business impact, inventing the new HR is more critical than ever before. *The Bahrupian Challenge: Inventing the New HR* is a timely book for professionals in the field looking at challenging the status quo.

– **Ester Martinez**
CEO & Editor-in-Chief, People Matters

It's a delight to see the articulation of a treasure of thoughts, experiences and directions of a galaxy of HR leaders with a golden touch of editing by you both in the form of a valuable book, *The Bahrupian Challenge: Inventing the New HR*.

Your proposition of aligning and integrating business and values is inspiring. You have rightly articulated the need, relevance and appropriateness to work of every aspect of reality and ensure a right mix of Bahrupian acts with value-rich Upanishadic colours. I am sure this treasure being curated by you both with the support of two great institutions—BIMTECH and Deloitte India—will bring happiness, contentment and excellence all over.

– Dr. G.P. Rao
Founder & Managing Partner, GPR HR Consulting LLP

The Bahrupian Challenge is a must-read because of the various perspectives of HR thought leaders that have been so well put together to make the book so very inspiring and relevant in the current context. The book offers many useful tips and practical solutions, challenging conventional thinking and pushing readers to try something different. I must compliment Professor K.K. Sinha and S.V. Nathan for their work in making a positive difference to the HR function.

– Gautam Chainani
President HR, Strategic Initiatives & Workforce Automation, JSW Group

I am happy to see The Bahrupian Challenge: Inventing the New HR, one more excellent book on HR management. The book will be an excellent guide for all executives.

– Gurdeep Singh
Chairman and Managing Director, NTPC

It is staggering to witness the culmination of Vedanta and HR. The ancient philosophy is much needed today, more than ever before as it trains and guides us to think independently and equitably. Linking our roots, rich culture and heritage to the workplace can enlighten us to channelize our energies most effectively, leading to success and contentment in all spheres of life. This trailblazing book by Professor K.K. Sinha and S.V. Nathan is a gift to all HR professionals and leaders alike. I take my hat off to both the editors for their valuable contribution to the culmination of this publication and my best wishes to both.

– Kamal Singh
Former CEO and Executive Director, UN Global Compact Network India

The wisdom from the Vedas and Upanishads focusses on the self. The indestructible, never-changing core of your being, the real YOU, is called the atman. The real YOU is luminous, magnificent, large enough to contain the universe! When you truly see this truth and embrace it is when you realize how inclusive life can be despite being so diverse.

The world of education is much different from the real world and when new generations set foot in the corporate world, they are lost and often they are not properly guided. We need to emphasize the brilliant concept of 'nishkama karma' (action without attachment), which our ancient sages conceived including Shri Krishna who explained this concept to Arjuna on the battlefield (Do your duty but don't become attached to the result of that action). The corporate world is not about luxury, money, power, etc. There is more to it.

This book is a compilation of revolutionary thoughts of today's HR leaders who have put their explosive findings in a manner to guide the coming generations. The world of HR is becoming invincible and extremely crucial to the weaving of a fabric of culture, competencies and values in our organizations so that the anchor is deep enough to face turbulent times. I am very happy to see that K.K. Sinha and S.V. Nathan tried to communicate with the HR leaders through our ancient texts. It is not easy and needs deep commitment, humility and focus. All the best to them in this endeavour.

– K.S. Bakshi
Group Head, Human Resources,
InterGlobe Enterprises Pvt. Ltd

When the business environment is so fast-paced and transforming in all its dimensions, can HR be left behind? Distilling the wisdom of an eminent and experienced panel of HR experts and anchoring the same on ancient Vedic wisdom, Shri Sinha and Shri Nathan have provided the blueprint for an ever-mutable and adaptable HR professional who can consistently create value for tomorrow's organization. My congratulations to both for this excellent work, which would immensely benefit the management practitioners.

– K. Sreekant
CMD, Power Grid Corporation of India

The Bahrupian Challenge: Inventing the New HR is a beautifully crafted book by Professor K.K. Sinha and Mr S.V. Nathan. It is a fine hive of pristine Vedic values which seeks to reorient HR to look within and realize the power of the self while looking out for scientific and technological mantras to succeed in life and business. The book is truly a unique gift to not only HR practitioners but also to people and organizations suffering a loss of meaning in life in times of the COVID-19 pandemic. I hope to see the book on the list of bestsellers!

– Professor (Dr.) Parameswar Nayak
Dean, Birla School of Management,
Birla Global University, Bhubaneswar

This unique book provides very compelling and valuable insights on change, strategy and the role of HR in making the business a sustainable success. The editors, namely Professor K.K. Sinha and Mr S.V. Nathan have done a commendable job by demonstrating that in order to be a sustainably winning organization in future, despite challenging times, it is imperative that HR needs to have a very strong commitment to values and ethics as enshrined in the Upanishadic Vedanta. The book is relevant and contextual and a must-read for all the stakeholders connected with management.

– P. Dwarakanath
Chairman GSK Consumer Healthcare Limited,
Advisor, Group Human Capital, Max India

This is a giant effort to link the fundamentals of our cultural and philosophical inheritance with the HR iterations of contemporary times. The range of perspectives from various leading lights of the HR fraternity, so wonderfully edited and sequenced, makes it an erudite treat for any reader. The collection surely is a moment to pause, reflect, appreciate and critique a lot of our rich legacy even as we throw the HR ball forward. Truly a collector's edition and more.

– Prabir Jha
Founder & CEO, Prabir Jha People Advisory

First of all, I would like to congratulate you for coming out with the book titled *The Bahrupian Challenge: Inventing the New HR*. Please accept my compliments for this wonderful piece of work. I am impressed with the kind of research that has gone into the various chapters outlined in the book and you have seamlessly interconnected the two aspects of Vedanta and HR Management, which would make it an interesting read. The book is aptly titled as *The Bahrupian Challenge: Inventing the New HR*, which captures the varied challenges being faced by most current organizations. I concur with the thought that if HR leads and plays the Bahrupian roles on the stage of society, there would be no looking back in creating a great organization and society even today. My compliments to you once again for this interesting piece of work and I am sure that many people across the spectrum will benefit from your work.

– **Dr. Pushp Joshi**
Director, Human Resources, Hindustan Petroleum Corporation Limited

I would like to congratulate Professor K.K. Sinha for his immense contribution to the academic fraternity. He is a shining example of an industry expert excelling as an academician.

The book *The Bahrupian Challenge: Inventing the New HR* seems very intriguing, to say the least. The title term 'Bahrupia', as I decipher, is derived from the Sanskrit words *bahu* (many) and *roop* (form or appearance). The social norm surrounding these appearances of a Bahrupia was that he/she takes varied roles and usually collected no money if he/she is detected as an impersonator. However, if he/she is able to successfully convince the audience of his/her identity, he/she would then reveal it and be awarded a 'baksheesh' (reward) for having entertained the group. So the title seems fascinating as businesses today have become multifaceted, multicultural and multinational; the leaders have to act differently under different circumstances in handling situations and people.

I compliment the editors for not just choosing an apt and topical title but also bringing together the views of stalwarts of HR across all ages. The wide spectrum of topics undoubtedly makes this book an interesting read for everyone.

I convey my best wishes to the editors, Mr Sinha and Mr Nathan, for the launch of this new and rich treatise on HR.

– **Ranjan Kumar Mohapatra**
Director (HR), Indian Oil Corporation Limited

The very interesting and aptly timed edition, *The Bahrupian Challenge: Inventing the New HR* being brought out by the most unique combination of Professor K.K. Sinha and Mr S.V. Nathan is indeed a laudable initiative. The word 'Bahrupia' truly reflects the diverse role of people managers and also adds a rustic charm to the book. I am sure this book will motivate HR professionals and people leaders to look into the multifaceted Vedantic dimensions of human beings and their harmonious coexistence with nature.

As we know, the Vedanta is ageless. The debate as to whether Vedas were brought by the Aryans or pre-existed will go on. But one should not miss the goal in the maze of endless debates. The truth is that our ancient culture was so rich that it takes a lot of convincing to believe it to be true.

In today's troubled times, when mankind is facing the challenges of the global pandemic of COVID-19 and human resource professionals are grappling with the issue, I am sure the Bahrupian dimension of HR will come in handy to give an insight into the future of this universe and the direction we should take.

My best wishes.

– R.P. Singh
Director (HR & Legal), IFFCO Limited

In the technologically determined contemporary world, mankind may have all the comfort, convenience and connectedness. Yet, in no other era of human history has man been so disconnected. The result is a tremendous amount of social isolation, psychological loneliness, ontological confusion and spiritual emptiness being felt by employees of all hues and at all levels. *The Bahrupian Challenge: Reinventing the New HR* repositions the workplace on the principles and values immanent in Vedanta philosophy. With his deep experience and knowledge steeped in the Indian philosophical tradition, Professor K.K. Sinha, along with his co-author Mr S.V. Nathan, the much-accomplished management practitioner, has brought forth many key learnings and insights for all managers and HR practitioners to inculcate in their day-to-day working. This book is a must-read for all those who are tasked with the onerous responsibility of making the organized world more productive, purposive and meaningful.

– Dr. Subir Verma
Professor of Organizational Behaviour, FORE School of Management

The book beautifully conveys the concept that while the world may be scientifically and technologically equipped for tomorrow, the new society lacks values and ethics and the higher purpose of life. Sustainable happiness needs to be created and this is possible if HR leads and plays the Bahrupian roles on the stage of society.

The authors, both accomplished professionals and leaders in their respective field, have chosen a very pertinent topic and this book will provide great insights to HR professionals and persons in leadership roles.

My best compliments for the tremendous effort and wishing you great success!

– Dr. S.V. Goyal
Whole-time Director & CEO, Model Economic Township Limited,
(Subsidiary of Reliance Industries Limited)

HR as a function is grossly misunderstood—both by the recipients of its 'service' and, sadly enough, by some of its own practitioners. Created on the foundations of the lofty ideals of the labour welfare movement, today it faces an existential threat of its own making. Geopolitical, societal and economic turbulence in the last 100 years has taken a toll on the spirit and soul of HR. Today, there is a crying need to reignite the guiding light and reinstall the moral compass within each HR professional and even business leaders who are people managers. The deep and rich spiritual legacy of India is a gold mine waiting to be rediscovered and exploited in a positive sense. This legacy belongs to the whole of humanity without regard to religion, race, community or nationhood. It is so heart-warming to see Professor Sinha and S.V. Nathan, both seasoned and expert practitioners of the profession, take up this task through their book. Through this book, they can gently remind the HR professional to infuse the spirit of Vedanta in their actions and, consequently, re-establish the function to its rightful place.

I congratulate Professor Sinha and S.V. Nathan.

– S. Venkatesh
Member, Group Management Board,
President, Group HR, RPG Enterprises

It's fascinating to know about this unique effort to put together the learnings from the HR Round Tables organized by the Birla Institute of Management Technology (BIMTECH), National HRD Network (NHRDN) and Deloitte India.

The deliberations by senior HR leaders being compiled in *The Bahrupian Challenge: Inventing the New HR* would be of great value for the corporate audience and especially the HR fraternity.

Integrating Vedic knowledge and its amazing relevance to life in general and specific learnings for leadership values, and HR function and role in future will be a very interesting reference to learn and align our basic approach towards the ever-changing business environment.

My warm compliments and very best wishes to both the authors for taking this unique initiative. Will eagerly look forward to the book release.

– S.Y. Siddiqui
Executive Advisor, Maruti Suzuki India Limited

It is my pleasure and privilege to compliment the publication of the book *The Bahrupian Challenge: Inventing the New HR*, a kaleidoscope of interesting perspectives created by interweaving the wisdom and experience of the thought leaders with ongoing management dilemmas.

In recent times, the focus on self-regulation to manage priorities has become even more important. . .this book provides deep and relevant insights on self-evolution and simplification for HR teams and individuals alike, while progressing professionally, often viewed as counter forces.

The challenges for HR professionals, by and large, have remained the same over the years, but have to be dealt with differently with the ever-changing business context and its paradigms. Whereas technology is accelerating work methods improvement, and speed and transparency, the human touch is somehow getting replaced by a digital touch. The book has touched upon the above thoughts and many more.

As one gets to read the book, I am sure all will immensely benefit from this treasure. Thanks to all for their contributions and especially to Professor K.K. Sinha, S.V. Nathan and NHRDN.

– Udai Upendra
Founder CEO, The HR Company

The world has been constantly evolving and so is the corporate scenario. Businesses are facing a challenging future—a volatile global economy, an increased need for innovation, talent shortages, technological advances and demographic shifts. To survive and thrive in the future, competencies and capabilities must evolve. The corporate agile movement so far has largely been an IT-driven intervention but this is not sustainable. Looking at the various agile frameworks, it is very evident that the greatest factor to agile transformation will be educating and enabling the people and leaders within the organizations. This requires a shift to a Lean-Agile mindset and culture throughout the organization. The HR departments in the organizations are accountable for the people agenda and will play a key and central role in transforming and enabling the organization to embrace agility.

Today, there is a doubt and debate going on about HR's contribution to organizational performance and there may be a reason for HR's beleaguered reputation. But the truth is, HR has never been more necessary. The competitive forces that managers face today and will continue to confront in the future demand organizational excellence. The efforts to achieve such excellence through a focus on learning, quality, teamwork and re-engineering are driven by the way organizations get things done and how they treat their people. These are fundamental HR issues.

HR needs to not only showcase its strategic role but rather it has to be the cultural, spiritual, professional and ethical ambassador of the organization.

I believe that the book *The Bahrupian Challenge: Inventing the New HR* will enrich people in the corporate world.

All the very best.

– Vijay Goel
Chairman and Managing Director (Additional Charge),
THDC India Limited

Highly recommend this interesting old world–new world approach to HR management to keep the function relevant in this evolving, changing world. The book leverages anecdotes and examples from the Upanishads and applies them to modern-day situations and at the same time calling out the role of HR specialist as the organization's 'Bahrupia'. The editors have attempted to connect the science or art of HR management with its value content. An enjoyable read, so go ahead and benefit from this practical narrative of Inventing the New HR.

– Vishpala Reddy
Head of HR, Indian Subcontinent, Philips

Preface

Vedanta and Human Resources (HR) have been drifting away from each other in society and its impact on HR or the way of life in an organization is also reducing. In our learnings and experience, society's rituals and rules guided and governed different segments of people management. Practices varied from one subculture to another. People also learnt from each other. Rituals and rules were developed on administrative needs and firmed up on philosophy, social ethics or principles founded by leaders.

We are attempting to connect this science or art of HR management with the Vedanta that should have been developing in society. As we have learnt from the roots, Vedanta has impacted this crucial people management area in the past. If this logic seems alright, HR professionals must learn a bit of it and take this journey of learning to connect to its rich philosophy.

In our history, we find so much knowledge which became the base of our culture and sustained it over such a long period. Even if we would have lost some of the values or learnings of this ancient knowledge, we would find that our civilization repeatedly wishes to explore and restore these values learnt from ancient cultures and history.

Aryan migration from Central Asia took place around 3,000 BCE. These migrants, who called themselves Aryans, are said to have also brought with them the Vedas and the early version of Sanskrit and related cultural concepts and practices, such as rituals, sacrifices and social rules from the Eurasian Steppes.[1] Many of these practices are reflected in the Vedas—especially in the earliest one, the Rig Veda. The Rig Veda seems to have followed the Indus and Harappan civilizations but had organised systems of kingdoms with organizational structure, armies and workmen. They had rules and rituals. They had gods, temples, ceremonies and priests.

The Vedanta, which means 'end of the Vedas', became gradually popular in building the society and its culture. The Aryans, generally distributed in tribes, needed to give identity to their culture and society and even not only through dialect, work styles, living styles but also through their way of dressing, painting their faces, etc. There also emerged a social activity called entertainment that became very popular over a short period. Entertainment, later on, would take the form of repeat plays or moving stories from whatever history they recalled, reciting and expressing not only history but also the process of knowledge that was going to become the foundations of civilization by recreating a certain way of life in the society over some time.

The Upanishads were the last literary products of the Vedic period. These mark the culmination of Vedic thought and these were taught and debated last in the student stage, which became and remained the foundation stone for all ways of life and work in society. However, while in matters of science and technology we have been growing the experiences of humanity, there is also a bitter disillusionment from the loss of meaning in life.[3]

Many of the Western learners have also turned to the East to explore what gives meaning and purpose to life and can stabilize humans and their learning and development for excellence. Most recently, the Japanese concept of Ikigai[2] reinforced one's hopes for giving humans a life worth living. 'Iki' means 'life' and 'gai' means 'value', which can be interpreted as finding value in one's life or discovering one's purpose. Exploring the concept of Ikigai and the simple looking questions that come with it can help people to find solid purpose through contentment and drive.

We are aware of the body, mind and intellect but not our real self. The Vedanta helps us unfold our self, which is the abode of absolute peace and bliss.

Humanity is unaware of the intrinsic wealth within oneself. People seek wealth and enjoyment in the external world. Few realize that there can be no fulfilment only through acquisition or enjoyment.

Life is defined as the stream of experiences. As long as experiences flow, there is life. An experience is, therefore, a unit of life.[3]

Scientists provide humanity with greater peace and happiness. Science has made a colossal contribution to human welfare. Nevertheless, people are not as happy as they should be. There seems to be only worry and anxiety, suffering and sorrow everywhere.

Philosophers discovered that the individual, the human, was unattended and neglected while the world was taken care of by science. They focused their attention on the human and gave out the sublime philosophy of the Vedanta, the knowledge designed to rehabilitate the human to perfection and hence bliss.

The Vedanta gives us a practical way of life to satisfy our material and spiritual needs and build on a good civilization. It trains and guides us to think independently. It helps us probe into the essence of human personality. The business world also must wake up from its slumber.

The knowledge of the Vedanta helps us evolve spiritually to enhance our self-discipline and regulate our desires. It also enhances the clarity of thought to gain success and progress in our field of activity, thus providing us with material well-being. Every human being tries to find peace and happiness. This is not something that we may draw from the external world. The enjoyment gained from there is transient and impermanent. It passes away, while true happiness lies within us.

The Vedanta guides us towards our inner self. Every human being is constituted of a supreme self within, enveloped by the material layers of the body, mind and intellect. The Vedanta has the formula for efficiency and productivity for success in career and life, acquired by attaining concentration, consistency and cooperation. We need to learn and practise them to gain success in our life and then become more efficient and productive in our field of activity. This is what the HR leads would have to intelligently and gradually utilise. Vedanta, therefore, presents us with the knowledge for our spiritual evolution as well as our material well-being, which is what all people in management sciences, including HR, keep searching for and re-emphasizing.

We need to link the Vedanta and its culture and civilization to the development of HR for building a greater human society—more value-based and more purposeful. The Vedanta has been providing this strength to develop social and personal values. A new society equipped scientifically and technologically for tomorrow but devoid of values and ethics may lose its human features. We would like to recall Sir Martin Luther King Jr who put it simply and forcefully: 'Our scientific power has outrun our spiritual power. We have guided missiles and misguided men.'

At the same time, HR is not just a role alone. It is about being human and helping in building a human organization. It has come to stay. HR are the main contributors to any kind of growth through innovation and development in business. It is no longer to be treated only as one of the factors of production. They have a strong sense of values and culture, which helps them to create an environment of ethics-based business. An attempt needs to be made to connect the science or art of HR management with its value content that is supposed to have been developing in society. If HR remains connected to the Vedanta, drawing out values in the organization, it has the potential to deliver sustainable happiness that is the real purpose of life. The native home of happiness is our own self and we can discover it through self-realization as taught through Vedantic teaching.

While with changing times, HR has been amassing and enhancing its roles happily, it still has to find the skill, knowledge and commitment required to remain effective. HR has to, therefore, be ready to undertake all roles which have been coming up with time and also make them work effectively, as businesses want an HR team that is versatile, multifaceted, ethical and courageous.

While there are scores of opportunities for learning, research and innovation in science and technology, making life easier in the organization and the society, we have been distancing ourselves from the deep learning that humans had received at the feet of the ancient gurus. We shall have to pause and rethink how we can prosper in the unknowable new world while retaining the deep teachings of continuous learning and creating value. We cannot see the future, and the impact of the radical changes that are taking place in society and the organization does not always very positively affect HR and humanity itself.

If HR were to lead and play the Bahrupian roles on the stage of society with the wisdom of Gargi, the focus of Kacha, the courage of Satyakama Jabala, the devotion of Aruni, the determination and commitment of Ashtavakra and the tenacity and fearlessness of Nachiketa, there would be no looking back in creating a great organization and society even today. We quote from Swami Vivekananda: 'If I get 10 or 12 boys with the faith of Nachiketa, I can turn the thoughts and pursuits of this country in a new channel.'

Our attempt should be to align HR and not let it drift away further. Only this can awaken the value of humans in society, whose ethics it is so essential to build and retain, to make a better and winning business world. HR, therefore, has a very big responsibility to work on this and help in achieving this quality of life. Working on all aspects of living challenges, including achieving the appropriate mix of Bahrupian acts with value-rich Upanishadic colours, would make living appreciably better and take us closer to the truth.

K.K. Sinha
S.V. Nathan

ACKNOWLEDGEMENTS

At the outset, we would like to say that this book is not by us but by those 60 leaders and professionals who were kind enough to be with us on our journey of discovering the complicated and multifaceted challenge of building Human Resource (HR) leaders. These HR leaders and academicians contributed their precious time and shared rich experiences as valuable gems of knowledge and wisdom during the 14 HR Round Tables (2014–2017) which we, as in BIMTECH, NHRDN and S.V. Nathan, Chief Talent Officer, Deloitte India, conducted. These were organized by K.K. Sinha, Dean, Executive Education, BIMTECH, in association with Dhananjay Singh, Director General, NHRDN and S.V. Nathan. These three partners relied substantially on the Deloitte Global Human Capital Trends Report in developing the themes and sub-themes of the HR Round Tables. Our heartfelt gratitude to Deloitte. They were like our Maharshi Veda Vyasa, narrating their stories and rich learnings to us. We were their Ganeshas, acting as their scribes to develop and deliver this book.

HR leadership has become a difficult and even a formidable subject. No constructive study with contributive and creative discussions can be delivered successfully without an enormous collective effort. *The Bahrupian Challenge: Inventing the New HR* is not an exception. This book is the result of the combined wisdom, experience and commitment of exceptional HR leaders from all types of roles in life but particularly from labour welfare, personnel management or HR. All the leaders who have been profiled here have contributed immensely.

This book belongs to BIMTECH and to Dr. H. Chaturvedi, our Director, who has been a constant source of inspiration during this journey. It was Dr. Chaturvedi who gave the idea and complete support for taking up important issues to research and deliberate upon through a series of Round Tables every year, with the pan-Indian involvement of CEOs, HR leaders and academicians.

This book belongs to the colleagues at Deloitte India who moderated and helped in shaping our thoughts regarding building HR leaders and their bunch of intricate roles with mountainous challenges in abundance. Dr. Chandrasekhar Sripada, Practice Professor (OB and Strategic Human Capital), Indian School of Business and Executive Director of HC and LI has been of immense help in developing the theme of the Bahrupia. He has such powerful insights that we would be remiss if we failed to mention his significant contribution to the chapter on the identity of the Bahrupia. Sushanta Banerjee, IIT, IIMA, the founder of Samuday Psycon and possibly the first organizational development (OD) consultant in the country, added a lot of flavour to the identity of the Bahrupia. Ashok Malhotra, another alumnus of IIMA, a brilliant leadership consultant and author of the EUM framework, and K.S. Narendran, an alumnus of Tata Institute of Social Sciences (TISS), an author and co-founder of Reflexive Lenses, were the reason that the Bahrupia concept and the integration of the role of HR happened and got enlivened in the dialogue process. We cannot thank them enough. They have an easy way of challenging the construct and engaging in a rich dialogue.

In the HR Round Tables, we partnered with the National HRD Network led by Dhananjay Singh. We were also supported by Krish Shankar, Group Head HR, Infosys and National President, NHRDN.

In the process of preparing the transcriptions of the round table discussions, we admire the inputs of Dr. Manosi Chaudhuri, Head, OB/HR Area and Dr. Jaya Gupta, Associate Professor (OB & HR) of BIMTECH. We are grateful for their valued knowledge sharing in the course of preparing this work.

This book also belongs to some of our eminent BIMTECH colleagues who shared their knowledge and well-researched ideas on various aspects of HR and its development. We particularly appreciate the devoted inputs of Dr. Rishi Tiwari, Sreevalsan K. and Abhinav Kumar in assimilating the content. The work could not have been completed without their help.

We were influenced by several contemporary studies and surveys which added a great value to this creation. Credit must be given to the relevant collection of articles and portions from books that acted as learnings to support our thinking on HR development as it grew in the past, present and also as it is very likely to be developed in a few years to come. These include but are not limited to the Deloitte Global Human Capital Trends Report, NHRDN's 'Future of HRD in 2030', *The Fourth Industrial Revolution* by Klaus Schwab of the World Economic Forum, the *Harvard Business Review* (HBR) and so on. We also express sincere gratitude to some great HR thinkers and Gurus like David Ulrich, Wayne Brockbank (Michigan Business School), Udai Pareek (IIM Kolkata) and T.V. Rao (TVRLS).

Bloomsbury India, an international publisher of repute, has been clearing our books for publication for the last seven years. We express our gratitude to Paul Vinay Kumar and Jyoti Mehrotra, the editors of Bloomsbury India.

Lastly, and most importantly, this book belongs to this country's illustrious HR Professionals and leading academicians, who have given us their thoughts and experiences on this topic and inspired us to take up the arduous task of studying Indian HR leadership through ages.

This acknowledgement would be incomplete without a big thank you to our families who stood by us even in those times when it seemed that we would never be able to finish this book.

Editors
K.K. Sinha and S.V. Nathan

CHAPTER 1

HR IN INDIA:
THE BAHRUPIAS

'We wear the mask that grins and lies,
It hides our cheeks and shades our eyes,
With torn and bleeding hearts we smile;
Still keeping happy and agile.'

– Paul Laurence Dunbar

THE WORLD BEYOND

Shvetaketu

Shvetaketu was the son of Uddalak Aruni. After completing his education from the Gurukula, he was further instructed by his father at home, and he became more learned than before. Shvetaketu always thought that he was the wisest among all. Once, he decided to go to the assembly of the Panchala. There, the Kshatriya prince Pravahana asked him, 'Have you had your full education, my dear?' To this Shvetaketu replied, 'Yes, indeed.' Then the prince started asking him questions in the following manner:

Pravahana – 'Do you know where all living beings go after death?'

Shvetaketu – 'No, revered sir, I do not know.'

Pravahana – 'Do you know how they return?'

Shvetaketu – 'No, revered sir, I do not know.'

Pravahana – 'Do you know the two paths—the path of light (devayana) and the path of darkness (pitriyana), along which the dead ones travel?'

Shvetaketu – 'No, revered sir, I do not know.'

Pravahana – 'Do you know why the other world does not become overfull though so many continue to depart from this world and enter it?'

Shvetaketu – 'No, revered sir, I do not know.'

Pravahana – 'Do you know how the fifth stage elemental matter in the oblation becomes the purusha or the living person?'

Shvetaketu – 'No, revered sir, I do not know.'

Pravahana – 'Then how dare you say that your education is complete? You seem to know nothing of these subjects.'

Shvetaketu was distressed and felt very humiliated at this. So he returned home and said to his father Uddalak, 'Revered father, you told me that you have instructed me well. But when prince Pravahana asked me five questions, I could not reply to even one of those. How, then, could you say to me that I was sufficiently educated?' Shvetaketu then narrated the whole story of the five questions and his awkwardness in the assembly of the Panchalas.

Uddalak, the loving father of Shvetaketu, listened to everything carefully and replied, 'Believe me, dear child. I do not know the answers to any of these questions. If I had that knowledge, do you think that I would have ever withheld it from you?' Saying this, Uddalak decided to go to the assembly of Panchala to gain knowledge from prince Pravahana.

In the palace of Pravahana, Uddalak was received with due respect. The next morning, when he presented himself at the assembly, Pravahana told him respectfully, 'Sir, I offer you wealth which is dear to all. You can demand as much as you please.' At this Uddalak said, 'O great prince, let the wealth remain with you. Tell me about the questions you have asked my son. I am thirsting for the knowledge of the other world.'

The prince was perturbed yet pleased with the attitude of the Brahmin sage. He then requested Uddalak to stay with him for a long time. At the end of the period, Pravahana said to Uddalak, 'O revered Gautama (another name of Uddalak), before you, this knowledge has never reached any Brahmin. It has been traditionally known only to the Kshatriyas. It is only now and for the first time that a Brahmin is receiving it from a Kshatriya king.' Saying this, Pravahana started giving Uddalak the answers to all the questions he had asked Shvetaketu.

The essence of Pravahana's teachings to Uddalak can be put in the following manner:

The elemental matter gets converted into life—or a person—gradually, by going through five different stages. These five stages represent five different sacrifices. There is the first stage where the elemental matter is the oblation offered to the fire and the sun, producing Soma, the life-giving sap, as a result. In the second offering, this Soma is poured into Parjanya, the power that brings rain. This results in the rain itself. The showering of the rain on the earth is the third sacrifice that results in food. The fourth sacrifice is when man consumes food, it gets digested and the Retas or the vital fluid is produced. This Retas takes up a different form in man and woman, and when the Retas of the man gets united with that of the woman as the fifth sacrifice, then the embryo is born and from this, the child.

The physical body of the man dissolves into the elements which constituted it. But the destiny of the soul depends on the actions performed and the knowledge acquired. The one who has attained real spiritual knowledge goes by the path of light and does not return to earthly existence. The one with no knowledge or partial knowledge goes by the path of darkness and falls into the eternal cycle of birth and death and suffers. Thus, some go to the world of Brahman and never return; some go to heaven, remain there for some time and return to the earth to complete their work; and numerous others are caught up in the ever-recurring cycle of birth and death.

In short, this is the knowledge of life and its origin, along with the knowledge of the destiny of the soul after death, imparted by king Pravahana to Uddalak, the aspiring learner.

(Chandogya Upanishad)

Editors' Treatise

HR in India: The Bahrupias*

BAHRUPIAS

A Bahrupia plays several roles. A loose translation of Bahrupia is 'many forms'. Bahrupias started out as street-side entertainers in Bengal and Nepal. Earlier, one could see their street plays, known as 'Jatra', in Calcutta during the festival seasons. The protagonists take on many roles and play them out with panache. The commitment and passion are visible. In a way, the Bahrupia is a 'meta' role. This 'meta' role bundles together the ethical living process of the person, the consciousness and an awareness that is developed over time. The identity of a Bahrupia in an organization is one of an HR specialist. A role that needs one to be the conscience keeper of the organization; a role that is acutely aware of the politics of the situation—not that of a head-butter but a master negotiator. At the same time, HR is not just a role alone. It is about being human and helping to build a human organization as well as being aware of the changes in the digital world, making it easy to absorb change.

A Bahrupia is a person who toggles multiple roles. The ability to manage a broad range of different themes is central to a Bahrupia. Given this nature, there is often a certain consistency at one end and a seeming inconsistency at the other. It is all predicated by the context and the response to the context. For

---

* The Bahrupias: Wikipedia defines Bahrupia as an impressionist in the traditional performing arts of India, Nepal and Bangladesh. Once popular and widespread, the art form is now in decline with most practitioners living in poverty. It was once common for Bahrupias to make a dramatic entrance at wedding or other festivities dressed as a policeman, priest, or other figure and create a commotion. The social norm surrounding these appearances was that the Bahrupia usually collected no money if he was detected as an impersonator. However, if he was able to successfully convince his audience of his fake identity, he would then reveal it and be awarded a baksheesh for having entertained the group. Due to their expertise with disguise and impersonation, good Bahrupias were recruited as spies by medieval Indian kings.

The mostly obsolete term 'naqqal', meaning mimicry or copycat, is also infrequently used, and Bahrupias are also simply called 'maskharas', a more general term for jester or buffoon, or 'bhands'. (Collated from Wikipedia)

instance, the role may be seen as supportive of an organization's policy, and at the same time, may be looking at it from a people standpoint and speaking to the 'management' about it. As an HR specialist, one needs to respond to multiple issues. In handling such situations, one may create either negative or positive outcomes. If positively deployed, the role has a great ability to turn the fortunes of an organization. However, if expedience is the predominant response, it will create serious repercussions for any organization.

THE CONTEXT OF ROLES

A Bahrupia plays according to a context. The context is central to the role of an HR specialist. It shines a light on the way one holds the role. Does one wish to make things so rule-bound that it makes it impossible to shift things around, or does one create broad swim lanes and allow for flexibility? In the past, policies were important. It made things easy for all to understand. How one exercises discretion depends on the context. Rule driven is far easier, but a Bahrupia is tasked with upholding the spirit of the law and going by the rule book as well. In a way, the Bahrupia is governed by the two accountabilities—the one to the organization and the other to the individual or the person in the system. In all that an HR person does, there is a responsibility to hold the conscience of the individuals' collective. This means a lot of tightrope walking in terms of action and comprehension and a deeper understanding of the situation.

The Bahrupia needs to be strongly anchored in themselves and the values they hold. They need to be part of the system and still look at it outside-in. They need an understanding of the organization along with the keenness to adjust, adapt and not get sucked into the politics of the situation. The ability to negotiate, be firm, fair and not be dogmatic are, therefore, the demands of this Bahrupia.

ROLE COMPREHENSION

A Bahrupia's role is difficult to comprehend. Why? Most roles manage the tangibles. How much production there has been, what the sales numbers are, what the customer complaint number is, the profitability and the like. The HR role manages and handles the intangibles. In a way, it helps people in the understanding of these intangibles and gets them to contribute to a wholesome environment. Culture is one such thing. HR plays a significant role in managing this intangible. Does the HR person collude with the business and forget their primary role—that of keeping the conscience of the organization, the culture and the intangible?

This brings us to the identity that an HR person holds. Many just amble into HR or accidentally find themselves in it. What is the professional identity of an

HR person? In marketing, it is about customers, sales and so on; for finance, it is about numbers and controls. All about tangibles. The HR person deals with the intangibles, and they bring in the same paradigms of the 'tangibles' into HR—the ones that are used in marketing or finance. The key performance indicator is now an internal customer survey (marketing) or cost of hire, etc. The context is left to be deciphered. This brings us to something even more important—the essence of the role. The finance person does not say he / she is a business partner. Neither does anyone else in the organization. The HR role does take on some interesting enabling functions of supporting engagement among people, energizing them and enhance cohesiveness. Much like a Bahrupia, who plays a role and steps back to see if the audience is connecting with the theme.

EVOLUTION OF THE ROLE

The nature of HR has progressed from welfare person to agony aunt, administrative backbone, business partner and other new labels and new coats of polish in some places. Yet, in all these, it is seen as an anchor of the soul of the company. HR is seen as a problem-solver of people. At one time, HR roles were much sought after and feared. What has changed is that some of these roles became less glamorous and some more so. A shaper-developer is a name it gave to itself. For some time, the Bahrupia felt a bit unsure of their standing in the organization. In comparison, other functions seemed to have a more solid footing. To ensure the legitimacy of the role, they started bringing out a 'scientific HR' and borrowed constructs that gave them a firmer footing, asking how they could be more like other functions and use the lenses that others used and feel better about themselves; how they could talk the language of the business. The business could be impervious to the toxic culture it was building, but this was something that the Bahrupia would know about. That is the edge of this master role player! The ability to make a difference to an organization by helping to shape the future of the organization.

The role at one end is also a master 'purchase manager' of talent, and a 'miner' of talent, depending on the circumstances. In today's world, the ability to marshal talent holds great value. The role also requires one to make opportunities for internal mobility. The need to ensure that talent remains in an organization is another role. The ownership lies here whereas the accountability lies somewhere in the HR leader's realm! At the same time, the HR professional is expected to help the organization get future-ready. The forms of the HR professional include a facilitator, a harmonizer, an anchor, a conscience keeper, the soul of the system, a minister and a friend. More like an interlocutor with the needs of the insider and like a coach with those on the outside. Given the multiplicity of the roles of a Bahrupia, it stands to reason that one needs to practice and build the capability over a long period. One needs to not get lost in the role but focus on the ability building that is needed to face up to the new and changing realities.

THE NATURE OF ROLE-TAKING

One of the dilemmas is what a Bahrupia goes though. The tension of the role and what happens to the individual. There are three stages here. One is during the time of taking on the role, the second is the question of how much of the script does the role demand and have to live with and the third is the extent of the authenticity of the role. In a way, it is about the sagacity of an HR leader in taking on such a role and the extent to which he / she extends their influence in this role.

There is a story of an actor who used to play a villain in movies. This role he played with such conviction that every time he came up onscreen, he was assumed to be the villain. One day, he decided to play the role of a hero. This was a bit of a problem. His producers did not agree to the proposal given the background. Between a role, a person and a need there is always a 'fitness' of purpose. The actor went ahead and produced a movie in which he played a lead role. As expected, the movie was a flop. So the question is whether in making a role, we have to find ways to set up a person for success.

How much of a Bahrupia can one be? It demands a lot from you. One fine morning you could be playing the role of a negotiator with a potential employee as a recruiter of talent, and in the evening, you could show up at an important meeting speaking of a strategic direction that the firm could be taking and the role of HR. The transition in the world of the new age work requires fluidity and an ability to don different hats seamlessly. This calls for competence and dexterity. One has heard of role-taking and role-making. Initially, one takes on a role and gets adjusted to the role. Over time, one finds their niche and finds ways to make their role count. Role-making is value additive to the organization.

The role-making part comes with a certain tension about the ability to live the role and the question of how they can impact a role, making it count. Some Bahrupias are really good at role-making. But even they have their limits. If the best were asked to take on a role that they would not be able to actually take on and if they were honest in admitting it, bringing in a certain authenticity, then they would be an honest Bahrupia.

A Bahrupia has three levels of investment in a role. At the lowest level, it would be to earn a livelihood; the middle would be to be a good entertainer; at the highest level, it would be an art. If this were to be translated to that of, say, an HR specialist—they would play different roles. The first level would be an operational role. The second level would be managing stakeholders, managing their expectations and acting as trusted advisors. The rare ones who play this at level three would be remembered as the Bahrupia of all times to come. They are exceptional, inimitable and unique. They take it to an artistic level and breathe life into the role. They are the ones who can do what the Vedanta speaks about—make the invisible visible, hear the unsaid and act the withheld. Let us take the example of an actor. A very revered actor and a national award winner went to his mother to take her blessings before he signed on a movie. All she said to him was take any role, play the role well, become the role in the movie, love it and live it and when you come home, shed it at the door. That transition will make you human and perhaps, humble. Tatwamasi—you are that. It also brings up the question of being authentic in the role and taking it to a different level of play.

In the world of HR, how does one play at level three? In the course of our work, it is asked of us to terminate the services of an employee. It is not an easy task. Yet, we are required to do it as this is part of our role. The test lies in whether the person could still be someone who will trust you after the separation. Will that person be your friend? If that happens, you have reached the third level of a Bahrupia. You are 'it' in the role and not 'it' at the same time.

Everybody's action has two levels of outcomes. First is the level of consequence and delivery in the immediate reality. The second is the level of making a difference to the context itself. The proportions vary. The decision that, say, a manufacturing head makes in bringing about a change to the process may result in higher output. Consequently, this would affect the quarter's results. The impact on the process or product is not necessarily high and the extent is reasonably predictable. The outcome of outcomes is the difference in the context. This is true for all the line functions.

The HR chief's actions in small or in large measure have a greater impact on the context of the organization. The context here dominantly includes the ambience and emotions—in other words, the sentient system that ordinarily lies unarticulated. The HR chief's impact on the 'culture' is probably more than that of any other role almost entirely because of his/her ability to influence the 'soft' sides. In other words, his/her contribution lies unmanifested most of the times. Hence, the criticality of the 'many roles in one' characterizes the Bahrupia (Sanskrit: bahu = many, rupa = visible forms). This role-taking does not come easily to everyone. So many amble into HR and find themselves at sea. If one understands the role and walks in with a commitment to make a difference to the role, there is a lot to do. If it is a matter of accident, the role will remain at a level where there is not much impact. It needs the commitment of a Bahrupia playing at level three, no less.

One of us (K.K. Sinha) recollects:

I would have been barely six or seven years old when I was living for some time at our Nani's (maternal grandmother) place in Dumka, Santhal Pargana, Jharkhand. We were more than a dozen kids or so in the same family, made up of my maternal uncles and us. It was mostly games and fun as few of us were going to school then, which only started with Class I after five years of age. Even if we were going to the primary school in the neighbourhood, we would all return by lunchtime and afternoons were the time for play and fun. There was no system of getting assigned homework from school. The times were good, indeed. During October–December, early winter, we would keep playing. Sometimes we would play games meant for boys or at other times, those meant for girls.

In those winter afternoons, we would all line up, sitting with feet dangling from the long verandah, waiting for the Bahrupias every Thursday and Sunday. There were four to five characters—a mix of males, females, old people and kids—mostly Santhals with a few Bengali characters. Sometimes the characters would change or would be replaced by others, depending on the story or play they would plan to enact in the market or the society. Once they reached a para or mohalla, at a chosen point, they would start playing their musical instruments which were mostly a dhol, damru, harmonium, ektara and a sort of trumpet.

They would, while playing several tunes, also sing songs—loud, powerful songs, sometimes created impromptu to recap the act they played last, connecting it to the act that they had proposed to play on the current day.

'Ta rara rara rara he…sss….

So on our last visit, you saw how Raavan persuaded Marich to agree and disguise himself as a golden deer in Panchvati to entice Sita, Ram's wife, and encourage her to ask Ram to bring its golden skin as a present for her…and the show begins… we all see a little boy with a cotton-made coat of a shivering yellow deer jumping around Sita, who attempts to catch the deer…and the Singer among them goes on:

Sita param ruchir mrug dekha |
Anga anga sumanohar vesha ||
Sunahu dev raghuveer kripala |
Ehi mriga kar sundar chala ||

And the actor playing Ram goes after that golden deer with his bow and arrow, ready to kill. The singer continues singing from the *Aranya Kand* and the music continues to play.

As soon as Ram slays the golden deer, he starts to return with the bow in his hand and the quiver at his waist. It is then that Sita hears the cry of distress and, out of fear, tells Laxman to go quickly to his brother who seems to be in great peril. Laxman replies with a smile:

Bhrikuti vilas shrishti laya hoi |
Sapnehu sankat parchu ki soi ||

And Laxman draws a line around Sita and the hut in Panchvati with his arrow and advises her not to breach it till they return. And further, the music goes on with loud drums and the damru....

Soon beech daskandhar dekha |
Awo nikat jati ke besha ||
Jinke dar sur sur derahin |
Nisi na neend din aana na khahin ||

When Ram returns along with Laxman they are shocked to see the deserted "Parn Kutir". Faced with Sita's disappearance, Ram starts crying, saying agonized words.

After coming to know from the vulture king Jatayu that Raavan had abducted Sita, Ram immediately advises Laxman not to tell Dasharatha, their father, of this on his return:

Sita haran taat jani kahahu pita san jaai |
Jaun maim ram ta kul sahit,
Kahahi dasanan ayee ||
Ta rara rara rara reh sss....'

Such episodes used to be delivered by this group of Bahrupias who would carry on and perform each episode in their determined area, para or lane of houses. All of us kids would flock around and see these performers delivering each episode. Often, we would recognize and be amazed that the same person who played Laxman in some episode, played the role of Sita in the next and often played it better. We would all giggle in the amusement of our recognition. Other times, none of us would be able to recognize the difference and would be very much impressed by their performance. After all, they were all seasoned and skilled Bahrupias doing a perfect job. We would also find, after a few months, the same family assigned to our street, now playing out a serial drama of a modern story with similar skill and effectiveness. They would keep variety and keep making changes in the story for different months and seasons. They would play stories from the Upanishads—perhaps the story of Ashtavakra or the story of Shvetaketu, son of Uddalak Aruni, or that of Nachiketa and the like. They would often repeat some of the stories, depending on their popularity or even the popularity of a character or a song.

As the Basant (spring) approached, these Bahrupias would also, on popular demand, get ready and present a serial drama on the 'Santhal Hool' (the Santhal Rebellion of around 1855). They would depict the conflict between Santhals and the British government, which was supported by the zamindars and sahukars—tools of exploitation of the Raj. The British proclaimed Marshal law for one year and the fight and rebellion was brutally ended by troops loyal to the British. It seemed that everybody in Dumka knew the story in all its detail.

We heard the resounding 'Nagara', the Santhal drums, and the names of the leading Murmu brothers—Sidhu, Kahnu, Chand and Bhairav. When our neighbours would come to know about the commencement of the Bahrupia episodes of 'Santhal Hool', there would be a large crowd of children on our verandah, gathered to watch this great show being presented by the same family of Bahrupias.

'On whose command Sidhu Kahnu
You slaughtered Sukurmuni
Bajal, you chopped Sukurmuni....
On Sidhu's order, mother
On Sidhu's command, mother
I slaughtered Sukurmuni
Your hands are tied Bajal
Legs are chained
You are taken to Sewri jail Bajal
You are taken to Sewri jail
Flute in my hands, mother
Bracelet around my feet
Going to Sewri, mother
To see the Sewri fair!'

(where they perhaps were hanged to death!)

I still remember a few lines of their song. It was pretty patriotic. These four Santhal brothers who led the Santhal Hool—Sidhu and Kahnu particularly—had characters that were dominant till they were killed by the elephant army lent to the British by the Nawab of Murshidabad to destroy the Hool....

We would all recognize the Ram, Laxman, Sita and Raavan of the 'Panchvati Sita Haran' episodes as the actors who played the roles of Sidhu, Kahnu, Chand and Bhairav effectively. Today, thinking of this in retrospect, I feel amazed at how the Bahrupias were able to play all the roles of heroes, heroines or even villains so successfully. While working in HR all through and decades after qualifying, I do realize that the HR role is typically an amazing 'Bahrupian' challenge! I often felt and assumed myself in the role of a Bahrupia—the Protean whose role would surprisingly change all of a sudden and who would still deliver the best, whether in acting, singing, music or dialogues, whether in roles of multiple characters with all their mixes and variations or even in sensitive roles, so dynamically atypical or opposite, to the extent of playing Sita or even Shurpanakha.

When I remember my childhood memories of the Bahrupias of Ekangar Sarai village (where I studied up to Class VI), who were attuned to creating impressions as acrobats, rope walkers and small trapeze swingers—demonstrating their capability to do the impossible—I am awestruck. There was so much to learn from them. Their changing roles that were played successfully, their ability to deliver that success with variety and diversity, their impressive and touching acts with music, singing, swinging and so on were all done with a tremendous amount of commitment and hard work along with a desire to exist and perform. It was, perhaps, a zeal for survival and delivery.

I remembered a gypsy who came to St John's School when I was in Class VIII in Ranchi. His sole activity was to dig a deep trench and bury himself in, asking his team to pack in the earth, without any air passage, pipe or hole. He claimed he could remain underground for three days without breathing air at all. The school guards watched the whole of the three days and when he was uncovered on the fourth day, he was not alive! Whatever happened, whatever he did, he was not alive and thus could not achieve his purpose, failing to impress people or even elicit any support or favour. There was complete grief and pathos on the school campus! No one was able to understand how this Protean, our Bahrupia, tragically failed, losing his life.

During my HR career, I continuously found us playing Proteans** again and again, delivering continuous success, leaving people both within our organization and outside influenced and mesmerized! Our success always depended on our readiness to pick up any role, irrespective of it being that of a hero or a villain; Ram or Raavan, Nawab or Sidhu Murmu, a musician or an excellent singer, I found only the versatile could rise to the challenge and, as an effective Protean,

** Proteans: They are more like our Bahrupias, multifaceted and versatile, adaptable and of varying nature. Proteans demonstrate a high degree of ability to access different forms as they proceed in life (or at work) and display a great diversity or variety. They are also referred to as masters of disguise and can even change their shape. He/She will be a performer or an actor, both mutable and adaptable. Mythologically, they have an ability to convert their shape and design from one to another at ease. They can comfortably play both comedy as well as very serious roles. Indeed, they demonstrate great ability and competence while taking on impossible challenges. (Collated from Wikipedia) be ready to deliver constant success with a clarity of purpose and an intense risk-taking ability.

In 1972, I was posted to the coal washeries of Hindustan Steel in Santaldih (West Bengal, Purulia). It was a hilly area with dense forests all around. Purulia was the poorest of the districts in West Bengal but had rich forests. Once, some of us decided to go for a picnic and after a lot of discussions, we agreed to visit Baranti Lake. This lake was primarily made by putting a mud dam on the river. It was a huge lake surrounded by hills and a couple of tribal villages. The lake was an expanse of exemplary beauty with a lot of migratory birds coming in the appropriate seasons. While this has now become a famous resort, it was then an isolated picnic spot with one or two guest houses or resorts which people from Asansol and Kolkata would visit occasionally. The staying arrangement was made by the security officer. The place was located at a distance of 35 km–40 km and took one and a half hours to drive by jeep. It was a beautiful ride with games, music and good food.

Captain Belliappa, a commandant, had organized through his contacts in the area to have some kind of dance and drama of Bahrupias. This was one of the tribals' avocations that helped to earn money from the neighbouring population. We were happy. The troupe came near the resort with their local instruments. When the show was about to begin, the *Sutradhar* (anchor or narrator) narrated a small story about a group of tribals who lived in a small village amidst wild animals like deers, tigers and boars. Apart from the problems faced by the animals that ruin the harvest, they also suffered at the hands of the greedy moneylenders—the Sahukars and police informers. Around this time, a newly posted British administrator arrived (in the story) who happened to be passionate about hunting. He befriended Ghinua, a native tribal, who was also an exceptional archer and a dancer. The two got into a deal where Ghinua would be rewarded if he brought down a 'big game'. The music became louder and the beats of the dance by the Santhals became faster and frenzied at this point.

The story moved on and focused on Sholpu, a young revolutionary who surreptitiously came into the village to meet his mother. Knowing this, the police informer chased him down till he reached the house, but had to return after seeing the whole village turn against him. However, he waited for his turn to punish Sholpu. Suddenly, there was a robbery in the village and one policeman was killed. The blame fell on Sholpu and the administrator declared a reward for his head. The informer took the opportunity and killed Sholpu, thereby claiming the reward. Sholpu's death created tension between the tribals and non-tribals. Around the same time, Dungri, Ghinua's wife, was abducted by a moneylender. Infuriated, Ghinua killed the moneylender to bring his wife back. Thinking that the time had come for the 'big game', he went happily to meet the British administrator, the Sahab. The British Sahab, however, caught Ghinua and hanged him for committing a murder.... The loud music became silent and affected the mood of the Bahrupian troupe and all the spectators as if time had suddenly stopped. Everyone looked awestruck in the informal audience there. Till his death, Ghinua failed to understand why for the same action one could be rewarded while the other was punished! This was converted into a famous 'Jatra' play by the Bahrupias and later, into a famous movie. Though it was a Bahrupian play, that evening at our picnic spot, it created a deeply pensive mood in every one of us. Surprisingly, we could still hear the humming of some soft songs and some occasional giggles of the Bahrupia performers as they started moving away towards their village, as though they were pretty satisfied with their challenging Bahrupian performance.

The globalization of business has amplified the intensity of business competitiveness to an all-time high. The new economy characterized by the predominance of service firms, Internet revolution, global competition and so on has placed a greater reliance on intangible assets for success. In this context, human capital has become the key component for survival and success. Unleashing the people power in the organization thus becomes imperative to achieve business success in the present business environment. As a result, people management has assumed a new dimension, bringing the function to the fore.

The function of HR has been evolving with the times, as reflected in the change in the nature of roles—going from being supportive with an administrative function to being a strategic function. The identity of the function has also been changing, from 'Personnel, Labour Welfare and Industrial Relations' to 'Human Resource Development' to newer titles such as 'Human Capital Management' and 'Talent management/Development', reflecting the shifting focus and priorities.

In over four decades of my experience in the people function, I have had the good fortune to see the growth of the people function through different stages—in the period of mega and radical changes taking place in the 1970s and later in the 1990s and also in the economy as a whole in India. We had to keep learning, planning and then again learning. This became a very dynamic process, causing a tremendous acceleration in the speed of changes, consequently demanding comprehensive transformation in HR and its people processes.

Though I have chosen the title of this book as *The Bahrupian Challenge: Inventing the New HR*, I must admit that the ideas and perspectives of a large number of Indian professionals and organizations have gone into shaping the concept of building people power and delivering results through it. The knowledge that created scores of innovative initiatives and experiments came from my team, my leaders, unions, books by thinkers in the field of contemporary HR, other organizations with whom we benchmarked or institutions of different kinds and perhaps many more people who, directly or indirectly, contributed immensely to my learning. The only thing that was needed was to always keep my mind open, explore and be inviting and generally tolerant towards mistakes while unleashing a culture of experimentation and readiness to carry out any new or challenging role in the organization.

I have chosen, at times, to write about parts of my personal journey and experiences of the odyssey of the making of an individual into a multifaceted performer through a meandering and rough lifetime. I have not been able to forget that experience of performing ever-growing new roles and delivering day and night, despite real-life problems at times.

At the turn of the millennium, the world started examining and exploring the challenges of the fast-changing, uncertain future. A major challenge that has emerged is that with the rapid change happening in all spheres of life, including technological, economic, political, social and cultural life, there has been an acute shortage of right leadership in the category of people managers—the HR guys. In a growing and transforming world, it is essential to develop the right types of HR leaders who steer, inspire and guide their people through challenges.

In the Davos Business Summit[4] at the turn of the millennium, (Leadership in Fragile Times, 2002) one of the issues that emerged as a major concern was the crisis of leadership predicted to happen in all walks of business and governance in the new millennium. The world would need to work in a focused manner to meet this crisis. We are already experiencing the leadership shortage in business, highly accelerated today by ever-changing business realities like a globalized market, demanding customers, availability of capital, regularity shift, changing workforce profile, rapid technological changes and so on. Under the circumstances, corporates, in particular, need to identify and work innovatively on critical success factors like cost, quality, speed, delivery, learning and social responsibility, along with factors like mentoring, guiding and developing talent and leadership.

Leaders who only live in the present and respond to its special pressures and demands would fail to achieve the quality of people leadership and change required in the future. In today's digital age, transparency and social awareness have to be the cornerstones of any organization. The HR teams need to align their current values accordingly. Some fundamentals like truth, humility, courage, energy, edge, equity, adaptability, realignment and social justice will have to be brought back into an organization's HR DNA.

All of us are aware of the sudden spurt in HR development activities in India in recent years. There have been frantic and dramatic efforts in Indian and foreign companies to quickly develop HR skills at all levels in an organization. The reason for this lies in the current growth trajectory of Indian companies. Many Indian companies are growing at a mind-boggling rate and so is the speed of change in organization culture, matched by the need for change and readiness in HR. In the last 10–30 years, several companies have phenomenally expanded to pan-India operations. This has put tremendous pressure on companies to develop their HR practices in the shortest possible time, trying to act as Proteans in such changes. HR had to, therefore, effectively adapt itself to the changing themes, stories, songs, dialogues, music and action styles and continue delivering like a Bahrupia.

What kind of HR do we need today in India? He / She should be ever ready to perform and deliver success because he / she is the people builder and the desired leadership developer.

When we explore our past, we expect our HR leaders to be present there in the form of a parent or grandparents or even in the form of a god, a king or an entrepreneur. We expect them to be 'sarv guna sampanna', which means, 'someone who has all the identified qualities required to be the "right" HR for a business'.

Today, the imperative for HR at all levels, senior or junior, is to enhance their own presentation and adaptation skills and foster those skills in various other talents in the organization.

Researchers have been researching and advising how HR needs to be developed or is getting developed in successful organizations. People have been identifying competencies that act as the basic ingredients in talent management and leadership. They have also been defining and penning down the roles, styles and attitudes of successful HR leaders.

For a long time, scholars have been grappling with various questions regarding organization structure, talent management and leadership. Who are leaders? What makes them tick? Is it their personality or education, or is it a result of their being good role models? Have they risen to be an HR leader, or were they just born with it? Is it life experiences that make an HR leader? How do they grow and help talent and organizations to deliver their multifaceted roles as HR?

BIMTECH, NHRDN and S.V. Nathan, Chief Talent Officer, Deloitte India, have been conducting some examination HR Round Tables and research on HR development in India during the post-liberalization regime. We have found that all those involved in the HR supply chain—companies, consultants, academic institutions, leadership coaches and trainers—have been busy with their respective agenda. There has not been much dialogue among these constituents.

The purpose of organizing HR Round Tables with this theme was to bring these stakeholders on common ground to collate their experiences, share processes, look at best HR practices and predict the future road map for HR development in India for the coming decade.

We started these Round Tables with a debate on the theme. Over some time, a few crucial sub-themes were identified and deliberated. To enrich the deliberations and churning of knowledge and experience, we adopted a process of capturing knowledge and experience by bringing in research on the subject—studies as well as cases. Business leaders and HR leaders responsible for developing talent and leadership shared their rich HR experiences and points of view in the panel discussions. We also involved academicians with the experience of leading business schools—ones who have taken the conscious responsibility of building HR leaders for tomorrow. Above all, we brought in CEOs, functional heads and the who's who of HR heads from both the old economy businesses (brick and mortar) as well as the new economy businesses, primarily dominated by IT services, financial services and retail. Consequently, we developed a blend of knowledge and experience coming from different fields of businesses, academics and research, which may give a very comprehensive perspective.

Keeping into consideration the factor of gender diversity, we elicited inputs, diverse experiences and views from a good number of women leaders, both from business as well as HR. We also explored the business environment or strategy building of the required organizational capabilities in terms of culture, competencies, process and also diverse practices of management and HR that are needed to examine the past, current, as well as future requirements. The diverse set of 60 HR professionals and business leaders appeared on our 14 panels in metros like Delhi, Mumbai, Pune, Bangalore, Hyderabad, Chennai, Kolkata and Bhubaneswar. They brought in clarity and since they belonged to diverse backgrounds, they brought in a holistic outlook to this topic. We found varying as well as contradictory experiences and views emerging on the platform.

This book captures and presents in brief rich experiences, successful and tested practices, learnings and brilliant insights of great business and HR leaders from varied sectors across the country. In the HR Round Tables, we found that this was the most appropriate and need-based theme to be discussed.

It was a very interesting bouquet of views and experiences and research that emerged in these discussions.

Vyasa[5] is a central and revered figure in most Hindu traditions. He is also sometimes called Veda Vyasa, the one who classified the Vedas. He is generally considered the author of the Mahabharata, as well as a character in it. He is considered to be the scribe of both the Vedas and Puranas. Vyasa is also considered to be one of the seven Chiranjivins (long-lived or immortals) who are still in existence according to Hindu belief.

According to the Vishnu Purana, Veda Vyasa is a title applied to the compilers of the Vedas, who are avatars of Vishnu. Twenty-eight people with this title of Veda Vyasa have appeared so far.

It is said that Veda Vyasa, who was himself an important character in the Mahabharata, asked Ganesha to write the story and work as his scribe. Ganesha agreed to help if Vyasa would narrate the story without any pause or break. Vyasa, in turn, set a condition that every part/shloka that he would narrate, Ganesha would write down only upon understanding the meaning well. And that's how the Mahabharata was written for us. So we editors of this book acted primarily as Ganeshas—the scribes of the Vyasas, or actors, in the story....

We have organized the articulations, letting them remain with the sub-themes of the respective HR Round Tables. This way, HR professionals can find a rhythm in the presentation as well as in the flow of knowledge and experience and in their story/play coming out through these articulations. Through these compilations, we offer the current and future thought of India that may trigger a proper, innovative and exciting process of developing HR leaders.

This book is for those youngsters who want to unleash the HR or even the business leader in them. Will this book help them to understand, adapt and become more successful? For sure. Will it help them to become successful? Maybe, maybe not. Will this book help them to be more loyal to their organization? Again, maybe yes or maybe not.

Will it make them more valued citizens of their organization? For sure. Will it make them contributing members of the global order? For sure. In essence, this book will help youngsters unleash their full potential for their organizations and the globe's greater good and give them strength, confidence and determination to commit to new roles and competencies and to adapt and display—perhaps even without rehearsals, like the Bahrupias. Let us be positive and deliver and keep in readiness for such roles that may seem challenging and even impossible at times—like the Protean challenges—and still do our best in the interest of the people in the organization and the organization itself.

HR roles have been expanding in the last 50–60 years in India. Many of the roles have been defined or redefined as they have grown in India but, at the same time, they have also been enriched by roles of HR that have travelled. I am going to dig out some history here.

Let me share a model which depicts the central role of competence for HR. It has emerged for me over the past few decades of experience in different organizations.

It portrays the evolution of a frustrated organizational development (OD) person who came to distrust the gap that still exists, far too often, between OD and HR. I concluded that we had to find a way to integrate good systems-thinking with the broad array of human dynamics in organizations. The solution was integrating HR practice vertically within the business and horizontally with each other in HR itself.[6]

1. Vertically within business
2. Competencies at the middle of the roles as their fulcrum
3. Strategic and tactical, well-connected and integrated horizontally
4. Business environment
5. Business vision, strategies, priorities and goals
6. Core capabilities
7. ER (Employee Relations)
8. Benefits
9. Reward and recognition
10. Performance management
11. Work and OD
12. Career and HR development
13. Diversity
14. Others

Every business exists in a given business environment which provides opportunities and challenges; it also provides the resources to capitalize on the opportunities and to overcome the challenges. HR leaders establish a vision of what role they want to play in that environment. With the vision in mind, they also establish a strategy. The strategy expresses the specific path the organization will take from the array of possible paths available to fulfil the vision. Every strategy assumes certain organizational capabilities—those abilities demonstrated by the system as a whole that differentiate it from others.

Building organizational capability requires very specific talent or competencies (at the centre of activities). Now we have the connection between the competence of people and the overall business direction. This is the *vertical link between people and the business*. No HR management effort can be entertained without a clear understanding of the connection between it and the business needs.

HR has been changing and adding on to its roles as well its competencies and education, much in the chameleon way. However, it has been demonstrating a lot of will and strength to build itself to deliver success in future. The adding of colours or topics and, consequently, competency list has perhaps not stopped anywhere. As a result, Dave Ulrich, at one point of time at the beginning of the millennium, observed that many argue that HR issues are increasingly salient to business performance under labels such as core competence, intellectual capital, organizational capability, high-performing work systems, process management, value-based management, empowerment, involvement, productivity, culture change and high-performing teams.[7] Underlying each of these labels or organizational initiatives rests an assumption that HR practices impactful executive thought and action, oriented towards an organization's better performance.

The people or the human resources that make up a company are its assets, and in organizations where effective human resource management has not been an integral part of management, it will have to be brought in for optimum success.

At another place, while describing the expanding role of HR, Ulrich has presented the role for HR professionals. He observes that HR roles could be perceived as a cacophony[8] that confuses the common professionals like us. He has the following HR Roles in that cacophony list.

A cacophony of HR roles:

- Coach
- Business partner
- HR leader
- Enabler
- Advocate
- Employee champion
- Change agent
- Initiative leader
- Strategist
- Operational supporter
- Rapid deployment specialist
- Internal consultant
- Human capital steward
- Manager of the firm infrastructure
- Competency practitioner
- Manager of employee contribution
- Knowledge facilitator
- Strategic partner
- Policy administrator
- Maintainer and monitor
- Programme coordinator
- Service provider
- Reactive problem solver
- Conscience

- Facilitator
- Relationship builder
- Architect
- Administrative expert
- Client relationship manager

The myriad of terms, concepts and metaphors for the HR role tend to dissolve into noise and confusion.

Rather than add yet another metaphor to the list, Ulrich proposed a simple framework in which he filters out the noise, synthesizes previous work and reveals five major roles:

1. Human capital developer
2. HR leader
3. Employee advocate
4. Strategic partner
5. Functional expert

HR professionals are *employee advocates*, charged with making sure the employer-employee relationship is one of reciprocal value. Besides advocating for employees of today, they build the future workforce as *human capital developers*. They are also *functional experts,* designing and delivering HR practices that ensure individual ability to create organization capability. As *strategic partners*, they help line managers at all levels reach their goals. And to tie it all together, they must be genuine *leaders*—credible both within their HR functions and to that outside. In the cacophony of roles, they show the evolution of these roles since the mid-1990s.

Ulrich focuses on the evolution of HR roles between the mid-1990s to mid-2000s. He suggests a synthesis of roles for HR professionals, combining employee champion, administrative expert, change agent and strategic partner, employee advocate, functional expert and leader.

Dr. T.V. Rao, formerly a professor at IIM, Ahmedabad, has the true credit of building HRD in the Indian industry / businesses while also introducing it—along with Dr. Udai Pareek in Larsen & Toubro—more than three decades ago. While Dr. Rao clarified the roles of the HR professionals' contribution as they have grown in India in his book *Future of HRD*,[9] he has been emphasizing vividly how he has travelled to his ultimate role of HRD manager. One can peek through a few of the roles identified for him, like:

- HRD manager
- Intellectual capital developer
- Human capital developer

- Positive qualities manager
- Performance manager
- People potential development manager
- Learning and development manager
- Human resource auditor
- OD specialist
- Organizational structure and dynamics (OSD) manager
- Chief knowledge manager
- Chief learning manager
- Chief of organization development and renewal
- Planning and development manager
- Holiday and recreation manager
- Leadership clinic

Dr. Rao, in one of his consultancy projects in Larsen & Toubro (L&T) in 1974–75, realized that the Personnel department did not have the required credibility to be able to create and implement a development plan for people. The Personnel department spent all their time on administrative tasks and if the development of people was to be taken up seriously, a new department had to be created that was beyond personnel management and should be called Human Resources Development department. Thus, an HR function originated.

A new function and department were formed, named Human Resources Development (HRD) department. Soon, others followed with an HRD function.

Now, the term 'business partner' is in vogue. The role of the HR function was to build organizational capabilities. Organization Development (OD) was conceptualized as a part of an HR's job—diagnosing the organization's health continuously. Thus, HR is not merely seen as a business partner but as a business propellant.

The term 'HR business partner' is a brainchild of the 1990s—the post-liberalization period. It was the need of the day to put it that way and hence, it became more popular. Dave Ulrich, and other HR gurus in the last decade and a half, promoted this concept. In a few organizations, it has shaped up reasonably. In others, HR is still a transactional function stuck in administrative tasks. Most of them do not understand the philosophy and the few who do are unable to push the agenda as they are caught up with administrative activities that demand immediate attention. Few depend on consultants to do the work for them. Consultants cannot create an HRD function by themselves when organizations have other priorities.

The HR function will become an integral part of the mindset, actions and activities of good leaders. HR will get integrated into business and it will take new forms. Most current HR managers doing jobs that can be outsourced will either end up as outsourcing agents or administrative consultants.

There will be no business without HR. Soft areas and intellectual capital building are bound to become focal points after the current turmoil is over and people start focusing on sustainable corporations and the role of competencies, culture, values, etc., gets more recognized.

While over time a plethora of roles for HR leaders has developed, Dr. Rao expects a set of five competencies:

1. Business leadership (vision, mission, values, etc.)
2. People leadership (people orientation, customer orientation, team orientation, interpersonal competence, emotional intelligence and empowering styles)
3. Change management (technological, systems, culture and other forms)
4. Integrating capability (ability to coordinate and integrate various departments and generations of people, diversity management, etc.)
5. Execution capability

Dr. Rao believes HR is not a career. It is a philosophy and a necessity, and a way of life. For those who take up HR as a career, it would only be a phase of their life, lasting for a certain period.

Dr. Rao, in a December 2018 article in *Business Manager*, said that HR should always focus on human resources. A human being is an integrated whole. Human beings act as a whole and not in parts. HR specialists, consciously or unconsciously, end up dividing a human being into parts. So in HR specialization, we have forgotten the integrated human being. How would you like to be treated? As a target or as a full human being? With growth in size, most organizations are making the mistake of dividing people by introducing specialization. HR facilitation strategies and structures need a sea change.

Dr. Rao tends to agree with that view in most cases. Means have become ends and what was originally thought to facilitate the building of the three Cs (competence, commitment and culture) has lost its original purpose and now focuses on the trivial. We are using the wrong measures for HR. That is why he feels the 'h' or human has been forgotten in HRD and development has got substituted by departments, leaving behind 'resources department'. Hence, I would readily agree with someone who says calling a human being a resource is a crime. A human is filled with possibilities while the term resource limits the possibilities and focuses on measurement.

We should be technology savvy. Technology does not mean only IT. Technology is needed in many other fields and we should appreciate and encourage the development of new technologies that solve or at least aid in solving human problems. It should be used to create more employment and entrepreneurship rather than unemployment and unrest.

An HR professional has many avatars. HRD is a philosophy of continuous learning (the three Cs). Therefore, it is spiritual. As a spiritual function, it can never become extinct. To keep themselves relevant in the changing world, HR professionals should learn to respect human beings first. It starts with self-respect. Discover more and more of oneself. Experiment with new ways of creating happiness at the workplace. Try to understand human beings and their enormous potential. Human talent cannot be fully captured by social media. In-depth and intense interactions and debates are a must. While reading books and blogs, listening to talks, watching movies and participating in debates and all kinds of research go a long way in making us experience the world, continuous self-reflection is a must. This understanding of the self is very important to understand human beings and their way of life can easily descend on us through sustaining the link with the Vedanta, easily transferring deep learning based on spirituality.

HRD managers of today do not have adequate professional preparation. They enter the work world ill-equipped, with a masters in social work or a diploma in training, personnel management or industrial relations. When assigned HRD tasks, they have an extremely inadequate understanding of business needs and feel comfortable reducing any job to an administrative job. They easily fall into the 'power trap' and 'administration trap' outlined in the HRD Missionary and then reduce their role to that of an Industrial Relations (IR) manager or an administrator of recruitment processes. The HR manager arranges campus visits for recruitment, liaises with recruitment agencies, maintains records and spends an enormous amount of his/her time administering recruitment. Also, he/she maintains files of appraisals, prepares proposals for commissioning compensation surveys and employee satisfaction surveys, administers townships, gymnasia and health clubs, makes travel and transportation arrangements, fulfils statutory obligations, organizes training programmes and sometimes, if lucky, writes the Chairman's speeches. He/She participates very little in policymaking, strategic thinking and real HRD activities. He/She holds very little credibility among the line managers and is often accused by them, privately, of lacking in human concern and the human touch and yet calling himself/herself an HR manager. Very few HRD managers have made a difference to their organizations in the recent past.

HRD managers play a very vital role, as they always have. Their roles have only increased in the recent past as we have been discussing right from the beginning, and HR officers are expected to be proficient in playing all the roles diligently in different avatars—be it Ram or Laxman or Raavan or Hanuman or even Sita for that matter. All the avatars that they have been playing are very critical and have been a challenge to them and, therefore, to the organization—the play by Bahrupias.

While several HR managers (which includes HRD) have grown disproportionately in the last few years or a decade, their knowledge base has remained very poor. Their credibility has shrunk along with their roles and, in some cases, they have become power brokers. Some of the relatively good HR managers have saved their image by restricting themselves to training and OD. But the plethora of roles and their demands has always been a challenge for the HR managers who have to immediately change themselves with the changing roles that they are faced with and perform or deliver accordingly. There have been major changes in HR managers' basic roles of IR of late. Thus, there is a new breed of HR managers in some organizations, trying to find out how they can do an HRD oriented IR. Outsourcing has come to the rescue and they keep themselves busy trying to find out agencies to whom they can outsource some of the specialized jobs like compensation service, employee satisfaction surveys, organizational climate surveys and so on. Today's HR manager in the new economy industry is, however, also busy establishing mundane things like gymnasia and swimming pools to keep the new generation of hi-tech professionals happy instead of merely looking at other trivial welfare matters or social security matters. There has been always a kaleidoscopic mix of roles emerging as challenges for HR managers while managing organizations.

We refer to Dr. Rao again, from his book *Future of HRD*. The kind of challenges that the HR managers have to face are not only challenges but risks when impromptu decisions are required to bring a solution, resolving the problem before the organization and the HR manager, resulting also in assaults as well as torture and death, at times.

We do not know, while we are writing over claims of HRD stalwarts and gurus like Dave Ulrich, Wayne Brockbank, Udai Pareek, T.V. Rao and others, we are ourselves lost when observations come onto the HR list as a cacophony. We are instantly reminded of our metaphor of the Bahrupias as the painted and multi-masked HR in their play, having tremendous flexibility of creating and finding new roles every time they encounter a new challenge, like a Protean or a Bahrupia. He/She operates to meet these challenges not only on the strength of one or two good diplomas or degrees but their rich experiences in their careers are amassed and stored well for future use. They also substantially stand by their own chosen and practised core values like integrity, courage, empathy, relationship and credibility.

CHAPTER 2

TALENT TODAY AND TOMORROW: PROTEANS IN BUSINESS

'We all wear masks,
and the time comes when
we cannot remove them without
removing some of our own skin.'

– André Berthiaume

NACHIKETA

Nachiketa, the son of the sage Vajashravas, is the child protagonist in an Upanishad story about a determined and steadfast boy who was as spirited as his father. He was taught self-knowledge by Yama, the god of death. Nachiketa is noted for his rejection of material desires and for his single-minded pursuit of the path of realizing salvation (moksha).

The name Nachiketa means 'the one who does not let his energy be lost in an endless loop'.

The Rig Veda talks of Yama and Nachiketa. The latter is also mentioned in the Taittiriya Brahmana and, later, in the Mahabharata. The primary story, dealing with the dialogue between Nachiketa and Yama, comes from the later Katha Upanishad, summarized below:

Nachiketa and Yama

Vajashravas, desiring a gift from the gods, decided to donate all his possessions in a ceremonial offering called 'Sarva Dakshina'. But Nachiketa, his son, noticed that Vajashravas was donating only the cows that were old, barren, blind, or lame; not such as might buy the worshiper a place in heaven. Nachiketa, wanting the best for his father's rite, asked, 'I too am yours, to which God will you offer me?' After being pestered thus, Vajashravas answered in a fit of anger, 'I give you to Death (Yama).'

So Nachiketa went to Yama's home but the god was out, and he waited three days without any food or water. When Yama returned, he was sorry to see that a Brahmin guest had been waiting so long without food and water. To compensate for his mistake, Yama told Nachiketa, 'You have waited in my house for three days without hospitality. Therefore, ask three boons from me.' Nachiketa first asked for peace for his father and himself. Yama agreed. Next, Nachiketa wished to learn the sacred fire sacrifice, which Yama elaborated. For his third boon, Nachiketa wanted to learn the mystery of what comes after death.

Yama was reluctant to answer this question. He said that this had been a mystery even to the gods. He asked Nachiketa to ask for some other boon and offered many material gains.

But Nachiketa replied that material things would last only till the next day. He who had encountered Death personally, how could he desire wealth? No other boon would do. Yama was secretly pleased with this disciple, and he elaborated on the nature of the true self which persists beyond death. The key of the realization is that this self is inseparable from the Brahman, the supreme spirit, the vital force in the universe. Yama's explanation is a succinct explication of Hindu metaphysics, focusing on the following few points:

- *The sound 'O'! is the syllabus of the supreme Brahman.*
- *The atma, whose symbol is Om is the same as the omnipresent Brahman. Smaller than the smallest and larger than the largest, the soul is formless and all-pervading.*
- *The goal of the wise is to know this atma.*
- *The atma is like a rider; the horses are the senses he guides through the maze of desires.*

- *After death, it is the atma that remains; the atma is immortal.*
- *Mere reading of the scriptures or intellectual learning cannot help to realize the atma.*
- *One must discriminate the atma from the body, which is the seat of desire.*
- *Inability to realize the Brahman results in one being enmeshed in the cycle of rebirths. Understanding the self leads to moksha.*

Thus, having learned the wisdom of the Brahman from Yama, Nachiketa was freed from the cycle of births.

Nachiketa has been one of the most influential characters and Indian monk Swami Vivekananda said, 'If I get ten or twelve boys with the faith of Nachiketa, I can turn the thoughts and pursuits of this country in a new channel.'

(Katha Upanishad)

Editors' Treatise

Talent Today and Tomorrow: Proteans in Business

A general question that comes up before Human Resources Management (HRM) is why companies succeed or fail. This is primarily due to the shortage of appropriate talent in the organization and their lack of development. Every company's journey is different though there may be some similarities and standardizations.

People are the most important assets in the organization and we feel that the main job of HRM is managing the talent required by the organization to deliver its work. HRM work has generally been in constant flux. This is not new but is true for most of the world that we live in, which is also in constant flux. This is always a challenge for talent, which is an opportunity as well as a threat for today and tomorrow. There is, thus, a direct correlation between an organization's success and the quality of its talent. The organization has to keep thinking about the requirement of talent, finding the talent from outside or within and developing them to deliver the results.

While experience says that expert talent is the order of the day, in practice, it is a better idea to develop talent that possesses greater diversity or variety and which is versatile—not the possessor of a single talent as a specialist. This talent is said to have a varied nature or an ability to assume different forms as a Protean in business. This is a kaleidoscopic talent. This talent is successful in delivering varieties of roles. He/She is capricious but very consistent in the kind of roles that HR leads are developing in today's business, in changing times.

The challenge for HR today is developing this kind of versatile talent within the organization and having an eye for identifying such talent from outside as well. Greater the ability in the organization to develop a Protean's talents from within, greater is the opportunity of delivering sustained success through this kind of talent management that is much needed for today and tomorrow.

For the roles that a protean talent has to play, the act to be delivered is scripted by the concerned line or HR leads or by the talent himself/herself. In similar situations, the HR lead has to be ready to deliver, irrespective of whether the role is tactical, strategic or that of a specialist HRM. This talent—along with the HR leads—has to continuously develop competencies of a versatile Proteus* who delivers all varieties of requirements with utmost efficiency.

According to K.K. Sinha:

I find that it is primarily learnt and developed through experience. I have, in my professional career, not come across theories or concepts on HRM which are always true.

Basically, I'm a storyteller. I narrate stories from my real experiences or experiences of people, melding their narrations and learnings with the required developmental needs in the organization. I have found them really useful and very powerful in delivering learning and performance success. Therefore, it is essential to build an understanding of the need for the right talent, comprising of required skill and attitude. HRM, therefore, has to simply understand how people create value and how they should and can be measured with a clear purpose. Talent depends on passion, belief, focus, initiatives, teachability, character and attitude. Generally, employees cannot be successful with talent or skill that focuses on IQ alone. Success is substantially dependant on EQ, which can help them to develop as better HR professionals. They must have a clear picture of the current and future state of business strategy, organization capabilities and HR practices. HR professionals cannot live and succeed in only the present but must align themselves and prepare for the future environment, developing their strategies and practices accordingly.[10] There is no shortcut for success as an HR professional, and the only key is to keep developing yourself and the talent in your organization. Therefore, there is a need to bring in experience to continuously develop available talent in an organization. Success depends largely on company leaders and managers' demands from their people and their expectations from the talent. HR must, therefore, inculcate this as a part of its culture after developing people appropriately and exposing them to opportunities to work on challenges.

HRM, therefore, has to create an environment where people don't assess themselves and fall into a trap of satisfactory underperformance and,

---

* Proteus: This Proteus was the original master of disguise. According to Greek mythology, the grizzled old shepherd of Poseidon's sea creatures possessed the gift of prophecy but didn't like to share his knowledge. Proteus would escape those who wanted to question him by changing his shape. The only way to get a straight answer from him was to sneak up behind him during his midday nap and hold onto him (while he frantically changed from shape to shape) until he eventually revealed what he knew. The adjective 'protean' describes anyone or anything that is as mutable and adaptable as the mythological shepherd. (From the Merriam Webster Dictionary)

consequently, start believing that they are the best. They begin to exhibit arrogance towards subordinates, teams, customers and suppliers as this stifles initiative and enthusiasm. Compliance and fear take over from enthusiasm and passion and the company and its performance starts slipping into satisfactory underperformance. This leads to stagnation and a lack of desire to change for continuous improvement, resulting in an acute crisis, happy incrementalism and more rationalization rather than optimization. HR's goal has to be to meet the gap between the potential and the actual. Therefore, there is a need to transform talent within the environment of an organization. Thus, the challenge is about changing behaviour at work. This cannot happen without changing the team's attitude to the right mode of performance.

India has a rich history of business and trade. The guild system is a perfect example of the efficient ways that work and workplaces were planned in ancient India. *Arthashastra*—an ancient Indian treatise of business, trade, political policy and so on—written by Kautilya around 300 BC decoded several facets of HRM. This treatise described ways of financial and trade management, business, commerce and people management. Chanakya, the great Indian brain, had three key areas of exploration—public policy, administration and utilization of people and taxation and accounting principles. These rational constructions were supported and backed by an intrinsically driven and long-embedded belief system with roots way back in the Aryan way of living, known as the Vedanta. This thought process affected the political, legal and social settings in India for a long time. Interestingly, the Indian thought process has a unique, dichotomous viewpoint, where collectivism and ideas of 'vasudhaiv kutumbkam' go hand in hand with an inner space of spirituality and connectedness with the supreme power.

These deeply indigenous but global ideas were present in Indian organizations' thought processes and value systems for a long time.[11,12] Historical evidence depicts regular interactions among the Indian economy, politics, society and public administration and global and international entities.

Administration and encouragement of rules and laws supporting a well-managed system are evident in India's past. India's managerial history was strongly affected by the 200-year-long British rule, which had sophisticated methods and processes of corporate organization and optimum utilization of manpower.

One of the most significant areas of values and cultural practices has been the 'Varna Vyavastha', which maintained social or organizational balance traditionally. This traditional social ethos underwent a substantial transformation during the British rule. Gradually, the factory system came into existence and later, industrialization and urbanization led to a greater emphasis on labour management. Globally, labour management was first known as labour welfare and also as 'personnel management'. Employees were treated as mere labourers and one of the factors of production that required constant supervision. The human element was not given due importance. Later, Elton Mayo's Hawthorne Experiment in 1928 gave rise to the human relations movement and the term human resource management was coined. Here, the 'human element' was emphasized. Workers were treated not merely as 'cogs in the machine' but as human beings, as individuals and as social beings. In HRM, the main aim was to encourage and motivate employees to identify their capabilities and use them efficiently. But the buzz term today is 'talent management'. Unlike in HRM, the main objective here is not just identifying an individual employee's existing potential but also the capabilities innate in him. Talent development aims at bringing out the hidden potential of an employee and helps him/her to develop as an individual. The Tatas are considered to be the pioneers of HRM in the country, much before our independence. They envisioned a holistic model of Human Resource Development (HRD) much ahead of the first dedicated HRD department in other organizations.

The liberalization of markets and global linkages has created a transformation of attitudes towards HR policies and practices. Today, in a globally competitive market, our world is changing fast; the presence and role of talent management is well understood. Thanks to technology, information flows rapidly around the world today and can dramatically change.

It is estimated that India will have a population of 1.45 billion people by 2030. It may be noted that half of India's current population is under 25 years of age. Though a demographic dividend for the economy, it also rings a danger bell for the country's ability to create new jobs at an unprecedented rate. But today's HR department has to be a business partner and even beyond. There are some unique changes that HR has to face with the changing kinds of employees. Today, the barriers between work and life have gone away and a large number of all workers believe it is only possible to get ahead in their career by significantly sacrificing time with their family and personal life.

Chanakya[13] had prescribed very clear tests for selecting ministers and had advocated for placing them in proper departments based on the results of the tests. The job-person fitment parameters suggested by Chanakya are so subtle and relevant that many modern-day psychometric tests would not be able to match it.

The hallmarks of a modern workforce include greater flexibility and agility, greater customization of services, more mobility, increasing influence of technology and social media and the effects of globalization. One of the ways to assess a company's competitiveness is to understand its talent and workforce capabilities. Companies that can attract, retain and develop deep, specialized technical skills are generally well-positioned to outperform their peers in nearly every industry. As the environment in which businesses operate becomes more complex, skills evolve and become obsolete more rapidly. Deep capabilities drive performance and take years to build.

Digital technology[14] is now everywhere, disrupting business models and radically changing the workplace and the way work is done. Technologies such as mobile devices, 3D printing, sensors, cognitive computing and Internet of Things (IoT) are changing the way companies design, manufacture and deliver almost every product and service, while digital disruption and social networking have changed the way organizations hire, manage and support people.

Innovative companies are figuring out how to simplify and improve work experience by applying the disciplines of design thinking and behavioural economics, embracing a new approach that we can call 'digital HR'. These organizations are integrating mobile and cloud technologies to build an app-based set of services designed to incorporate HR programmes into an employee's daily life. The barriers between work and personal life are dissolving through the use of mobile devices.

Integrated apps on mobile devices can deliver on-demand video learning to participants in a new project, send messages to a team when someone is running late for a meeting, monitor stress levels and recommend when it is time to take a break and offer intelligent recommendations. This is the new vision for digital, HR-integrating SMAC** technologies—to redefine the employee experience and make work easier, more productive and more rewarding while hopefully improving work-life balance. The all-digital world is changing how we live and work.

As networks and ecosystems replace organizational hierarchies, it is time to appreciate that building the organization of the future is a very important issue. Organizational design and change are complex. Many organizational redesigns fail because they are reduced to an exercise to cut costs. Others face resistance from company leadership and suffer from a lack of appropriate talent and its development.

In the past, most organizations were designed for efficiency and effectiveness, leading to complicated and siloed organizations.[15] The resulting business models, which were based on predictable commercial patterns, are unsuited to an era of unpredictability and disruption. Instead of mere efficiency, successful

** SMAC: Social, Mobility, Analytics and Cloud

organizations must be designed for speed, agility and adaptability to enable them to compete and win in today's global business environment.

Top companies are built around systems that encourage teams and individuals to meet each other, share information transparently and move from team to team depending on the issue to be addressed. For a company to stay agile, teams must be formed and disbanded quickly. Some companies are already designing their organization to be more adaptable and team-centric.

The concept of career is being shaken. New business realities are forcing companies to rethink the way they manage careers and deliver on learning and development (L&D) opportunities. Leading companies are moving to overhaul their career models and L&D infrastructure for the digital age, though most organizations are still in the early stages of this transformation.

Learning technology[16] is changing rapidly. Traditional learning management systems are being complemented with and replaced by a wide range of new technologies for content curation, delivery, video distribution and mobile use. This upheaval in learning and careers is becoming a catalyst for radical change.

As companies build the organization of the future, continuous learning is critical for business success. For today's digital organizations, the new rules call for an organization that can deliver learning that is always on and always available over a range of mobile platforms. In many instances, employees themselves are pushing for continuous skill development and dynamic careers. Yet, several millennials also say they are likely to leave because they are not learning fast enough. Companies worldwide are scrambling to catch up with employees' desires.

Companies are facing disruptive changes driven by digital technologies. Skills are also becoming obsolete at an accelerating rate. Software engineers must now redevelop skills rapidly.

Furthermore, in most companies, the learning management system (LMS) is among the oldest and most challenging to use. Today, a new set of learning tools for building talent has entered the market. The fastest-growing segment in HR technology spending is now the adoption of new employee learning systems. The goal is a learning environment adapted to a world of increased employee mobility.

Here, a Bahrupia's role is that of a prompter hiding below the stage, not visible to the audience but enabling the performers to continuously make acceptable deliveries. This requires the Proteans, the Bahrupias, to be masters of all roles or even the entire acts of all trades—an impressive feat.

Strategies of talent management (TM) and engagement, much talked about in terms of the ultra-modern HR, substantially impress employers at times, depending upon the skills, language and support and resources used by smart HR professionals who understand their roles and the expectations of both their employers and their customers and present strategies and plans convincingly. Generally, they use excellent logic but miss the philosophy needed for TM.

There are several stories and biographies of a host of entrepreneur leaders in India who were putting much thought into identifying talent and teams who could deliver success in challenging times. They would intently look for basic values emphasizing integrity and trust, with consequent reflexes and the ability to use common sense. They would pick up young people and allow them to learn and practise these values and senses, distancing them from the basics of the human persona.

A habit in leaders to take responsibility for the organization in challenging times and situations emphasizes that radical performance is possible in organizations at all times.

We are reminded of a famous proverb relevant to this context: 'Experience is a comb that nature gives to a man when he is bald.' Experience does teach, train and build leaders but it does take time. The Vedanta also emphasizes that life is defined as 'anubhava dhara'—the stream of experience.

I have been a management student but I repeat that no management theory or concept is absolutely true. If there is any—I have not come across it[17] so far, especially in the HRM area. HR has to continuously keep learning and renewing itself to keep pace with changing times and knowledge.

HR has to integrate with business. Therefore, HR is to move away from HR administration to proactive TM (acquiring and developing leadership and talent). Therefore, HR needs to be ever creative and credible. HR may lose the ability to integrate themselves with business but it must not lose the human touch due to excessive target obsession and poor connect with subordinate or long-term goals! Therefore, there is a need to see millennials in these times as humans rather than only as measurable resources.

HR and business are two sides of the same coin. There is no business without HR and vice versa. There is a very famous saying that goes 'nothing succeeds like success'. To justify this, we may quite often speak of people with an ordinary upbringing, from ordinary schools or colleges, who later had tremendous success in life. We may limit this discussion with some very good research on known talent to prove this point. Most of them were not always identified as so-called child prodigies but primarily due to intense hard work, commitment or even due to their being fortunate enough to get a great mentor, they received an opportunity that opened the road to success.

We are very convinced by most findings of Geoff Colvin.[18] In *Talent Is Overrated: What Really Separates World-Class Performers from Everybody Else*, a book written by Colvin, he very convincingly argues that top performers in business, as well as in sports, music and other walks of life, were not seen as typical child prodigies always.

The mystery of TM is the question of where does it really come from. Sometimes, we refer to child prodigies as little ones who demonstrated excellent talent in either art or science right from the beginning of their lives. We generally hear names of music lovers, sports and games players or other achievers like Mozart, Tiger Wood and more. In India, we can recall among the current talents people like Ravi Shankar, Sachin Tendulkar, Mahendra Singh Dhoni, Rahul Sharma, Anoushka Shankar and many such. People think that they were born with talent. I have heard of a proverb that says 'the son of a rich man or a woman inherits the riches from a parent'. But this may not be the case in the inheritance of talent.

In terms of inheriting talent from childhood, I would endorse Geoff Colvin's research that we may give up branding young talent in music, sports, science, mathematics as child prodigies; these are generally not inherited by birth but are developed by deep interest, focus, commitment and very hard work on the part of a little child. Most of the music maestros, whether vocal artistes or instrumental, choose to start training their little ones from a very young age. They infuse the interest, focus and habit for hard work in the little ones, which gradually inducts them into the life of what we call prodigies, achieving excellence in whatever they are learning right from the beginning.

Some of the prodigies who had been trained in a particular art or music or sports or science changed their interest with time and still excelled. The experience depends upon the pandit, guru or mentor, who is investing time to inculcate interest and focus, and elicit commitment for hard work.

Pandit Ravi Shankar,[19] who was a famous Indian sitarist—acclaimed and rewarded substantially—was not exactly a child prodigy, for that matter. He started his training and career, surprisingly, in classical dance and singing, right from the age of five years. After he had been performing in these areas for a while, he changed interests and a fresh mentor helped him develop his skills in sitar—a talent he pursued vigorously after the age of 18 years. Hence, we find that there have been intense developments or even changes in the identified talent of a person and we find at times, people diversify from one branch of talent to another as a youth and still excel in the new talent field. These are some brief experiences that we are narrating to primarily emphasize that talent is something that can be developed at different ages, depending upon how sincere the interest and focus is in the individual and how much hard work and time he / she is prepared to give to sharpen the learning every day.

In the field of business, particularly in management and leadership, we often come across several characters who have been excellent in terms of academic and startup roles; however, they do not persist in the long run. On the other hand, people who have been simple, honest and not a high flyer initially, with experience, commitment for learning and hard work, rise and prove their ability as excellent performers.

TM involves anticipating the needs of human capital and setting out a plan to meet them by identifying easily, deploying effectively and quickly developing critical abilities.

There is a need to align Talent Management Architecture (TMA) to the changing times and business environment. I would choose to be guided on this by Peter Capelli of Wharton.[20] Further, there is a need to simplify TMA and its process to achieve high effectiveness of use. I would be guided by Marc Effron and Miriam's work[21] in *One Page Talent Management*, for this.

There is a bureaucratic and legacy support system needed that was developed in the second half of the last century. This worked well in a highly predictable environment when assessment, forecasting, development, banking and so on were possible and easy. This fails now in a highly volatile environment. The new TM strategy, with practices like layoffs, changed the culture.

In the 1980s, there was a dearth of long-term employees. They found that TM, except in 'academy organization', changed. White-collar layoffs emerged as a new practice but the practices in the large scale 'academy companies' sustained. In the decades of the 1990s and even of the 2000s, huge growth emerged in the global economy and also in India. As there emerged a talent shortage, it also absorbed surpluses with high hiring speed.

Sudden emphasis also shifted to hiring readied talent from competitors in the market. Talent attraction, retention and engagement became a business concern. Succession planning became short-lived.

TM was not an end in itself, and business results were balanced. In rapid-fire changes in the business world, structuring and demands required frequent restructuring. HR's Bahrupian act changed suddenly. HR had to see the cost-benefit analysis of long-term TM support.

There may be a new way of looking at TM, new architecture and framework—as driven by market and operation strategy. It could be Talent on Demand (ToD) in line with Just in Time (JIT). It may be in line with the supply chain management of the 1950s but developed and adapted further.

Supply Chain Management (SCM), with today's adaptations, allows businesses to anticipate shifts in demands, including an easy forecast of TM/TD, cost-effective TM/TD, hiring and strategic talent pipeline and package with retention and engagement.

But there is a need to plan the development of critical succession positions and parking of different challenges such as adapting to uncertainty, high ROI on development of employees and also preserving investment by balancing employer-employee interests.

There were efforts to optimize TM frameworks by simplifying needs as done in the 1950s or 1960s.

There was also a need felt to optimize by simplifying, as Marc Effron strongly suggests, also talking of HR players as 'Feature Creeps' in TM. He also said that at the other end of the product chain, some consumers or users suffered from 'Feature Fatigue'—those who were not able to put all features in use as in the case of a mobile, cameras and so on. The business world understood that while complexity was easy to make, innovate and sell, it did not work so much with users who were immensely fatigued by the constant enriching of new features in HR systems.[22]

Most companies continue to battle complex and bureaucratic TM processes. Several consulting companies demonstrated low abilities to grow talent. Line managers blamed HR. All of them developed the capability to develop TM. On the other hand, HR blamed line managers, saying that the architecture and processes that were best suited for business needed to be developed and made user-friendly. Thus, there developed a need to balance complexity with value and a need to simplify it for the users, not loading them with huge process manuals and questions banks.

One cannot venture to suggest an ideal type, with a general optimism, and take a risk to recommend a TMA for all professionals. They will have to recreate the business- and time-specific architecture and framework of TM relevant for their own business.

Our only humble suggestion is to restructure based on business realities and environment volatility today and to be sensitive to make the strategy, framework and process simple for consumers and users like the average line managers and employees. Hence, no standard structure needs to be developed that can fit all requirements and businesses, optimally.

As K.K. Sinha recalls:

My encounter with the then great HR leaders in TISCO, specifically Russi Mody[23] happened in the late 1960s when I was entering this profession. The economy was performing poorly in the mid-1960s. The growth of national income during this period was slow. The commodity-producing sector was lagging as an industry, the basic and capital goods sectors were suffering and, more importantly, the production of mass consumption goods was also lagging behind. The growth of non-farm employment was deplorable, with higher rates of inflation. When I got the University Gold Medal, I cried, 'I didn't know how I got this.' Having won the ILO Day Award in 1967, organized by IIPM-TISCO, I had become popular in my campus a year before passing out and was invited as a guest of the Tatas at XLRI, Jamshedpur. I still recall how Russi Mody, in his hilarious but serious message delivered to the students as chief guest, spoke about the changes that were taking place in the business world. He narrated his story saying that learning was his passion. He got admitted to Oxford and wanted to go to England but his mother would not agree. However, after great and repeated efforts, he was able to persuade her to let him go. Mody added that till the time of his departure, she kept on giving him tips. She once said that the people in England were very sensitive and had a lot of weakness for good etiquette and culture, and ladies expected a lot of respect, courtesy and chivalry in particular. Further, she advised him to remember to be courteous to the English ladies, demonstrate chivalry by taking out the cigar and taking off the hat, mischievously adding that anything else he was able to take off depended on his luck! The auditorium resounded with laughter. The people present there—Industrial Relations (IR) students from XLRI, faculties, and many personnel professionals of Jamshedpur itself—least realized that Russi was making a serious point for future personnel and IR candidates, though in a lighter tone with the usual Russi pun. Later, while congratulating me personally during tea, he promised me a job after a year when I passed out with my degree. I recall, when I received the gold medal, I was very encouraged and wrote to him several times in the 6–8 months which I spent without a job but there was no reply. I started appreciating the 'Russi pun' over time.

In TM, one of the fundamentals is to work on developing employees' and our own Individual Development Plan (IDP). We must make our own IDPs and keep preparing and updating ourselves, enabling continuous improvement. Change is a door that can be opened from inside. As a change breaks open the door and enters, we have little time to manage the complexities most suited to meet the challenging goals, unless we have anticipated and prepared ourselves and the organization appropriately in good times.

HR exists as an HR profession if we add value, keeping the external business realities and the business context in mind, making HR solutions relevant and realistic for business. Furthermore, HR must focus on its deliverables rather than doables. Not the menu but results. Stakeholders must perceive value from HR and its solutions and HR practices, such as in the way HR professionals hire, train, pay, organize work, assess and reward. HR must give a varied menu of choices of applications created but they must make sense and deliver value to businesses.

HR also needs HR professionalism, ensuring genuineness in terms of roles.

HR personnel, hence, need to invest in themselves, keep updating their competencies and upgrading their knowledge, skill and, above all, their positive attitude. How do they do these and deliver? HRD needs to organize itself and keep developing as part of the business and align to its structure and strategy in a way that will deliver value.

NEW WAY TO TM

Unlike models of TM used by HR to deal with dynamic Bahrupian challenges, the models of supply chain management have improved a lot since the 1950s. No longer do companies own huge warehouses to stockpile components and nor are they needed to assemble years' worth of products because the competition is muted and demand is eminently predictable.[24] Since the 1980s, companies opted for JIT manufacturing processes and other supply chain management innovations that allowed them to anticipate shifts in demands and adapt products even more quickly.

The proposed ToD framework is in line with JIT. Principles drawn from operations and supply chain management were used by ever-changing Bahrupian HRs for developing innovative approaches in TM. Companies cannot take risks of long-term forecasts as employees leave so easily now.

What is the accuracy in your needed predictions of talent and the current cost implications? Quick movements of employees will need the organizations' readiness to take on cultural change with a new set of employees. Organizations will often miss having and retaining one robust culture with all its strength and consequent advantages.

The other approach could be to adapt to uncertainty in talent demand and prepare to break up the developmental programs into shorter units in place of long-term GET / MT at this juncture. They would also need to change less time-consuming training programmes, which have lower cost implications and also have a tendency to lose value. This would, therefore, be another risk reduction strategy of HR in TM.

HR has been developing and using the principle of portfolios, especially in large corporates with separate divisions. HR has used this smartly to combine and optimize both cost and risk. HR in large corporations have also developed general competencies that are effective in most positions.

Yet another approach has been to improve the return on investment in developing employees, in which an organization's HR wants employees to share in the cost of development, their absence and so on. HR has also started working for alumni approvals, making an effort to bring back investment. They have also developed and relied on bonds for cutting down risks and cost.

Another approach has been to preserve investments by balancing employer-employee interests; this is the downside of talent portability. It makes the fruits of TM/TD perishable. Till recently, employees left if they didn't have a choice of job. High internal job postings were kept in design by HR to match interests and reduce exits. HR prepared itself to negotiate solutions to match the interests of valuable talent, who tended to leave organizations. With ruthless changes during and post the Covid-19 period, along with its impact on jobs, industries, businesses and institutions, a drastic scenario change is expected, to which Bahrupias will have to adapt.

Talent problems of the employer, employees, society and economy, we have found, are closely knit and intertwined. Employers always want the right talent at the right time and at an affordable cost. Employees want prospects for advancement, control over their careers and best compensation. The economy and society need higher levels of skills and competencies in management that are best developed inside companies.

These often conflicting desires have been attempted to be addressed by existing development practices by HR professionals to the best of their knowledge, experiences, experiments or innovation. HR professionals attempt to play their roles, trying to script the roles of all the synergetic partners and even the conflicting ones.

The existing TM model's language and framework persist through a few companies' HR teams who use them. Bahrupias keep adapting to the roles of Raavan or Hanuman or even Ram by changing the needs of the roles rather than the entire play on the stage of business. Often the language, deliveries, lyrics and quotes change as per the demand and need of the people/customers—both internal and external. This language comes from engineering and planning which is not accurate any more in the long term.

The new language and framework are driven by customers, markets and operations-based tools better suited to the challenges of uncertainty. HR is seeing through these rapid and dynamic changes, enabling not just its roles, dialogues and languages but those of everyone else involved—most particularly, the viewers who assess not only one or two actors but the entire play of business performance. Hence, ToD gives HR professionals a way to manage their talent needs and recoup costs and investments in developing a way to balance the interests of both employers and employees, in the context of the delivery of a whole business on stage.

Valli 2.01

Leaders (Particularly HR Leaders) Recognizing Potential and Sponsoring Talent

NARENDRA KOTHARI

I am not a specialist in HR but a technical man from the steel industry. After graduating from college, I joined SAIL and worked for 37 years in the steel industry, till I was brought by the government to NMDC in 2014. We need talented and skilled employees to perform our work. The business has to run on a profitable and equitable basis and in an integrated way. In any profession, we need skilled people whom we have to retain. Nowadays, a lot of people are changing jobs frequently and it is a big problem for us and the HR department. So we need to introspect seriously.

Earlier it was not so. Very few people, only about 10%, left the company to join other companies. The PSU culture was like that, particularly in the steel industry, probably because the number of opportunities available was low. But nowadays, this is not the case. We recruit people. After training them for two to three years, a lot of employees switch to other companies. We need to take adequate measures because trained employees leave to go to other companies. We tried to analyze the reasons for this and found that higher wages and salaries were an important factor and comfort of the place was another consideration. For instance, a few years back, we recruited new ITI engineers at Burnpur and trained them but later we found that within one year many of them left to join railways or defence because the wages were higher there.

To retain employees, we have to see that people are reasonably paid and basic things are taken care of. I come from an industry that operates in very remote locations. At NMDC, my present company, we work in very remote locations notorious for Maoist activities, which we often read about in newspapers. If we want people to go and work in those areas, we have to give them good skills training to motivate people to work. That could help in their retention.

At NMDC, we are doing a very good job. We are a lean company with 5,000 people and are producing 30 million tons of mineral, which may be regarded as one of the most efficient as far as iron ore or the mining industry is concerned. We take good care of our people. People have to be trained and skill development has to be undertaken regularly. New people have to be appointed and trained. In the manufacturing industry of steel and mining, there are not many dynamic changes. Things are the same. The blast furnace has been continuing for the last 100 years. The fundamentals have been there for a long time though some modifications may have happened, which are mostly in automation. But still, regular capability building and upgrading are required.

Another emerging development is that highly educated people are coming in for class three and class four levels of jobs, which is creating a major difficulty. When we advertise in the papers, we will enlist the minimum qualification required for applying but would never put the limit on the highest qualification. Suppose, I need a person at the level of class three. If an engineer applies for that post, we cannot deny them and we would have to appoint them. For instance, in 1983 or 1984, I was a young officer at the junior level in the Durgapur Steel Plant. I was the shift–in-charge, and I found that a young person who had joined our organization as a semi-skilled worker had an MSc in physics. When I enquired about what he had been doing before joining the company, he said that he was a lecturer in some college and had left that job to join as an unskilled worker in Durgapur Steel Plant because the salary was higher than that of a lecturer. I found that he had a lot of enthusiasm and skills and motivated him to sit for the AMIE exam in another two or three years. Thereafter, he competed for higher positions and became the junior manager and subsequently, he became an executive and joined REC Durgapur. He did his MTech too, after that.

Valli 2.02

Devise a Sourcing Strategy—Simplicity and Effectiveness

RAJESH SAHAY

In this rapidly changing environment, where we are so exposed and accessible, everyone needs to manage their reputation because becoming a successful professional counts a lot, going forwards. Talent is mapped and invented. The management of the reputation of talent is very important. The reputation of talent is not about the standard reference check which an agency can perform for somebody. The important thing is that if someone is a frontline salesperson, then probably the reference can come from the dealer or the distributor and can impact the reputation. In the case of campus recruitment, the reputation can come from the seniors who have watched the candidate's performance earlier. If someone is a marketing person in the FMCG space, the creative agencies that work with the marketing people can help to make or mar the reputation of the individual. I maintain a very active database of all ex-employees and the reputation of all these ex-employees is very critical, in case they choose to come back to the organization.

Regarding the global workforce, organizations today may be regarded as IPL teams. In IPL teams, there are people from the Bermudas and Barbados and so on. They are all experts and they form a team. The onus is on the management of the teams to instil a sense of purpose into them and make them perform. On the surface level, if we compare all the eight IPL teams, there is very little that distinguishes the teams from each other. But finally, one team is the winner. Similarly, the ongoing challenge is in the composition of the workforce, involving people from different backgrounds, knowledge and capability who come together and are required to perform. The purpose-driven organizations, which are the winners, are the ones where though the skills may not be at a premium, the complementarity of the purpose exists. It would remain a challenge for HR leaders and business leaders to ensure that we create purpose in the organizations to bring people together.

Individuals and organizations need to manage their reputation. The workforce is very disparate, and we must bring a definite purpose so that employees may prove to be winners in their fields of operation. When we go back to the database of employees who have left us, we consider it an accountable reference. We have schemes to get talent through monetary rewards, but we always focus on an accountable reference. When a reference is made, we ensure that it contributes to the competence of the organization, is culturally compatible and adds value to the organization.

When we devise the sourcing strategy, we need to ensure that we utilize the most effective mechanism for it. The tracking of references is fairly simple. We have something known as a source-mix tracking system, wherein all the sources of references—including consultancies, social media, direct websites and so on—are periodically tracked by using data. We all have heard about various job sites such as naukri.com, shine.com, monster.com, wisdom jobs and the like. There is one job site called IIMjobs.com. We find that the quality of this site is far better than other job sites. Probably, the title of the source has created an aura that the best of the jobs and best talent seekers hunt there. Sometimes, we need to alter our hiring strategy depending on what is available in the market and we keep experimenting as well. In any sunrise industry, there is always a demand and supply issue that spirals the cost because we are typically in the auction game. We have seen it in the airline industry, the IT industry and financial service companies. When it stabilizes, these kinds of madness go away.

VALLI 2.03

THE TRANSITION FROM A MANAGER TO A LEADER—NEED FOR CONTINUOUS INTERVENTION

SUDIP BANERJEE

There has been a globalization of talent. As has happened with businesses, the same thing has happened with the talent. Businesses have moved from being local to global; much before that happened, the employees moved from being local to global. The people who may be regarded as high achievers in their careers are the ones who have not restricted themselves to working in one city or one country. By the same token, the smarter companies and smarter organizations have done the same. They have got people from all over the world to fill in the positions which they have empty.

Talent is not local; it has become global, whether it is in schools or company boards. There are a lot of schools in Bangalore where the school principals and teachers are foreigners.

The educators have come from overseas and are teaching here. In companies and organizations, the board and management teams across different levels would have several professionals who do not belong to that particular city or country. This is important from the perspective of talent acquisition and talent access.

Problems are more at the senior levels. We have a lot of managers but not enough leaders. In the last 20 years, we've grown a lot of managers, but unfortunately, there has not been a commensurate growth in the number of leaders. This is suggested by surveys as well, which mention the gaps in leadership. The growth from being a manager to being a leader requires continuous interventions. Initially, there used to be training when we entered the job and training when the job profile changed. However, training is now imparted as a part of the regular curriculum. The best organizations mandate 7 to 10 days of training interventions, particularly for senior levels, which transforms their managers into leaders.

In terms of leadership or talent access, the context has changed significantly in the last 20 years. All context in the past was seen relative to a particular industry, city or country. This paradigm has changed and all contexts are now global. The industry itself is global, the competitors are global, markets are global and the talent is also global.

The concept of building employee branding implies that people find a company a relatively easier place to work in. There are small elements that contribute to achieving this objective. For instance, when a person comes into the office and is received well, it creates a positive impression or going through the entire interview cycle and being informed about the progress at each stage creates a good impression. The thing about feeling comfortable is such that people want to continue to work for that organization. Some companies have consciously built that image and reputation. Whether somebody works for them or not, people are likely to say that it is a good company to work for. That is what we call the employer brand. For this, we need to walk the talk and provide an environment of continuous learning and be a listening organization. Some organizations are getting there, striving hard to reach the goal, and some organizations are pretending to get there. Not only would it give a competitive advantage to a company, but it would also give a business advantage. Suppliers would like to deal with such an organization, customers would like to deal with such an organization and employees would like to deal with such an organization. Therefore, all the stakeholders at 360 degrees would make for competitive business advantage.

VALLI 2.04

THE NORM FOR TALENT IS CONSTANT DISRUPTION

SURAJ CHETTRI

The global war for talent suggests that the future has a very strange way of becoming the present suddenly. If we feel that we have taken adequate steps and now we can sit back to relax since the trend is going to roll on, we are in for a rude shock because the norm for talent is constant disruption. We need people with a global mindset. It requires a completely different way of working, and there is a lot of shortage of people in that area. We need to work in global teams that involve modular work, dealing with hands-off points between different countries or project work based on continuous service. In a global company or an Indian company that has regional R&D centres in one country, manufacturing facilities in another with the supply base in a third country, we have to be someone who is a 24 × 7 person.

We are going to see a lot of changes in computing capacity, data analytics and complex domain learning where an individual will not only learn from one's own domain but will need to learn from different domains and different technologies. There will be no comparisons. Two things that are going to be important in the present context are the HR ecosystems and the HR bounty hunters. In terms of ecosystems, if we seek to map the trends around the globe, we will find resources in abundance. If we start mapping human resources or talent of a particular type found all over the world, we will have to map the HR departments of the globe. We will be able to pin down the details about a particular type of talent available in some country, not today but in the future.

If I try to draw the skill map of our organization today, we need to anticipate the changes that are likely to happen in the next three, seven or ten years within the organization. If these changes are going to take place in the sphere of technology or in the way we need to work, we will have to link them to the available talent. When we need to find sources from which to avail the right talent, we will have to identify the organizations from where we can source the talent by giving them huge salaries. Or will we build them inside?

At the same time, we need to know what other companies, that is, the competitors, are doing in this area and the circumstances in which these people will join our organization. Such is the ecosystem that one should be aware of for the specific areas of talent procurement.

Suppose a reputed employee, such as a principal scientist, suddenly leaves the organization. What should be the right approach to deal with such a situation? One is that we start searching for a substitute immediately after the employee leaves. Otherwise, we can identify someone today itself. They are called the POWs, that is, persons on the watch, included in our list of talent. This implies that we would have to map every person who works in our organization, in India and abroad, to see who can match that profile and whom we can approach immediately after the news has been disclosed. We in HR will have to keep a tab of such situations in the future.

The role of HR as bounty hunters does not involve any rocket science. We need to know the talent requirement for the future and the source from where we can get them. There is a huge amount of data available on the Internet, on social media, on LinkedIn, on websites and so on. A knowledgeable person can extract every single detail about the person—their backgrounds, preferences, likes and dislikes, life history and aspirations. The task is not very difficult and we need to develop ourselves to stay updated with the technological developments in our daily life so that we can deal with our talent requirements. Many companies, including our company, are doing this.

No one strategy fits all. Some areas are at different stages of maturity within the same organization. There could be some areas of work in which we have attained a very high maturity level, whereby we know exactly where to get the people from, what needs to be done and the strategies are in place.

Valli 2.05

There Is a Chronological Age and a Psychological Age for a Leadership Position

Dr. Vasanthi Srinivasan

The gap between the global and local is increasing rather than decreasing. Peter Senge once said that, 'All today's problems are an outcome of yesterday's solutions.' Therefore, if we consider today's talent challenges, they largely stem from the rapid growth context. Interestingly, the last article on HR rapid growth was written in 1976 from the developed world because since then, the rest of the world has seen 3%–5% growth. Very few sectors have seen double-digit growth. Therefore, a lot of people-related challenges, particularly regarding talent and its acquisition, are a local problem because we have very few answers to them from the global context. There have been several innovations that have happened in India and to scale those innovations is a challenge as far as talent acquisition is concerned.

Organizational demography has changed drastically in the last 20 years in terms of talent acquisition. Corporate India has been forced to become more diverse in the last 10 years. When talent shortages happen, the queuing theory becomes pertinent. The primary reason was the labour shortage in terms of men, and more and more women started to enter organizations. So as we exhaust the top and outstanding talents we have, we need to move deeper into tier one and tier two. The level of access, networks and capabilities that are needed for them to compete do not stand at par with what is available amongst the top talent.

If I look at the census of 2011 and try to predict what Corporate India would look like in 10 years, a large part of the young population would appear in industrial jobs. Banking and financial services, pharmaceuticals and other industries which are sales-driven would find that a large proportion of the population would come from Jharkhand, Uttarakhand, Madhya Pradesh, Uttar Pradesh and Rajasthan. This would be a major challenge. When we bring resources from economically well-developed states of India, we need to make very little investment as a company. So if we have to hire from Tamil Nadu, even from a fourth tier college, the quality of talent would be better because Tamil Nadu has had stronger infrastructural support historically.

There is too much hype about Gen Y and millennials. I have just completed a survey for a study conducted by the Society of Human Resource Management, India. My study contradicts several stereotypes that exist. There is no one, homogenous Gen Y that exists in India. The economic and social development, along with other factors like social mobility, implies that there are multiple generation Ys coexisting within our organizations.

We need to look into social mobility to understand the fundamental questions about work values, talent identification and leadership development. Also, we need to understand the impact the new generation has on the existing generations. In our research, we found a large 'Gemini twin generation'—the confused generation. They aspire for all that is material but, interestingly, when it comes to the way they behave with others it is the opposite of what they profess. During the rapid growth phase, when organizations try to get the businesses going and when they try to scale up, it is quite likely that a large number of employees from the Gemini twin generation have ended up in positions that are maybe two levels higher than what they ought to be doing.

When people are paid more and are given higher responsibilities, they know that they have earned it. But when we give more money to people, there is a tendency for people to believe that even though they may not have the skills, they have made the company believe that they do because the company has given them a much larger amount than what they deserve. And if they change five organizations, then their salary is quadrupled and they might believe that they are good which helps to cope with the higher salary and the designation that they get.

There is a chronological age and a psychological age for a leadership position. The leadership crisis today is not the absence of leadership but more in terms of whether our leaders can stretch to the kind of demands that the context places. Performance is not static. While the organizations' demands are changing, the performance criteria are also changing. The crisis of leadership probably exists because the right chronological age exists amongst the people but the psychological age may not be as high. Therefore, the leadership crisis is not about having an adequate number of leaders but about the fact that they are less prepared and they don't even realize this.

VALLI 2.06

BUSINESS DRIVING PERFORMANCE MANAGEMENT SYSTEM: THE PURPOSE IS GROWTH, PROFITABILITY AND PROFIT

A. THIRUNAVUKKARASU

Every company has a performance management system that is either driven by business or by HR. This is a debatable question. In my view, the business should drive the performance management system. In my current organization, we initiated a differentiated workforce concept where, in the senior leadership, we distinguish an 'A' category customer or 'A' category jobs from others. We may term it as critical or strategic and those people are going to make a significant difference to the business. Then, we evaluate them separately and provide coaching and development inputs in their IDPs. The Chief Human Resource Officer (CHRO), along with promoters and directors, look at this section. It comprises approximately 3% or 4% of the performance appraisees at the top levels and provides them with input and continuous feedback.

It is a cultural decision regarding whether we are willing to differentiate between employees in terms of rewarding performance. If we declare some employees as critical resources, we might lose them to the market. But as long as the system is transparent and meritocracy exists, we should have the guts to declare and differentiate performance, long-term incentives and variable pay.

However, once we declare this for a particular short-term period or a couple of years, then it remains in the appraisers' heads that that particular employee is a permanent high-potential employee. This needs periodic checks to see if the situation has changed, the market has changed and business has also changed. Irrespective of individual development plans or growth plans, if a role or work ceases to be significant, then I should be shifting my focus to another, who may be 10 or 15 years younger. The managerial mindset is more important than the various systems and processes.

When we go to the campus, we should be going with a positive mindset of selecting the pupil and inspiring people to join. Similarly, in the performance appraisal system, irrespective of our level in the organization, as an appraiser it is important to know whether we are going to evaluate or enable better performance. If we are intending to enable the performance of our subordinates, then there are changes required in body language and the dialogue of performance appraisal. Instead of telling people what they should do, we should introspect from our side about how to inspire people to perform better.

Whether we like it or not, performance and rewards are inseparable. Perceived value is very important. In my previous assignment, we wanted to implement a stock options scheme for all levels. We also wished for management trainees to be recruited as per the Graduate Engineer Trainee (GET) scheme. It was a London listed stock options scheme. There were concerns raised about these GETs all being young people and about our offering them this scheme when other companies were offering this to GM and above only. There was a suggestion that we give them a fixed retention pay, say five lakhs or six lakhs, after three years since they would leave the organization after three years. We debated this issue and decided that we would talk to the stakeholders, the young trainees. We asked them whether they would want cash or stock options 6 or 7 lakhs after 3 years that is guaranteed or 40% of the 6 lakhs or 0 if TSR does not happen, which may go up to 10 lakhs or so. But nine out of ten young people, including newly joined candidates, said that they would like to avail stock options.

We have been trained to say that people will retire at 55 or 60 years. Long-term careers have declined and show slow growth. Today, people are willing to relax at 45, and they want to create wealth quickly. We need to be ready to create good opportunities for young people and then the average age would be brought down. Who am I to plan their future career up to the age of 60 years, because probably they will move out after 45 years and become entrepreneurs? Are we ready to take this kind of bold challenge?

Please don't complicate things further by adding one more appraisal form related to leadership dialogue or performance dialogue and so on. I have seen many guidelines such as we should spend 70 minutes on leadership dialogue, out of which 20 minutes we should talk about family, followed by other concerns and so on. HR heads have got this idea that paperwork surpasses all important matters rather than purpose. Sometimes, the purpose is forgotten and processes start driving us. Let us go back to the purpose due to which all these things are happening. The purpose is growth, profitability and profit. We need to reinvest for stakeholders and convince them.

Valli 2.07

Workforce Transformation Happens in a Deliberate Way for Strategic Reasons

L. Prabhakar

Workforce transformation happens in a deliberate way for strategic reasons. Often, HR leaders believe that they are responsible for leading the transformation and take great pride in owning this. However, a specific set of dimensions determine whether such transformation is primarily driven by HR leaders or business leaders or whether is it more a case of co-creation. There are three such specific dimensions.

Firstly, the context. This includes competitiveness, capabilities and customers. For instance, the context might be related to a major IR challenge in the business, wherein the workforce transformation has a significant element of employee relationships, engagement and, eventually, contribution. In such cases, the primary responsibility for transformation would be with HR. However, in case the context is a launch of a new product category or a merger and acquisition, then the primary ownership for co-creation would be with the CEO, with HR needing to play a very proactive role.

The second dimension is the time horizon. The co-creation ownership tends to shift more towards the CEO when we are looking at a longer time horizon. The more distant the horizon, along with a lack of clarity, the ownership and lead for co-creation rests with the CEO. The more immediate it is, with a focus on execution excellence and agility, it is for HR to take the lead for co-creation.

The last dimension is in terms of the execution hierarchy or execution criticality. When we have to build workforce capability at the senior levels, then the co-creation has to be owned by the CEO. However, if we intend to have the workforce capability creation at the frontline levels, then HR can and should take the lead in terms of co-creation.

Many organizations pursued a philosophy of predominantly building capability. But given the dynamic changes happening both in the business and talent context, organizations are now being forced to work on a blended model of build and buy. The blended model also has a significant component of partnerships with specialized agencies, either for speed, specialism or scale or because of a belief that such capabilities are not necessarily core.

We need to inculcate the habit and practice of proactively building business scenarios and then matching the same with talent scenarios to identify gaps, the consequences of the same and the best way to mitigate the risks or possible negative consequences. The concept of new-age learning is showcased when the individual says: don't tell me anything already available on websites. And what is not available on the Internet is experience and insights. An HR professional who can bring his/her experience and insights, along with functional expertise, is more likely to be part of the co-creation of workforce capabilities. Hence, the key requirement of new-age learning is creating an ecosystem where HR professionals go through crucibles of experiences, ideally through different business cycles and are guided by seniors to reflect on such experiences and convert them into insights. Insights so gathered then need to be further discussed, deliberated upon and deployed to evolve both a robust strategy and strengthen the competency. This, when shared within and outside the organization, helps build institutions. This has to be a 'deliberate' process.

VALLI 2.08

CAPABILITY BUILDING—EXPERIENCE WITH MENTORING AND COACHING

RACHNA MUKHERJEE

Corporates all over the world are realizing the dynamic nature of today's workforce and that it is the 'new reality'. Multiple factors contribute to this phenomenon, such as the workforce which has rare competencies, bigger ambitions and expectations. They are young, more diverse, extremely well-connected and technology savvy. And while these millennials are the prime workforce, so is the older workforce, also known as the baby boomers, members of which continue to front-end as leaders in various organizations while mentoring Gen X employees.

With new competencies and skillsets that are rare, companies are being compelled to effectively incorporate these diverse generations into the work environment. They are being forced to develop innovative training programmes, where Gen Z can closely work with the leadership, and offer opportunities for long-term growth and personal development. After all, a company can only be successful if it establishes strong workplace relationships for the long haul.

In line with the global trend, India has witnessed the most rapid technological evolution with the proliferation of social media, smart devices, analytics and the cloud. This has led to organizations and HR leaders realizing the need to craft well-defined policies to help the baby boomers effectively cope with the influx of these new technologies. Organizations that had long foreseen these changes were well prepared to deal with the technological effects on their workforce and current and future recruitments.

An important aspect of today's recruitment process is to ensure the right balance between generalist and specialist workers in a company. Potential companies are more likely to be distinguished by a diverse array of T-shaped employee skills that aim towards the integration of generalists and experts. While the top line represents the generalist with good basic knowledge and understanding of operations, the vertical line reflects the skilled professionals—supposedly, the domain specialists. As such, it becomes imperative to fine-tune a scientific perspective for different work aspects that support a boost in performance quality and work productivity.

The aspirations of today's skilled generation are going beyond measures, and companies are under constant pressure to implement creative HR approaches that offer greater convenience and flexibility. Organizations are running well-defined leadership programmes catering to all generations to help them become future leaders. Policies like family leave, long maternity and paternity leaves and sabbatical leaves are being introduced and implemented successfully. Such initiatives are not only smashing the adage that says 'leaders are born, not made' but also producing new-age leaders of tomorrow. This augments employee satisfaction and increases efficiency and retention.

Employee expectations are changing dramatically. Corporates are increasingly committing to and introducing innovative programmes to not only attract but also retain talent. While adapting to new technologies is certainly crucial, having motivated and talented employees is an absolute must! The 'ideal workplace' is no longer a myth but a reality that has transcended conventional corporate paradigms.

VALLI 2.09

MULTIGENERATIONAL AND HIGHLY DIVERSE WORKFORCE

UMA DEVAGUPTAPU

I proudly represent the manufacturing industry and speak for the manufacturing industry. The major challenge in modern times is to attract talent to the industry. The workforce today is not only multigenerational but is also highly diverse. There is gender diversity and also socio-economic diversity that we see at the workplace. Things that we, the baby boomer generation, took for granted are not even thought of as basic requirements by the workforce that comes in today. And similarly, things considered very important by Gen Y were perhaps not even on the horizon or on our radar at any point in time.

Though the demography is in our favour, the paradox is that we are also seeing that people are working longer. At any point in time, even in the IT and IT Enabled Service (ITeS) industries, we have at least four generations of people working together at the workplace. And when we have so many generations working together, we cannot gear ourselves to work with one particular generation. Today, Gen Y is perceived to be different; probably in earlier times, the baby boomers said the same for Gen X and the earlier generation said the same about the subsequent generations. The important aspect is adaptability. When we talk about transformative interventions, the Indian experience or situations dealing with acquired companies in Africa, Asia or even in developed markets like Australia, the key factor is enterprise contribution. At some level, workforce capability is very strongly linked to enterprise capability.

If the enterprise stands for a certain standard, the workforce capability will follow. The major leadership challenge is about enterprise capability benchmarking—setting the bar—so that all the investments then easily come forth. The transformations that occur in workforce capability building are gradual steps that are very closely linked to other flex points in organizational life. When the organization decides that its enterprise capability needs to be enhanced to survive or to grow in the markets that it operates in, workforce capability will follow. The important thing with the multigenerational workforce is to recognize that the people are marching to different drummer's tune. We need to find means to personalize the enterprise capability experience, building them into each individual's question of what is in it for me. The organizations which can synthesize this are the successful ones.

I think the strategy in our case regarding whether to buy or build talent is borrowed from biotechnology; the idea is to create for every new skill, a nucleus which we may buy and then let the cells proliferate by building along that nucleus. It is fundamental to human nature and natural for everybody to like people who are like them. So we need to look for that commonality so that we can establish it in an organization that has people from all walks of life, belonging to different genders, different socio-economic strata, different language groups and different dressing styles. In the organizational context, therefore, we have a great opportunity to create that organizational identity which allows for inclusion and then allows people to build capability. We need that common factor that says that you are like me so that it can bring us together and we can all grow.

Valli 2.10

The Way Forward—Coaching and Development; Positioning PMS to Bring about Desired Change

BARTTANU KUMAR DAS

We need a good performance management system to create a performance culture in the organization. We cannot completely abandon whatever systems exist, irrespective of whether they are bad or good. We need to move from a bad system to a good system.

We need to consider the various challenges for the future, especially when we talk about leadership challenges, learning and development challenges and so on. Information related to these is gathered from various surveys and reports. The performance management system should be an enabler for meeting these requirements of leadership and learning and development. We have made it bureaucratic and more process-driven and have not looked at the real power of the performance management system. We need to look at the subject holistically for ways to make performance management 'management by target' instead of 'management of targets' or objectives. We have to position this performance management system as a powerful tool of management of achievements, which constitutes a major shift.

HR leadership needs to work with business leaders to create this shift and transformation. Today, the employees, managers and even HR folks hate the current performance management system that has been revealed by various surveys. We need to change this into a process that they like and appreciate enough to use as a tool for self-development. Getting feedback is a powerful tool in terms of the quality of discussion we engage in. In my 25 years of experience, I have not seen the quality of discussion on performance management systems amongst the reporting managers. People do not have such amounts of time.

Initiatives that we had launched in our organization to position and bring out the development focus include an executive development review or a development dialogue for the managers. This process was ranked as the best by around 600 managers and we were forced to wonder why we had not done this earlier. Direct involvement of the business head and HR facilitator or the HR head and the reporting manager gives excellent feedback about the kind of open and transparent environment we have been able to create. This initiative has been adjudged the best or the highest-ranking HR process in the company.

I am convinced that the way forward is coaching and development and positioning the performance management system to bring about the desired change. HR has to work and invest more in talent development.

Valli 2.11

There Is a Need for Increasing the Pitch and Frequency of Dialoguing

GAUTAM CHAINANI

Processes like goal-setting are no longer static and need to be reviewed every quarter, even in the manufacturing sector. This is similar to financial services.

The second issue happening is in manufacturing where more and more cross-functional teams are working on different business projects. Today, the supervisor could be from the finance sector or technology sector or an alternative field. We need to get feedback from these resources as part of the performance management process.

The third thing that is happening is that structures are no longer static and are getting revised and reviewed every year. At one point in time, in the manufacturing sector, we could review structures once in 10 years but now we need to work on them every year. The new millennials that are entering the manufacturing field are similar to the millennials in the services business. They are looking at growth and feedback development. At the same time, they are looking for multiple career opportunities.

There are a few things we must do in this space to increase the pitch and frequency of dialoguing and to increase the level of engagement feedback that we are getting. After every performance review process every year, we reach out to over 7,000 employees of our organization seeking actual feedback on various parameters. One of these is the quality of discussions with the manager; another is about the preparedness of the manager—whether he / she is prepared as per the perception of the subordinate; yet another relates to the time the manager spends with the subordinate for the review of performance—does he/she spend 30 minutes or 15 minutes, and so on. Further, we try to find out the degree of satisfaction with the entire appraisal process amongst the employees.

This data is being fed back to managers and is being sliced and diced into regions, verticals and functions so that more and more feedback starts to flow in. People are getting more and more sensitized about what the organization is seeking feedback about. After a survey, someone came up to me and informed me that his manager had done his performance appraisal while they were standing and waiting for the security check-in at the airport. It was a long line and the manager suggested that they complete the appraisal process now itself because by the time they would check in their baggage, they would be able to finish the whole exercise.

We took another initiative from the services side. We wrote to all our employees that they can click a selfie with the manager at the end of the appraisal process and send it across. Many of the diehard folks from the manufacturing sector said that this will never work. But to our surprise, out of the 6,500 people that we have, 3,500 actually posted selfies back to us with their managers. There is a huge amount of engagement and there is a huge amount of dialogue that needs to set up the trends, going forward.

The growing role of technology is going to be very critical. With all the analytics and data mining, the sharper focus that we have with numbers and data is going to ensure that a lot of information going to be available to both manager and employee. But no matter how many texts we get or how tech-intensive we get, culture and engagement derive from high touch. Dialoguing will continue but the level, calibre and discussion will be much different from what was happening today. So for example, while Gen Y or baby boomers just swallowed everything that the boss said, conversations with the new millennials are going to be quite different. They will not hesitate to point out whatever is wrong based on what the results suggest. Millennials may come and inform the boss that they are unable to find a career in the present company and so would be looking for it somewhere else. This is the level of frankness and transparency that may come up and we need to be ready to take that kind of feedback.

If we look at the correlation coefficient between pay and performance and run it over for a period of five or seven years, then we will not get the coefficient of correlation beyond 0.35 or 0.4. This is a fairly weak correlation coefficient. So while we talk of pay as a great differentiator, actually, many other overriding factors play a role and these different variables add to the whole thing.

VALLI 2.12

NOTHING SUCCEEDS LIKE MEETING EMPLOYEES FACE TO FACE WHILE WORKING ON ENGAGEMENT OR CREATING CULTURE

DR. RITU ANAND

Recently, we had an executive education programme just for women leaders. I am not going to go into its diversity but it is about engagement, and we have a substantial number of international employees who are non-Indians. Every other month I call them but I always feel sceptical. How do I engage with Americans? How do I engage Latin Americans who don't understand the language that we use? English is not their first language. We are a global and multicultural company, and we are committed to becoming really inclusive.

But what we find is that they actually need the same kinds of inputs, stimuli, engagement and drivers that Indians need. So the myth is actually broken. I do believe that nothing succeeds as well as meeting your employees face to face.

About 20 years ago, there were no malls in India and mobile phones were just coming in with costs of about ₹16 or ₹20 per call. In those years, if anyone went to the US and you called that person, they would often send a message saying 'please leave your message and we will call you back'. So I wondered what this voicemail was. I had never heard of this voicemail concept in India. How do we talk to this person? Why is he / she never available on the phone?

So I learnt the art of engaging with those employees through voicemail. I learnt the art of leaving a voicemail in an engaging voice, nurturing, caring, without asking questions about leaves or their competency gaps to give you a development plan or an intervention.

Your children should not blindly go for HR degrees but they should specialize in something that makes them feel important and adds value to their lives. Then, that becomes the fulcrum and the basis for you to have a conversation with the other person. Why are we spending all our lives trying to tell the operations guys how to engage? They will know how to engage because they will give value to the employee.

So there are three learnings that I take for myself. If I go to office on Monday, what can I do? What will I do in this new scenario? I will link the engagement with the individual while the guidelines and framework will be common for the company. However, when I am implementing or connecting with the employee, it will be uniquely made for him/her. So do you dare to do it or can you do it? Or will you wait for the orders from your boss? I leave that to you.

Secondly, start accepting the fact that he/she knows more than what you do. So in that scenario, reward and recognition are going to be very big players. Thirdly, I have understood that the way we measure our performance is not the way to measure it in the future. Today, the number of people hired, the average cost of hire or the number of people who resigned is not going to define the success of the organization because our employment models have changed and we want a more flexible workforce.

BNP Paribas is a global organization. They are now experimenting with and going for project-based hiring. It was very impressive and it was written in a book and I am sure some of you must be doing it already but doing it on a pan-organization basis requires an extraordinary commitment. In that scenario, the metrics of the performance of our department and our company have to change, and that is where we need to work. Whether we call it analytics or some other way, I leave that to you, but this is something about which you should get disturbed. Either change the way we are working or change the profession that we are in and move ahead.

VALLI 2.13

THE NEW AGE PERFORMANCE MANAGEMENT SYSTEM—OLD WINE IN A NEW BOTTLE

T.K. SRIRANG

It is too early to declare whether the new-age performance management system is old wine in a new bottle. We need to understand this new age performance management system that is being proposed. A lot of focus has been on feedback or 'check-in', the new jargon that is being used. The big shift requires managers to meet the subordinates and team members regularly and provide feedback on an ongoing basis.

In my opinion, the old performance management system did not hinder the giving of regular feedback. Indian organizations jumped onto this bell curve bandwagon in 2000, not fully realizing what could be its consequences. And the worry is that a lot of us are focusing on doing away with the bell curve.

Therefore, before we rush into this new wave of discussion, we need to think about what is so new about the performance management system.

A performance management system is always a business process and not an HR process. This is something that needs to be reviewed. We tend to focus disproportionately on rewards as tools for managing performance. Over the years, we have seen that if we give people incentives and offer more money as a bonus, automatically the performance is good. This brings us to some fundamental issues. Traditionally, the concept of incentives was largely used when there was an adverse relationship between the management and the workers. Incentives were used to release their efforts.

Unfortunately, over the years, we have blindly used it across sectors. Today, I believe the major challenge in organizations is about the release of ability and not effort. But we use incentives for that. Rating is largely a process of distribution of rewards. Doing away with the bell curve is not synonymous with doing away with the performance management system since the bell curve is just a small part of performance management.

The discussion which most organizations are struggling with is the challenge of differentiation. It has nothing to do with the bell curve or normalization. Instead, it relates to the dilemma of whether to differentiate or not to differentiate. We know that if we differentiate there are consequences; if we don't differentiate, then also there are consequences. The fundamental framing of the issue is related to an understanding of the more acceptable consequence amongst these. And as long as differentiation continues, all the consequences that are associated with differentiation would continue to exist.

We need to challenge some of the discussions that have happened. We all follow some distribution but we never follow a bell curve. As we go up to senior levels, no distribution is followed. Yet, we believe that we will follow the bell curve concept in India. Most organizations follow a very loose distribution, which may sometimes be left-skewed or right-skewed depending on various market conditions.

Performance assessment should be done once a year to be fair because we cannot judge performances in anything less than that. The new performance management system proposes to increase the frequency of feedback.

Formalizing these feedback sessions would make it bureaucratic and create systems around it. We should give more feedback but I don't think we should leave it as a loose structure, foregoing formal reporting systems. Otherwise, after five years we will be doing away with this as well.

The life cycle of employees is changing. In every organization, there are a set of people who inherently invest in their teams and do it very well. We can have some systems and processes to ensure the threshold or minimum delivery. It is a challenge that has existed for a long time. For instance, when I initiated a programme on coaching and mentoring employees in 1996, some people did it brilliantly while some people struggled to do it. That struggle continues even after so many years.

Valli 2.14

Will the Human Resource Function Be Needed at All?

S. PARASURAMAN

It seems that we are now ready for deglobalization. All that was built in the last 30 years, in terms of integrating the world, will have to be dismantled. I don't know whether HR will be needed at all or whether HR will be meaningful at all in the days to come, fundamentally because of the way technology is replacing people. More and more people are being put out of work; they are not needed to work in the economy or by society. And what you are dealing with at this point and in the coming days will be a very small fraction of the people who contribute to your production process, because most of them are out of your range.

This is why I see the coming era as an era between the First World War and the Second World War, where much of the deglobalization took place, thereby redefining the economic paradigm. It is going to be an extremely disruptive process. And it is disruptive fundamentally because about 62 individuals possess 50% of all the wealth of the world. Now, you cannot have such a concentration of wealth. Only 1% of the whole population accounts for 90% of the world's wealth. We have created a context whereby people are irrelevant. Some people get paid abnormally at the cost of displacing a whole lot of people and that is not the sort of process by which societies can survive. So we are entering a phase where we are going to see a whole lot of bloodshed. The organized sector is going to become irrelevant because they are not cared for. Deglobalization is going to be similar to climate change. Climate change is going to have highly unintended consequences as well, and we need to be prepared for that process in the context of deglobalization.

CHAPTER 3

ORGANIZATION OF THE FUTURE: THE NEXT YUGA

'We understand how dangerous a mask can be.
We all become what we pretend to be.'

– Patrick Rothfuss

UPAKOSALA

Upakosala was the son of Kamala. He dwelt as a brahmachari with Satyakama Jabala, living with and learning from Satyakama for 12 years. At the end of his study, when he was about to leave the house of Satyakama, he was not allowed to depart. He became very sad when he came to know that all his friends were allowed to go.

The wife of Satyakama was very kind towards Upakosala, and she pleaded with her husband to allow Upakosala to go home like the rest of his disciples. Satyakama not only refused to do so but also went off on a journey. At this point, Upakosala was so sad and sick at heart that he could not eat. The teacher's wife treated him with tender affection, offered him food but to no avail. She kept insisting that he must eat otherwise he would not survive. At last, the boy cried out to her saying, 'O mother, my heart is still so impure; I am too unhappy to eat!'

Satyakama knew that Upakosala had not yet learned all that was necessary for him to know and was not ready to lead the life of a householder as per dharma. Upakosala, too, was aware that his was not an academic failure but rather one of interior disposition. He kept saying to Satyakama's wife that in him there were many desires which tended to focus on many things. Upakosala understood that the desires may not be negative or foolish, yet they pull one in many directions, whirling one around and confusing one's mind and consuming all of one's life energies. He was determined to develop focus and commitment, engage in true hard work and keep meditating on truth. Only when the mind is fixed on the One can the many be safely attended to. Upakosala kept aspiring to attain this oneness with the One.

One day, he heard a voice from the Brahman or Agni, the yajna's sacred fire, say to him, 'This life is Brahman, the sky is Brahman, bliss is Brahman, know thou Brahman!'

To this Upakosala replied, 'I know that life is Brahman but I do not know that the sky is Brahman or that bliss is Brahman.'

Again came the voice from the fire, this time explaining that sky meant the lotus of the heart, wherein dwells Brahman, and that bliss meant the bliss of Brahman. 'Both,' said the voice, 'refer to Brahman.' Continuing, it taught Upakosala, 'Earth, food, fire, sun—all these that you worship—are forms of Brahman. He who is seen in the sun—that one am I. He who dwells in the east, in the north, in the west and the south, he who dwells in the moon, in the stars and water—that one am I. He who dwells in the sky and makes the lightning his home—that one also am I. Know well the true nature of the world that it may never do you harm.'

Thereupon, the fire, which had been only an earthly fire with which to prepare sacrifices, assumed a new aspect and became the Lord himself. The earth was transformed; life was transformed; the sun, the moon, the stars, the lightning—everything was transformed and defied. And thus, it was that the true nature of all things was revealed to Upakosala.

In due time, Satyakama returned home. When he saw Upakosala, he said, 'My son, your face shines like one who knows Brahman. Who has taught you and how?' 'Beings other than men,' replied Upakosala. 'And intense commitment and hard work.' Then said Satyakama, 'My son, what you have learned is true. True also is this that I teach you now. Lo, to him who knows it shall no evil cling, as drops of water cling not to the leaf of the lotus. He who glows in the depths of your eyes—that is Brahman; that is the self of yourself. He is the most Beautiful One, he is the Luminous One. In all the worlds, forever and ever, he shines!'

Thus, Satyakama explained more about Brahman to Upakosala and finally declared him as a worthy disciple.

(*Chandogya Upanishad*)

Editors' Treatise

Organization of the Future: The Next Yuga*

na ekam cakram bhramayati[25]
(One wheel cannot make a cart roll)
sampadya atmanam anvichhet sahayavan
(After equipping oneself, seek helpers)

The organization structure defines how activities such as tasks, coordination and supervision are directed towards achieving organizational aims and objectives. The organizational structure affects the actions of the organization and provides the foundation on which Standard Operating Procedures (SoPs) and routine rest. This is a very basic requirement for organizing business and delivering results. Over time, there have been several types of organization structures, being a hierarchical structure, matrix structure, horizontal/flat structure, network structure, divisional structure, line organization structure and team-based structure.

* Yuga: A yuga in Sanatan Dharma is a large period of time, as it relates to the past, present and future. It is mostly used to describe one of the four dharmic ages—Satya yuga, Treta yuga, Dwapar yuga and the Kali yuga. A yuga cycle is a cyclic age (epoch) in Hindu cosmology, where eternal time repeats general events. As the cycle progresses, each yuga's length is often related to the condition of the Earth and humanity's general moral and physical state decreases. Near the end of Kali yuga (the current time), when virtues are at their worst, a cataclysm (a Pralaya) happens and reestablishment of dharma occurs to usher in the next yuga cycle. Kali yuga, which is believed to have started in 3102 BCE, when Lord Krishna left for his heavenly abode, is expected to last for 432,000 years. It might be thus appropriate to make the calculation that Kali yuga will end sometime in 2025 CE. With another 500 years of the sandhi period (overlap period,) it should be complete by 2525 CE. The overlap period of 500 years is a period when Kali yuga (the outgoing yuga) and the Dwapara (the incoming or the ascending new yuga) will together present a portion of yuga, improving and entering into the new yuga. (Collated from Wikipedia)

The hierarchical model is the most popular organizational chart type. In a hierarchical organization structure, employees are grouped, with every employee having one clear supervisor.

In a matrix organizational structure, the reporting relationships are set up as a grid or matrix, rather than in the traditional hierarchy.

A horizontal structure is an organizational chart type mostly adopted by small companies and startups in their early stage and many levels of middle management are eliminated in this structure. This enables employees to make decisions quickly and independently.

A network organizational structure is not only less hierarchical but is also more decentralized and more flexible. It is viewed as more agile than other structures as it has fewer tiers, more control and a bottom flow of decision-making.

A divisional structure has divisions that correspond to either products or geographies. Each division contains the necessary resources and functions needed to support the product line and geography and the main advantage is its independent operational flow, in which the failure of one company does not threaten the existence of the others.

Line organizational structure is one of the simplest types of organizational structures. Its authority flows from the top and each department head has control over their departments, whose main characteristic is a self-contained department structure.

A team-based organizational structure is made of teams working towards a common goal while working on their individual tasks. It is less hierarchical, with flexible structures that reinforce problem-solving, decision-making and teamwork. Manufacturing companies that work together with suppliers around the globe and need to keep costs to a minimum while still producing high-quality products prefer this.

Time and again, we have been talking about 'change'. Business people have also been examining change from time to time and working fervently to align themselves to change.

It is very interesting to go through *The Fourth Industrial Revolution*, a book by K. Schwab,[26] founder, World Economic Forum. In one of his presentations, he said that we are at the beginning of a revolution that is fundamentally changing the way we live, work and relate to one another. Going through the history of business in the world, everybody can understand change and how it has been developing disruption as well as allowing growth. The First Industrial Revolution used water and steam power to mechanize and improve efficiency, speed and productivity. This was around 1784. The Second Industrial Revolution developed and used electric power to enable mass production after around 90 years. The Third Industrial Revolution used electronics and IT to automate production. This was around 1960 and the whole business world was impacted tremendously by this change. We know how the world has changed thereafter by using IT, Internet, WiFi and so on, improving the quality of work-life as well as speed and productivity at the workplace.

We are always reminded of a reference from the Manusmriti: '*Parivartanaiv Shashwatam*'. Change is the only permanent.

Schwab suggests a Fourth Industrial Revolution, caused by a fusion of physical, digital and biological change. He refers to this revolution as 'cognification'. We are now talking about megatrends happening, significantly impacting the world, business, society and people.

In terms of physical megatrends, he mentions tangible change like autonomous vehicles, 3D printing, advanced robotics and a host of new materials being developed, which are lighter, stronger, recyclable, adaptive and smart.

For the second megatrend, happening on the digital front, we may refer to IoT (Internet of Things), which is the relationship between things (product, services, places and so on) and people all around. Blockchain is also a bridge between physical and digital platforms getting developed with matching supply and demand in a very accessible way.

The third megatrend, developing on the biological front, involves genomes, synthetic biology, customized organisms formed by writing DNA and data to increase medicine precision that targets therapies.

The above changes have greatly impacted the economies, businesses, nations, society and individuals, creating opportunities as well as threats.

In terms of impact on the economy and the critical dimensions we see, growth in technology and innovation has the potential to unleash a surge in productivity, change the face and nature of employment and enable the emergence of new skills and nature of work, while helping the workforce create a portfolio of things to generate income. While the velocity of disruption will increase, there will be a certainty of the acceleration of innovation. Impact on business will be tremendous, particularly in the areas of customer expectation, development of data-enabled products, new collaborations and a new operating model with a philosophy of always being in beta, which means one will always be evolving. There will be an impact on the national front, where disruptive changes are redefining how public institutions and organizations that operate in cities will need to act like entrepreneurs and compete with others in attracting talent. Talking of impact on societies, the biggest challenge of society will be how to absorb and accommodate the new modernity while still embracing traditional values. There will certainly be an emergence of a self-centred or a 'me-centred' society.

As far as individuals are concerned, the Fourth Industrial Revolution is not only what we do but also who we are. This megatrend is going to change our identity as human beings in various aspects like behaviour, privacy, ownership, consumption, time for work and time for leisure.

Schwab's interest in the Fourth Industrial Revolution is quite revealing but at the same time, it shares the possibilities and opportunities of growth through efficiency, quality and productivity, which have been the desire of humankind in all spheres. Things will drastically change with this revolution. Technology like IoT can create a network of physical objects or things embedded with electronic software sensors and network connectivity, which enables all these objects to exchange data. This allows objects to be sensed and controlled remotely. The existing network infrastructure creates opportunities for more direct integration between the physical world and computer-based systems, resulting in improved efficiency, accuracy and economic benefit. The business world seems to be going towards high speed and radical revolutionary change in the economy, society and people. This will require an overall change in work-life, procedures and systems.

Deloitte Global Human Capital Trends Reports in 2017[27] and onwards have been raising several issues about the need for organizations of the future. BIMTECH, in partnership with Deloitte India and NHRDN, has been bringing out these issues via several Round Tables all over the country—particularly in major metros—and sharing with professionals ideas on how the organization of the future may need to be changed.

THE ORGANIZATION OF THE FUTURE

High-performing organizations operate as empowered networks, coordinated through culture, information systems and talent mobility. Companies are focused on redesigning the organization itself with nearly a half actively studying and developing new models. And many organizations are not only designing but also building this new organization. As networks and ecosystems replace organizational hierarchies, the traditional question of 'For whom do you work?' has been replaced by 'With whom do you work?'

The way high-performing organizations operate today is radically different from how they operated 10 years ago. Yet, many other organizations continue to operate according to industrial-age models that are 100 years old or more, weighed down by legacy practices, systems and behaviours that must be confronted and discarded before true change can take hold.

As organizations become more digital, they face a growing imperative to redesign themselves to move faster, adapt more quickly, facilitate rapid learning and embrace the dynamic career demands of their people. Leading organizations are moving past the design phase and actively building this new organization. Still, many business leaders seem to have little confidence that they will get the process right.

This concern is warranted. Organizational design and change are complex. Many organizational redesigns fail because they are reduced to an exercise to cut costs. Others face resistance from company leadership. Many consulting firms anecdotally report that up to 70% of reorganizations fall short because of 'creative disobedience' from the executive team.

Frustration is also common. Designing the organization of the future is a difficult and, sometimes, messy project of trial and error; not an exercise on paper. It is a continuous, dynamic and, in a sense, neverending process. Yet for companies that rise to the challenge, the payoff can be immense in terms of financial performance, productivity, employee engagement and a host of other benefits.

It requires trust in yourself, particularly as a leader and HR of the organization where managing change and creating a transformation for the success of the organization in the future becomes a Protean challenge or a Bahrupian challenge. Today's times need to drive excellence and continuous improvement for competitive advantage. This requires a continuous renewal of the organization, its processes, its vision, mission, values and also a creation of it as a learning organization. The success of the company depends on this.

Change has been professed by not merely management professionals and academicians but everyone who is a philosopher or a scientist. They have all talked of change as an imminent feature in the life of mankind. There could be anticipatory change, which is slightly comfortable; there could be aspirational change, which is planned as per your desire; or, there could be a tsunami change or a surprise change, which is shocking and destructive. Change is imminent but if we want to deal with new change opportunities with old thinking we will be running on the spot like Alice when she goes to the giant chessboard with the red queen in Wonderland. We don't want to do that, and we know that if the change outside us is faster than the speed of change within us, then we will be gone. There is no way of survival or success. In so far as people are concerned, it is fundamentally difficult to change people and if it is possible, it will be by changing the context. E.M. Goldratt, a businessman, talks of transformational and holistic change as contrasted to segmental change and talks about managing change and execution of plans as complementary roles. HR professionals have a big role as they have the easiest access to the people in the organization. They can easily develop credibility and contacts, therefore, making the role of HR very critical. Success will depend upon creating leaders at all levels and all teams as leadership is latent in us and we have to only energize this as an instrument of managing change or creating change.

Often, we start thinking that we are the best. That is the ordinary and most common rationale of belief in the minds of people. So HR will have to contribute substantially to the organization's vision, mission, values and holistically the culture of the workplace. If we miss out on this, we are missing an opportunity and undermining the challenge. Leaders, more particularly HR leaders, will have to keep thinking about the question of how they can inspire their team to become energized and deliver a sustainable organization with continued success.

We remember the story of eight blind men and the elephant from the Jatakas. We will, as HR professionals, ensure that our appreciation improves our perception to understand every aspect of business holistically and not like each of the blind men did. Today, HR is taking people and teams of people to a higher level of excellence, inspiring them to actualize the direction and goal of the organization and then motivating people and teams with the strength of personal character. This favour or advantage is available to HR because leadership and success influence each other. Generally, leadership development or motivation of the team is based on performance and potential assessment by others, which depends largely on a company's expectation from their leaders. The Pygmalion effect works and works very well. People live up to their image, their expectations of teachers or coaches or leaders and bring a continuous zeal for improvement. HR will have to teach and develop meta virtues in the heart of the teams within the organization. Meta virtues would consist of action plans like 'if I don't know, I will explore'. These are critical and essential virtues for people who want to develop themselves regularly, and HR has to generate a feeling and confidence among the team of people that they can develop themselves independent of others if need be.

This will all depend on emotional leadership, which will require the team to be optimistic, authentic, high-energy, sincere and very resonant. This emotional leadership is laden with control, zeal, persistence and the ability to motivate oneself. In simple words, this is an intelligent and careful use of your and others' emotions for business results.

One is reminded of Dr. Sumantra Ghosal's idea of radical performance, which came to him from one of his mentors. This progresses on the belief that ordinary people can create extraordinary results. We must look at our vision—whatever we may create, whatever an organization puts before us. But somewhere, we are missing out on the optimum potential.

While dealing with the idea of change or transformation, Dr. Sumantra Ghosal speaks of a framework of cooking sweet and sour.[28] He says that a successful transformation in an organization is possible when both sweet and sour cycles are completed and not merely one of them—a very rare key to success. This is what he clarifies as radical performance improvement in an organization. Clarifying the sour part of the cycle, he speaks of improving resource productivity, which generally hurts the people, the team and the organization as it involves portfolio choice, improving labour productivity, improving operating per employee, improving capital productivity, ROCE and so on. This is generally disliked by employees and teams as it is quite often hurtful. On the other hand, the sweet of the cycle is creating and exploiting new opportunities. This covers growth opportunities like working on new products and markets and expanding the share. It also involves building competencies and developing new capabilities and resources and organizational capabilities—revitalizing the organization and its people. Such a transformation is complete and delivers excellence even though the journey is sometimes fairly painful. While it sounds exciting, it also involves a great deal of fear and acute pain. This is a metamorphosis—the pain that a caterpillar goes through and the fear that it has to face. It is like a roller-coaster ride, emotionally draining and almost like a journey to the valley of death.

ORGANIZING FOR SPEED, AGILITY AND ADAPTABILITY

As previously discussed in Chapter 2, in the past, most organizations were designed for efficiency and effectiveness, leading to complicated and siloed organizations. The resulting business models, which were based on predictable commercial patterns, are unsuited to an era of unpredictability and disruption. Instead of mere efficiency, successful organizations must be designed for speed, agility and adaptability to enable them to compete and win in today's global business environment.

THE POWER OF NETWORKS OF TEAMS

An important part of designing for adaptability is shifting away from hierarchical organizational structures towards models where work is accomplished in teams. Indeed, only a few executives believe that the traditional organizational model—with hierarchical job levels based on expertise in a specific area—makes their organization highly effective. Instead, leading companies are pushing toward a more flexible, team-centric model. As organizations make this transition, they find that smaller teams are a natural way for humans to work. Whatever a hierarchical organization chart says, real, day-to-day work gets done in networks. This is why the organization of the future is a 'network of teams'.[29]

Top companies are built around systems that encourage teams and individuals to meet each other, share information transparently and move from team to team depending on the issue to be addressed. Different networks can have different specialities, such as innovation or getting to market quickly, but the principle is the same.

For a company to stay agile, teams must be formed and disbanded quickly. High-performing companies, today, may build a 'digital customer experience' group, select individuals for the team and ask them to design and build a new product or service in a year or two. Afterwards, the team disperses as team members move on to new projects. This ability to move between teams without risk is a critical attribute of today's high-performing companies.

High-performing companies[30] often first develop these flexible models at the 'edge' of the company. To make further progress, they focus on building a new leadership mindset that rewards innovation, experimentation, learning and customer-centric design thinking. In short, if what a company needs to know and do is constantly changing, then the organization's structure must change as well.

Many new tools and techniques offer valuable contributions to building the organization of the future.

One promising technique is Organizational Network Analysis (ONA),[31] which uses specialized software and methodologies.

Only a few companies are using ONA today but usage is growing rapidly. One company used this technique to redesign its sales organization and found that many experts were underutilized.

Simplification of work practices and new work tools are critical as well. While a networked organization makes sense for agility and responsiveness, it also increases the need to coordinate teams and can lead to an overwhelming number of meetings, emails and communications channels. Cognitive overload can dramatically reduce productivity.

New organizational models would also require a new approach to leadership. Leaders of networked teams in agile organizations require skills such as negotiation, resilience and systems thinking. In some cases, the most experienced leaders and business unit heads may be the wrong people to take charge of digital, agile networked teams.[32]

Empowering people to make decisions[33] and relying on networks of interactions does not mean that people are no longer accountable for results. In fact, one objective of an agile network is to use goal-setting to support success.

In teams, accountability becomes more transparent. Individual and team goals and metrics should be shared for everyone to see. The sense of accountability this can create is critical to team and corporate effectiveness.

LESSONS FROM THE FRONT LINES

One key capability of the organization of the future is the ability to form teams rapidly. This requires a clear understanding of each employee's skills. Most fundamentally, the organization needs to restructure itself to enable greater collaboration, communication, employee empowerment and information flow.

Programme entities set up a variety of ways to enable anyone to raise and view issues, escalate decisions when required and, ultimately, facilitate a collaborative environment. From a talent perspective, continuous coaching, learning and teaming employees with other types of workers (such as contractors) allow for a diverse and collegial environment, increasing agility and removing decision roadblocks.

The legacy organization engages with the programme team to support the design and delivery of the programme. The interactions between the legacy organization and new entity are defined in advance, and while it takes effort and time to reach the point where the model works effectively, it is critical to the success of the programme.

As we move forward to the new aeon—the novel yuga—we need to structure a new organization that brings undeterred challenges onto the new path of the coming yuga.

As this new type of organization takes hold, working in teams will likely become the norm in business and dynamism will become an organizational hallmark. Building and supporting teams will be leaders' principal tasks. Software to help companies benefit from teaming may also become standard.

Leading organizations will offer dynamic developmental opportunities for employees to build their careers, while companies that continue to operate in the old manner will likely struggle to keep up. In this new world, nimble organizations will have certain advantages but the successful large organizations will keep pace by building stronger ecosystems and partnerships that broaden their workforces and capabilities.

Valli 3.01

A Deluge of Information but Lack of Knowledge: The Paradox of the Technology Invasion

SHIVAKUMAR VENKATESWARAN

I am from IIM and CHRO Bangalore. It is a complex organization that looks after both employee experience and stakeholder experience. In the last five and a half years I have seen five directors in the institute. Despite this, we have been ranked 25th in the world and that is because of people across all the segments.

I think it is important to talk about experience holistically. I wish to point out the paradoxes of the millennium.

There are issues of a niche appeal, pervasive information technology, security issues and so on. We are grappling with these issues. Next comes faster processing—complex processes. Everybody is running fast and everybody wants to be on top. Another issue is growing non-employability. For the last two decades, the employability quotient has been quite low. This has caused a rising income but growing disparity—you might have seen the per capita income distribution graph that has grown significantly.

In most countries, due to income disparity, income is receding enormously. However, as a sequel to this, there is a growing number of millionaires. Some customers are easy to reach but difficult to retain. Lastly, there is a deluge of information but a lack of knowledge. This is the paradox of the technology invasion. And in this context, if we rewrite the rules for reinventing HR, we need to speak a lot on the holistic stakeholder experience in any organization.

Today, we are looking at vendor experience, customer experience and employee experience. It's not completely narrowed down. In the last 44 years of our institution's existence, how are we doing things correctly? What is the magic we are creating? Is it only because of HR policies? Is it only because of the digital process? It is because of a variety of factors; one such factor is humanity, which is critical.

The next big thing is a major longitudinal shift in career choices. Now, employees of each organization are looking at options like that, be it in the pharmaceutical industry, retail, public sector, consulting or in an academic institution.

Regarding technology, you either do it or perish. There is no other choice. There are no global solutions for local problems. There are solutions in our own backyards. Our role should change from reactive to proactive, from standardization to customization, then from linear to non-linear and from convergent to divergent. Thus fundamentally, we have to think about reinventing ourselves. What matters is a complete stakeholder experience. If I have to stay up front, I should be proactive.

We have to accept our incapability also. The realization that 'I don't know many things' is important. I think that once we get this realization, we will start to see a lot more reinvention happening in this digital world. The digital is just a medium for us to deal with it. We sometimes overemphasize bots or the so-called digital revolution. So how do we continue inventing?

Learning is not a very easy habit. So are we truly learning and are we in HR trying to reinvent ourselves to look at disjointed experiences?

Let us also look at inclusivity. What is an inclusive organization? Work culture, for us, is very critical and everyone in the organization contributes to the nature and growth of the administration. We look at innovation, and here we are, trying to be innovative within the constraints we have. And the question we are asking is will we stay relevant 10 years from now? Next is integrity—fundamental and professional integrity in terms of the purpose of the organization. Integrity is not about signing any CVC pledge. Integrity refers to whether you are practising what you truly believe in.

I come to the last issue of the three Ps. These are people, planet and profits. I will end by saying that HR is equally relevant, equally critical and equally important. But in different kinds of organizations, there are different purposes and they are not just about profit alone.

VALLI 3.02

DIGITAL—THE MEDIUM THAT BINDS A DISTRIBUTED WORKFORCE

SMITA SAHA

I come from Astra-Zeneca Pharma India Limited, and pharmaceutical companies are viewed as a little more traditional than others. We are actually transforming the company to a large extent. So we have decided to regroup ourselves to see what we are good at and what things are needed to bring our company's business back on the right track.

At present, we are a reputed biopharmaceutical innovation company and also a biotech company, and we are less of a pharmaceutical company. But we still embrace the DNA of the organization. We have moved away from a lot of high revenue therapy areas and moved towards chronic diseases or speciality areas like oncology, respiratory diseases, metabolic diseases like diabetes, renal failures and several others.

To make the shift and to attain expertise to produce acute disease medicines for infection, we felt a huge change was needed in the organization. In a very simplistic way, as HR people, we can understand that selling cough syrup and selling oncology medicine is completely different. The science is different, the complexity is different, the audience is different and research is different. So when we all decided to bring forth a shift three to four years ago, there was huge rework in the organization—a transformation or a re-engineering.

To understand the DNA of the company, you can depend on the basic ethos and values of our organization. Our transformation was seamlessly done, spread across the world, and a lot of it occurred through digital means. We had Town Halls and jam sessions, just rallying the whole organization across several hundred countries to come together to contribute to the transformation of the whole organization over the last few years.

Of course, our efforts translate locally. You would understand automatically that in the pharmaceutical industry, the workforce is distributed and largely dependent on the influence of the market. They sit somewhere and business takes place elsewhere. Our entire connection with the employees is through the virtual medium. We have blended models, we discuss virtually and meet face-to-face as well.

First line managers may see the concerned employees for three or four days a month. A second line manager probably sees them once a month or twice a month. And they will see the team once every quarter and all of them will come into direct real contact once a year. So the entire digital medium is such a means and mechanism for us that it keeps this entire distributed workforce together, not only in India but also globally. Our entire workforce management is completely in virtual mode. It is not just the HR—the entire business runs virtually as well.

VALLI 3.03

HR—THE NEED TO CONVERT THE POTENTIAL TALENT INTO ACTUAL TALENT THAT IS INDUSTRY READY

PRAMOD MAHATME

Many changes have happened from the time of industrial relations to talent management. One of the most fundamental changes we have seen has been in the role of HR functions—from the one defined by Edwin Flippo to that outlined by Dave Ulrich. Personnel management in the 1970s was a line management responsibility and the role of the personnel manager was to aid, advise and assist the line manager in procurement, development, maintenance, compensation and separation. In this role of an advisor, the personnel manager had to have expertise in at least one or more of the portfolio of functions that he/she had been assigned. The role was one of a strategic partner.

The multiple HR roles model proposed by Professor Dave Ulrich has made HR co-champions, with the focus on deliverables. There are four quadrants in which he talks about HR as a strategic partner with a metaphor added about employee champions that has completely confused HR managers. This is the major change that has created confusion. Calling an HR manager an employee champion is as ridiculous as calling a marketing manager a consumer champion.

India can be regarded to be in a very enviable state today. It is one of the potentially most attractive places for investment that the whole world is looking at. We have a huge potential talent that is available. I think one of the important tasks that HR has is to effectively leverage this potential. The students applying for JEE are students securing distinctions and are potential talent. Every year, more than 700,000 students appear for 7,000 seats in IITs. In IIMs, students who score above the 99th percentile are preferred. This means that there are more students available than those that are getting selected. In a large country like ours, we are still working with a shortage mindset. We have a huge surplus and we have every reason to transform this potential talent into actual talent.

Real Corporate Social Responsibility (CSR) is to run an ethical business, have profitable growth and create employment and employability. That is why the greatest contribution of HR to the nation would be to focus on contributing to and converting the potential talent we have into an actual talent that is industry ready, rather than expecting institutions to create industry-ready people.

One of the major transformations that have happened in HR is our movement from recruitment to talent acquisition. Recruitment is the process of making a large pool of people available for HR departments. It was the task of the industry to induct them, train them and make them ready for the job. Talent acquisition, on the other hand, involves poaching people from one another.

VALLI 3.04

TECHNOLOGY CANNOT BE A BANE: IT IS ALWAYS A BOON

KRISHNAMURTHY SHANKAR

Indian HR is very strong with strong foundations. Indian HR professionals are among the top three or four in the world, as per nationality. In many multinational companies, we have Indians playing key roles in HR. If we look at the practices many Indian firms adopt, they are very much at the forefront in their practice, thanks to people like Dr. T.V. Rao and Dr. Pareek.

If you look at Unilever or GE, for instance, many Indians are doing a great job in the top leaderships.

The role of HR is changing. One of the key things is the rate of change happening in the industry. The dynamism in the industry is changing the way HR has to act. Earlier, the change could take place gradually. One prominent change that has taken place now is that HR has to react very fast to situations. HR has to predict what is really going to happen. Businesses today are people businesses. I think the role HR has to play has to be much more strategic and needs to predict the changes in the industry in terms of skills required, the kind of workforce needed in future and also the ways to build them. This requires a thorough understanding of business, strategy, geopolitics and economy and also the ability to work closely with business leaders. If any organization has to survive in these turbulent times, they should be able to predict the future in a better way than their competitors, and that is where HR plays an important role.

We need to enable each individual to achieve their potential. We need to do this in the context of the business as well as in terms of the challenges of the industry. It is not an easy task. Some factors differentiate the IT services industry from others. Foremost amongst these is the scale. Secondly, it is very dynamic. Technology and skills are changing constantly in the industry. Further, it is a people-intensive business and requires that we keep the customer at the forefront. Therefore, the HR practices required would be different.

HR has to lead the ability to predict what is happening. For example, automation, new technologies coming in, startups coming in and what they are likely to be doing should all be predicted. There is a range of activities that will happen in the new frontiers. We are at the centre and so we need to look at things happening around us. We need to be a lot more in touch with customers and employees in terms of what they see or perceive. We need to take clues from the skills that people are looking for to hire or from what the consumers say that they want.

To be able to predict what is happening, we need to be updated about the changes happening around us in the industry. We need to keep in touch with the leading edges of the industry, know how the customers are changing and how technology is changing. It has to be in our DNA to be at the forefront. Technology cannot be a bane. It is always a boon. A lot of intellectual capital has gone into building something and it needs to be seen in the ways that we are using it. Automation is affecting the way work is being done. Automation is having an impact on the work. It is amplifying the quality and quantity of work that people are doing. Technology is going to be a big enabler that is enabling us to do more. In the next few years, we will see an exponential growth of technologies that will enable us to do a lot more. Technology has enabled HR. It removes the middlemen. Technology is being used in various jobs and enables people to move across different spheres.

VALLI 3.05

HR FUNCTION WAS CREATED TO IMPLEMENT HR PHILOSOPHY—HAS IT LEFT THE PHILOSOPHY BEHIND?

DR. T.V. RAO

In 1974, when we started the first HR development department, it was started with a certain philosophy. I would like to underline: HR is a philosophy. To implement the HR philosophy, we thought of a function. A function is created in an organization to use some tools, instruments or systems to achieve a certain kind of goals. The goals are themselves indicators of the philosophy and values. The HR philosophy is that every individual dedicates a major part of his/her life to the service of an organization. The organization is the first family and it should make the work more exciting and make the employee feel like he/she is in the family. It is the responsibility of the organization to create happiness in the workplace. It is the organization's responsibility to use a variety of mechanisms to understand human potential. To do this, we have created HR departments and have identified HR as a function.

Over a period across the last few decades, a lot of change has taken place. HR has become strong as a department but philosophy has been left behind or sidelined. The human part of HR has been sidelined.

Nowadays, many HR departments seem to work for their own sake and multiply HR staff for their own sake—sometimes to promote the philosophy and sometimes not. There are examples of a few cases where HR executives have lived and promoted the HR philosophy. They have done a lot of good work for the corporation, won the credibility of the CEOs or group chairman and have become business heads in some of the companies. The HRD network provides many examples of this sort among its leaders.

To understand the HR philosophy, we need to go back to the basics of Designing and Managing HR Systems by Pareek and Rao. The first three chapters lay down the principles and philosophy of HR functions. These chapters suggest that HR's job is to integrate and differentiate employees, to manage specialization and to manage growth and manage happiness. The basic competency that is missing in HR professionals is working for the larger goal of creating 'happiness at the workplace'. Some companies recently stated that they have done away with employee engagement surveys. They have done away with the surveys because the surveys were serving only the interests of consultants and business magazines rather than that of the company. However, in the case that companies conduct their internal surveys and make necessary changes in them, the surveys could still be used because they are philosophy driven. They aim at enhancing employee engagement by working with individuals than merely tinkering with policies.

Competency models have been developed by SHRM, NHRD network and so on. Certain things are common in them. All of these have stressed the credibility of HR managers. They have also talked about HR values. This is very important. At the same time, they have also talked of the HR function as strategic business partners. We forget the first two but look at the third one and that becomes very important for us. So the change is there.

Many changes are happening in the country today, at least in 'thought'. Many innovations are happening. HR is not only for the corporate sector—HR is for the entire country or the entire world. I am a strong believer that HR is not a strategic business partner. HR is business. There can be no business without HR. We cannot do any business, whether it is clean India, manufacture India or startups. These are all talent-based, people-based and human capital based. Therefore, HR's job is for everyone and every individual should take care of his/her HR role. The CHRO's job, in case that role exists, is to make everyone believe that an individual is responsible for his/her own HR and the job is to treat HR as a business.

Organizations recruit individuals with the hope that he/she will be human capital. They don't normally recruit a role-holder although they may emphasize that. But once we recruit, we must treat this person as human capital or treat him/her as a role-holder. This implies that we are creating but not integrating. Organizations should take care of individuals and reciprocal relationships should exist.

We must prepare ourselves for the uncertain environment of the future. In my latest book, I have mentioned that our PMS orientation should shift towards planning for the present as well as future and selectively forget the past. Every individual KRA and KPA should selectively forget the past and should ask themselves what is it that I am supposed to do in my capacity. Every individual should introspect about what he/she can do better than in the previous year. The organization gives guidance but every individual has to be involved in managing in the VUCA world.

Vijay Govindarajan has said that we should spend 70% of our time on managing the present, 10% or 20% on selectively forgetting the past, while 10% we should spend on predicting and working for the future. Not only corporations but individuals at all levels need to become change managers. That is a big challenge for HR.

We are still struggling with forced distribution, which is outdated. In the 1974 report, while creating the HRD department, in L&T we had suggested delinking performance appraisals from rewards. Because the moment we link them with rewards, a vicious circle gets created, focussing on rewards rather than development. L&T implemented this for five years and then gave up. We have not learnt our lessons from this. Now after 35 to 40 years, we are reverting to what had been said earlier.

The biggest challenge for HRD in an academic institution is to facilitate learning among the faculty. Students today are well-read and have a good network.

Technology can give a lot of assistance to the HR function. HR people need to become more technology savvy. Technology can be a great aid in recruitment and performance management. Seven years ago, SAIL computerized the entire PMS operations. Consequently, the KRAs and KPAs of every single manager were available to everyone. So someone sitting in Bhilai could see the KRAs of the assistant manager in Bokaro. They could start comparing, learning, contributing and competing with each other. We have not recognized the importance of modern technology in treating human beings as human capital. Today, the world is moving fast by using e-learning modes of technology. People are learning on their own and not making HR facilitate learning for them. In case a certain skill is important for the employee, they learn it on their own before they are sponsored for the training.

As a member of the Khandelwal committee, I came across a very interesting case on knowledge management as we were dealing with public sector units. Normally, when a senior manager is promoted as a vigilance DGM, he/she is posted in another bank. We came across a vigilance DGM who was posted in a bank. He collected all the business-related cases for the last few years and started to analyse them and create case studies. He intended to use these details to educate people on how to avoid future vigilance cases because this vigilance orientation is preventing people from taking any decisions. This is knowledge management. Business newspapers these days are talking about bad loans/ NPAs (non-performing assets). We need to put the relevant data for the last few years on the computer, ask a series of questions and have the focused attention of HR personnel for six months to do some research. Therefore, knowledge management can be facilitated by an HR person to learn from their own experiences, which can help to improve the credit assessment ability and even convert the NPAs. HR, in the post-1990s, lost a great opportunity of being the knowledge managers in the IT sector. They passed this to others without our knowledge and a separate category of knowledge managers came into existence. And we were left helplessly concentrating on recruitments and retirements. Knowledge management should be the field of HR managers because they are human capital managers.

Valli 3.06

HR Learning to Be Lean and Smart

DR. CHRISTINA AUGUSTINE

In my opinion, 'being' digital is much more important than 'going' digital or implementing digital solutions or using a digital platform. We should go back to the period of the 1990s—a peak period when the age of automation cracked up. We presumed that operational tasks and recurring activities were to be automated as an element to salvage operational costs. Thereby, we grasped that change is certain to happen but this transition is not radical. The first thing is that we need to realize that HR needs to be followed with the indispensable need of HR reskilling. This impetus makes companies concentrate on how quickly they can indulge in reskilling, otherwise becoming prey for the extinction game or sunsets.

The focus needs to be on technology enhancement for substantial business outcomes and then people should have the acumen for number crunching and statistics. Upon building a new talent pipeline, we should be hiring people who excel in competencies of data analytics, statistics and so on. For existing inhouse employees, umbrellas for reskilling to future new roles and transferable skills should be thought of. The skill enhancement and job roles need to be tailored as per the organization's needs, vision, culture and growth plans. For example, earlier titles like human resources—finance or vice versa have now been relabeled as HR data scientists, HR chief data officers, HR designer and more. Perhaps, organizations will come up with more enriching roles with automation and artificial intelligence at play.

HR would not be completely sidelined but we will be a lean and smart HR. That means we would enumerate the percentage of recurring transactional activities that would be shelved to bring in a much more efficient mode of operation and thriving. Perhaps, these analogies should urge us to review our current HR practices and tenets. If one has the immediacy of Uber, experience like Twitter or visibility like Facebook, such an HR workplace would matter more to any candidate. These experiences can be catapulted within any workplace as well. These days WhatsApp group engagement is more in than even email communication. The big world of future work will crack; you will see through the wall and we all should be prepared for this.

HR experts now work on what kinds of new structures, tools, processes and solutions enhance talent experience, efficiencies and effectiveness. Today, if anyone can directly approach the CEO, then we cannot stick to a 'box approach' that promotes red tape, toxic culture and inefficiencies. There is an end to linear channels of workstyles and there is a directional change towards non-linear workstyles, promoting multiple, integrated and personalized digital solutions. We see it already with the implementation of agile leadership models and structures across organizations. How can HR escape this whirlwind?

Valli 3.07

Digitalization, Yes: For HR Is Here to Stay

GANAPATHI SUBRAMANIAN

HR is becoming like a mobile device, introduced for the sake of communication and now, a mobile device does everything. Being digital in HR is about focusing on helping the business by being an active business partner and working closely with the organization's leaders, making the right choice and taking the right decision timely. All the operational issues are solved from digitalized solutions. It gives a lot of insights about high performing talent and what to do in terms of engaging them. What we should do in terms of developing those future leaders is where digital support helps. And HR also will be helped by this in terms of more time to work with full focus and with the top leaders.

Despite the digital increase, I don't see a situation where employees won't exist. The digital world can support us with AI and comprehend the levels of stress and fatigue and mood and emotions among humans, but at the end of the day, you would want to meet face-to-face. And this human and personal touch will always continue. For example, my daughter listens to stories on YouTube but she enjoys it more when her grandmother narrates the stories to her. It's about being human and establishing that human touch. So I will say, HR professionals and the HR profession will continue to touch the nerves of people. Some upscaling or upgrading will be required and that might take away a few regular jobs but HR is here to stay.

VALLI 3.08

CONTEXTUAL ROLE OF DIGITAL

NAVEEN S. PILLAI

HR practices are subject to change in different sectors. When I was in the corporate area, I used to get instant gratification and feedback on employees' performance. We did all the functions in an automated version and then we moved into the digital mode to see how our people would take it up. One of the things we have seen is the usage of inefficient measures, and it is very common nowadays on all platforms being used.

The years 2010–2011 and 2011–2012 saw mobile revenues go up because of digital and location-based services. It was a healthy step that led to many new ideas in the new mobile space. In 2012, we wanted to get into something like having an intra-mail web page and we wanted to have a much more robust web page for on-the-spot jamming sessions. With adequate feedback and quorums, it took less than six months to convince the management and senior board members across the organizations to have this integrated entry into workplaces. So this is one of the ways how constant change in the organization takes place. Because when you talk about digital, it has to be very contextual. It cannot be that somebody is doing something and we want to copy it. I think what we realize from this is that it is important to have the contextual condition and we need to understand cultural differences and introduce the system accordingly and not get entangled in the entire gamut of things here. We need to do things that will help us take it to the next level.

Coming back to the organizational context, here, we cater to the farming sector. Mobiles might have reached them as customers but maybe not. We have done automation and we have reached our goals and most of our processes have worked out. But how much and how long we should have to go with automation will be the question of HR.

Next is the impact of all this on the work of HR. I think we need to realize this as we have done a great deal for our own creative space and because it needs constant engagement. When you take away mundane activities and make them automatic and digital, it throws a lot of space into the lives of employees, managers and HR. How will you then very specifically engage with those individuals? IDPs will have to be a little more rationalized and more personalized because this is where the platform is opened. Learning is open and the employee does his/her job but he/she does not know how to do career planning. So then what does an HR person do? Do they take it a little further and come out with offerings that are very selective and very personalized?

It is also about the content. I think we, in the HR arena, shy away from taking the bull by the horns. We find ourselves struggling and wanting to go into the digital mode when we talk digital. The pushback would be there given the context in which we operate. But strength and efficiency in this can push back the organizations and these are few tips that I fully endorse as the way forward.

I have never worked as a recruiter. I only do 30% of the job and that is the way forward for HR. It is better to be a generalist and attend to particular functions. But having said that, the time, space and areas that are eaten up by software like chatbots and Ammyy in the field of HR is the zones where professionals should step in. They should understand the talent of each individual and realize how they work with talents and skills that are required for particular jobs. They have to ensure that there is a faster growth in this sector.

Today, it is about instant promotions and faster movements as millennials are coming in. Most of our conditions are structural and productive. There are different parameters under different dimensions. We cannot give everything to everybody.

I believe the HR element will be very important there because we still talk to the person and understand his/her emotions, perceptions and attitudes, value systems and potential.

Valli 3.09

While Technology Will Grow, HR Has No Reason to Worry

RAMKUMAR CHANDRASEKARAN

A couple of years back, there was this personal assistant that was introduced by the name of Siri. Since then, a huge amount of improvement has been made to Siri. Next came Google's Allo. The founders of Siri sold it to Apple and went on to found a new company called Viv Labs. Samsung acquired it at a huge price and they will surely bring out their own version of a personal assistant with whatever name they choose to call it. So there is a revolution in personal assistance, wherein various kinds of non-existing scenarios would be put together, which will then provide help with artificial intelligence.

There is a new personal assistant in the market (the founders have named it Amy) that will connect with whomever you want for a chat. If you want Amy to set up a meeting with a contact of yours, Amy will search your contacts or find their email id from your inbox and send a mail and check for an appropriate time. Then, it will check both parties' calendars and fix up the right time. Then if it is going to be at a restaurant, it will contact the restaurant to fix up the meeting at the restaurant and then send the reminders. The point is that it is so good that your contact will not realize that he/she is chatting with a software program.

The interesting point to note here is that 60% of the organizations that have evinced interest in Amy are recruitment companies. What does a recruiter do? Asks the prospective candidates some basic questions and shortlists the names of candidates based on the responses and profiles. He/she contacts the hiring manager and fixes up interviews, finalizes results and forwards it. Amy will do all these things. So anybody who is doing recruitments or running a recruitment agency will have a real big threat in the next two years from now. And we are developing products which have helped HR. There are a large number of companies where people travel across the world. For any policy related queries, they can call the concerned person and they will answer or they can send an email. This kind of important work will get settled smoothly. In six months, HR assistants will be gone. It will be a chatbot and you will be able to chat with this chatbot. If any query is posed, it will immediately check the database and respond in microseconds.

So in the future, how is this huge revolution in technology going to impact HR? HR operation personnel and anything under HR operations will have to reskill very soon. Anything that is an operation under the HR system will be done by software programs. In a couple of years from now, technology companies like ours will sell products to you at cheap prices that will take care of most of your HR needs. There are areas in HR, like the coaching and mentoring process, leadership development programmes and so on, which involve a high threshold of learning. When you evaluate the future of HR practices and processes, you must realize that a large proportion of HR practices are still operational. HR professionals must constantly reskill themselves to move from the operational space to the actual human development space.

VALLI 3.10

MAKING SMART USE OF TECHNOLOGY, YET MAINTAINING THE H IN HR

DR. AQUIL BUSRAI

When I look at AI, it gives me déjà vu of the late 1970s. When computers came in and everybody said how it would make jobs disappear and how it would be anti-workforce, anti-labour and yet, nothing like that happened. Jobs increased, computers lived and grew and so did jobs and careers.

When people talk about AI today, there is a similarity in the dialogue, with questions of whether AI is going to take over and replace human power. So I would use different words altogether. I wouldn't use the words artificial intelligence; I would rather call it augmented intelligence. This means that we, as professionals, will get an extra tool in hand, to work differently.

That brings us to the question of whether HR people should step into the world of AI just because everybody else is going for it as well. There are two applications of augmented intelligence. One within HR, where HR activities will be augmented by AI, involving things like predictive analysis. Second is the use of AI in the changing business scenario, where AI will be used to benefit the business. For doing that, we have to make sure that HR professionals understand business.

At the end of the day, we are here to make sure that the business runs efficiently and effectively. To augment the running of the business efficiently, we need to provide skills proactively. We must train people and make them accept and embrace technology, be it augmented intelligence or machine learning, rather than trying to find ways and means of convincing them that this is nothing to be afraid of. I would rather take the route of facing technology and helping the organization move forward in preparing its growth plan.

The only part that I would add is that whatever augmented intelligence we use, at the end of the day, I do not see the H in HR disappearing. It will remain. The H in HR will predominantly remain because it is our stock in trade. I feel very proud to be an HR professional helping to maintain that H.

On the other hand, I can share a live example from one of the major IT organizations in the world. We are using a considerable amount of technology for performance management. The goal-setting itself uses technology to see how much alignment there is with the purpose and the strategy. It measures the percentage. Then, simple things like notes of discussions that we have had with people are recorded technologically in such a way that you can go two levels above regular access when you deal with 52,000 employees. That is a smart use of technology. Somebody reports to me and that person's appraisal or comments can be viewed by my boss sitting in New York, without even going through any channels but by simply looking at it. Technology does not mean that we convert everything into non-human activity. The touch and feel must remain. In fact, with the use of technology, there will be more emphasis on skills like empathy and maintaining relationships. If we use technology as an aid to pursue human resource management, then we will have made smart use of it.

VALLI 3.11

HIRE PEOPLE FOR DEFINED AGILITIES, DEVELOP INNOVATIVE PRACTICES TO BRING ABOUT DIGITAL SAVVINESS

PAVITRA SINGH

In today's world, everything is changing. We are living in a VUCA world. Therefore, when we are hiring, the first thing that we look for is agility. Agility is a huge word.

If I bring it down and dissect it a little bit further, firstly, agility is about learning agility. Are you constantly learning? Are you reskilling yourself and shedding what you learnt earlier and relearning? Do you have learning agility? Do you have a curious mind? That's the first thing that I would look at in terms of learning agility. Secondly, I would look at result agility. Do you have a bias for action? Are you a self-starter? And, therefore, do you have the agility to demonstrate and provide results? Thirdly, I would focus on people agility. It is about really working with diverse people and, therefore, leveraging the results. The fourth factor is mental agility—whether one has the agility to look at problems and unlock them with very different solutions. Especially in a VUCA world, if one has mental agility, it is a bonus. The fifth factor is change agility. With the number of changes that we are facing today, are you adaptable? Do you challenge the status quo? Because it is all about breaking barriers. It is all about innovation. Therefore, if one has the agility to make a difference by changing things and challenging, he/she has the edge. These are the five things that I would look at while hiring.

One can say that the traditional methods of developing talent honestly don't exist today and may not be very relevant. In the past, we have focused on classroom training. Today, it is all about choices. If you look at the millennial talent coming into the workforce, they are not going to have the patience to sit through a training programme. It is about giving them choices.

I can give you examples of how we function at PepsiCo. We follow the 70-20-10 learning model. So the 70% is 'on-the-job', 20% is mentoring and 10% is training in the classroom. The 70% 'on-the-job' learning should be filled with various types of learning. For mentoring, we also have a concept called externship, where you actually go to a different market. If I need e-commerce skills or if I need high-end digital skills, I may not have them inside my organization. I can send somebody as an extern to another market and acquire those skills.

The third could be the one that we recently experimented upon with Levers, where we broached this concept of career JV (Joint Venture), which is about going to a different organization and learning. It is all about experiences and providing them in different ways.

I would also like to say that a leader should demonstrate listening skills. Gone are the days where the leader could dictate. With the new generation coming into the workforce, people need to look up to the leader and they need to be convinced by what the leader is saying. For the leader to inspire others, he/she needs to be a good listener first and needs to understand others. Listening skills are a new trait that a lot of leaders are now learning so that they can listen to this new generation.

Since the focus is digital experiences, I wish to describe a few exciting kinds of work that we are doing. We have got a youth committee board comprised of millennial. They elect themselves and their main role is to bring about digital savviness in the organization. They do a lot of reverse mentoring for our leaders and help them become digitally savvy. You have the experience of our people, the executive committee, and you have the experience and aspiration of the young generation. Our system brings the two together.

VALLI 3.12

DIGITAL TECHNOLOGY IS ONLY AN ENABLER FOR ORGANIZATION PROGRESS, BUT HUMAN TOUCH SHALL ALWAYS REMAIN

P. DWARAKANATH

I always quote: 'A leader is one who can cope with change.' Are you willing to change with time? When you talk about digital proficiency, I would say it is a measure of how effectively individuals organize and engage with digital technology. As long as you have the right bent of mind, you are willing to change, you don't resist the change and you don't have misconceptions or apprehensions against digitization, you will progress.

Digitization is something that cannot be forced on anybody. The easy advantage of technology is needed to be demonstrated to establish how it makes one proficient—helpful for individuals as well as for organizations—and only then will it be easily accepted.

It is the ability to engage and execute; the ability to leverage strategy to improve service and communication. If you can drive that compelling communication, people will be ready to change. I think the issue of whether you are a baby boomer or Gen X or GenY or Gen Z is very incidental and it does not matter which generation you belong to; you will be able to use technology like any other youngster if you are interested in it and convinced about it. It is a question of applying your mind. It is like the 'art of tough love'.

The 'H' element or the human touch always remains. Digital technology is only an enabler for you to progress, in terms of leveraging the best advantage in the competitive environment.

I do not believe that due to technology, you lose touch with people. It all depends on what sort of a technological structure or architecture you develop and how you engage with them. As HR professionals, I think we need to generate awareness and bring about compelling communication.

Last but not the least, technology should become only a means to enhance organizational effectiveness and make the right business decisions. It is not a substitute for the human element. In nutshell, it is vital to create the right balance between technology and touch when managing employees, especially in the VUCA work environment.

Valli 3.13

The Potential of Digital Technology Is Immense

SAPTARSHI ROY

I think we all recognize the fact that technology is causing a profound impact on the way organizations work, their workplace and the entire workforce. Gradually, we all realize that the organization of the future is going to be vastly different from the typical organization that is conventionally there in our mind. The organization of the future will not be enclosed within a boundary wall. It will be very difficult to perceive that employees might have to come to a certain location to work and that there can be certain sets of codes of conduct or guidelines which can govern and regulate their employment.

We are witnessing the emergence of the new or alternate work arrangement for those who are in the quadrant of 'off-campus' and 'off-balance sheet', which means the employees that are not on the payroll of the organization. At the same time, many of them will have not even witnessed where the organization exists or where the campus of the organization is. So in that kind of scenario, the only thing which can connect and regulate processes to ensure proper governance is that we need to have more service level agreements. That means that delivery will take more prominence than the process. Secondly, it will be important to have this set of workers—who represent an organization but have never seen their campuses or are not on the regular payrolls of this organization—demonstrate a certain set of behaviour. Therefore, the core value will assume paramount importance in terms of creating a broad governance framework.

I think the potential of digital technology is immense. Conventionally, in a typical organization, we consider that communication is one of the strongest backbones for developing commitment and culture. But now, communication has undergone a sea change. It is no longer unidirectional. For example, you send out some circulars which take time to reach the people for whom they intended and, by that time, the content becomes almost stale. Today, people expect instantaneous communication. At the same time, people also expect instant reactions to that particular communication.

In NTPC, we have done away with house journals, newsletters and magazines. We have developed an app that is something like the social network tools we use, where anything that happens is instantly captured and communicated to the entire workforce. People can also comment there. Maybe if some of the new initiatives of organizations were to be posted on this kind of communication module, people could directly comment with their responses and comments. So it is about bidirectional communication.

Another thing is the excitement of learning. Particularly in an organization like ours, we use technology for learning new skills that are required and for developing competence and new skill sets, allowing people to learn 24×7. And they need not go to a predefined place to learn. These are the kinds of changes and excitement which is going to be part of the future.

Valli 3.14

Technology Is to Be Harnessed Carefully and in the Right Way in Order to Progress

S.Y. SIDDIQUI

In my understanding, in addition to the emergence of the digital era, there are two more very strong variables that will be affecting the future of the workplace, people processes and the overall transformation of HR functions. The first variable is the impact of globalization, which has brought in a strong global connect, intense competition and also global turbulence. The second variable is the demographic shift of the workforce towards millennials, which is something we are all experiencing already. This demographic shift has also posed the challenge of the coexistence of multiple generations in the workforce, including gig workers. Currently, Maruti is working with four generations of employees. This will again necessitate reinventing HR with flexibility, innovation and shorter shelf lives of HR policies.

The impact of the digital era will vary in different industry sectors. It will be wrong to make a generic assessment that in every business sector, digitization will have a uniform impact. Manufacturing will be different while IT/ITES, FMCG and Telecom will be different. So we will have to keep that in mind when we explore the relevance and impact of digitization on the future of HR or the workplace.

In my way of thinking, the impact of technology on the work culture of any company will start with disruption, discomfort and maybe a basic tendency of resistance. There will also be a clear advantage of technology. Organizations will benefit with increased speed, responsiveness and a much bigger reach and measurement, leading to high performance. People will be able to work from different kinds of geographies and locations, maybe from home. That will bring in new thought processes for redefining or reinventing HR and workplace options, along with great flexibility.

I think the biggest impact of technology on Maruti is the instant connect with the entire employee audience of 15,000 people. Our reach to our people in 20 regional offices and 6 zonal offices, including communication, training and information sharing, has increased multiple times. This dictates how we acknowledge and recognize that they are doing a great job or how we ensure that they connect with the culture and the top management philosophy, strategy and directions to increase overall company performance. Enhanced technology will also significantly impact communication regarding key company events and periodic communication meetings conducted by the top leadership. In this way, it will enable us to connect with employees across work locations. If we increase the people connect and decentralize access to HR processes through enhanced technology, that will become the fulcrum of higher engagement. Digitalization will also have huge potential to transform the learning and development offerings through e-learning modules and e-games, leading to higher involvement, internalization and flexibility in the capability development process. De-learning, relearning or reskilling will become relatively more effective and relevant through digitalization.

There are a few very obvious benefits that technology has brought in. The one most exciting shift which has happened is that the annual increments just flow in on your email within five minutes. Wherever you are, you can see how much you have got. There are many such perspectives. When we look at training and development, in our experience, the introduction of learning and skilling through e-games is very exciting for shop floor workers and it makes them learn hands-on, via enhanced technology, which is more absorbing and effective than classroom training. At the same time, it is also extremely important to maintain a balance between hi-tech and hi-touch.

The future of HR will also entail the following significant shifts:

- New employment contracts—short term, freelance and project-based—will emerge.
- A team-based organization structure with low/no hierarchy and low designation focus will form.
- There will be a transnational workforce with global teams and a digital work net.
- Flexible working with flexi hours will become the norm.
- AI and robotics will leave an impact on HR processes

Because of the above, we may bring in some key changes—new perspectives for redefining HR to address future challenges:

- HR must lead to the future.
- We must selectively delete the past
- Flexibility, risk-taking and experimentation must be key.
- Speed, responsiveness, transparency and measurement must also be deemed important.
- Retain a personal touch and sensitivity to people's aspirations and well-being must be prioritized.

VALLI 3.15

CONSUMER BEHAVIOUR IS LEADING TO CHANGE WITHIN ORGANIZATIONS

DR. ARVIND AGRAWAL

Consumer behaviour is leading to change within organizations. Now, employees want to be treated as consumers. If you look at the base of consumer behaviour, you will find it leaves transparency, consistency and choice in the hands of the consumer. Employees want the same thing. And that's the big shift. Earlier, the power resided traditionally in the organization. It resided among bosses. It resided inside the HR department. Now, it needs to be reinvented in a way where the power actually resides in people. They will decide what careers they choose, what learning opportunities they want to pursue, how they want to learn and when they want to learn, and that's the big disruption.

In time, it will further evolve and like everything else, it will get settled. In this unfolding scenario, there is a possibility that employees will largely become contractual, which could be a challenge. In that case, the soul of the organization may get destroyed.

The second challenge is contextually relevant to India. On one hand, several evolved organizations are early adopters of emerging practices. Then there is a vast proportion of corporate India that consisted of small proprietary companies when HR was evolving in the country some 20 years ago. These companies did not worry too much about formal HR processes. Now, over time, many of them have grown successfully. They are globally competitive and have an international footprint. They have formal HR functions to put the people architecture in place. They are currently preoccupied with introducing basic HR processes such as performance management systems based on KPIs and goals. How will these companies embrace the new, disruptive and technology-enabled HR processes? They perhaps have to leapfrog to provide that.

If we continue businesses as usual, then we are denying ourselves the opportunity and power that technology offers us. To give a very simple example: I was recently approached by a very large public sector unit. They wanted to train their people on 'how to give performance feedback effectively'. They were searching for an appropriate training programme for this. Nothing unusual. We said we would do it. We enquired about the number of people who were to be trained and were surprised to find there were 1,200 people. It was clear to us that traditional classroom sessions, delivered in batches of 20 participants, would be very time-consuming and would not be the best way to go about it. We proposed a technology-enabled gamified version of 'how to give feedback on performance'. This would be of 90-minutes duration. We would train 10 HR people. They would become subject matter experts so that if people faced any difficulties, they could approach one of these 10 internal HR professionals. This, to our thinking, was a quicker and more interesting way to train people. Also, it gave people the freedom to choose what they wished to learn, rather than the HR department nominating them for the programmes.

Likewise, quite often we need very strong analytics to be able to analyse attrition, employee engagement and such issues in the organization. That can be done many times more effectively with the use of appropriate technology like machine learning. This is very similar to marketing using technology where one would use consumer-related data to engage consumers.

By embracing the appropriate technology, organizations will be in a better position to meet growing employee aspirations of being treated as customers with flexible and customised solutions. If companies do not adopt such solutions, it will be tougher to stay in business and to stay competitive.

Of course, in all this, we should not lose sight of continuing to provide the 'human touch'—the glue that connects people to other people, organizations and society at large.

Valli 3.16

The Need to Remember the Human behind All the Technological Change and Not Get Carried Away

RAJEEV DUBEY

We are in an environment that is volatile, uncertain, complex and ambiguous (VUCA), and anyone who thinks he / she has all the answers and can teach others what to do is making a great mistake. So if I could focus only on the learning part, I would say that the following things are very important.

- The context for learning, especially because that context keeps on changing
- The attitude towards learning—the ability to continuously learn, relearn and unlearn
- The pedagogy—and here, we are moving away from the old, one-way instructive style to multiple, out-of-the-box and innovative styles of learning and teaching

All of these three things are undergoing a huge transformation. Technology plays a very crucial role in bringing about this transformation. I sometimes worry whether technology has become the master and whether we have forgotten the purpose behind using technology, which is to serve humanity and human beings. While using technology in the forms of artificial intelligence, robotics and so on is the need of the hour, at the end of the day, we should not forget the human being that is behind all this technology.

VALLI 3.17

THINGS ARE CHANGING AND EVEN GETTING DISRUPTED: WE HAVE CHANGED OURSELVES AND THAT IS WHY WE HAVE SURVIVED

DR. RAJEEV UBEROI

The one word that is used often in today's world is change, and when the change is fast enough, it is termed as 'disruption'.

But the crux of this is that change is something that all of us are living with. We have accepted it and have changed ourselves and that's why we have survived. And that is the most important thing for anyone who comes and joins us in the workforce. Changes have happened and we have accepted them; we have survived and grown. But we have also adapted ourselves to meet those challenges and requirements that could be termed as capability enhancement.

Changes have two objectives. One, the system wanted to be changed. Two, your aspirations are to be changed. And when you change your own aspirations, you need to work for them. We can try to link it with the objective of HR responsibility or functions. That purpose may be in the form of capitalistic terms, for money. But you can only make money if you are successful. And you can only be successful if you have the right resources, and if you have the right resources, you have to take them to the right path where they meet the corporate objective. It may be a social objective or whatever you may call it.

If we have to meet the challenges of so-called change or disruption, we have to guide the employees, give them enough opportunity to align their capability to the need of the day. We cannot just leave things to them, though I was in a school where people felt that my career is my problem. It is perfectly fine but if my career is my problem then I don't think I have loyalty to you. You need loyal employees. You need people who move to your organization to be successful. All those companies, all the institutions who have built core employees are the survivors. Everywhere, you will find that if a company has a very strong employee base, they survive much longer than others who have no such base.

Banks are supposed to be old stable organizations that need stability. On the other hand, the workforce we get—especially the millennials—is more than mobile. You change their workplace from east to central and they are ready to go. It is a huge challenge, even in the quality of work. We have been taking people up on contract-basis but that does not work either. When you are taking them up on a contract basis, you are giving them project-driven work which has no anchor. So in the financial sector, it's very important to build and develop talent which is to be useful for a certain purpose within the organization for at least some time.

Having said that, it is very important to have our organizations be receptive and responsive to the needs of people who are coming to work and to understand their problems and give them what they need, in the interests of the organization.

Valli 3.18

Preparing to Meet the Challenges of Real Disruption

DR. TANAYA MISHRA

We are at the microcosm of the environment. It is about disruption, and it is about being new. And also, it is about rethinking and reimagining what we do as a function. We are definitely changing the way we are hiring. We are talking of variables like workforce and liquid workforce. The workforce has different skills to adapt to the changing technology and space which is constant.

A lot of organizations are rethinking their way. The paradigm shift in performance achievement is about you or it is about your own matrices, your own performance and how you are going to move in that direction.

Compensations and benefits are also undergoing a sea change. The thoughts of the workforce are some things that have a distinct meaning. Every organization has different talent resources and they are wondering if they have future-ready people. Also, we don't know the kind of employee that is going to come through our doors next time. All these changes lead up to what kind of future it is going to be. And every organization is grappling with this reality and trying to adapt in some ways.

I would say it is relevant to discuss longevity and longer opportunities for an individual to work. It is about how quickly one can know how agile you are. An agile workforce keeps abreast of changes that come their way. The core value of this kind of reaction to the change is that we are all human beings.

Today they are talking about co-sharing of particular jobs, and they are talking about contract employees. This is because they don't have liability in their jobs. What was earlier looked at regarding the workforce was the quantity but now the onus is on their deep skills and quality of work they perform. So the norms are changing. The other spectrum of challenges related to the millennial workforce is quite alarming. Their conditions of mental alertness or wellness are a matter of concern. You can look into the statistics of our company through annual reports, and you will find that one in two professionals is suffering from mental disorders or abnormalities of different kinds. They could be stressed or suffer from obsessive-compulsive disorder. They carry these issues to the workplace. Most often they have personal problems and work issues, making them feel physically insecure, and suffer from human psychic and neurotic disorders.

So to what extent are we engaging services or assistance programmes to cope with these kinds of stress-related issues prevailing among the workforce? Counsellors and buddy system executives can help to identify the disorders and treat them with proper guidance and care. Thus, the overall HR function depends on this periodic guidance in overcoming mental stress. Today, everybody needs some sort of psychic counselling or else these disorders will get aggravated. Take, for example, the Blue Whale game phenomenon, popular among adolescents. The game is about trying to identify the people who are not mentally strong enough, or who are weak in their consciousness, to eliminate them from this planet. The anchors are missing here and hence, are to be provided.

VALLI 3.19

THE CHANGE TODAY IS INDEED REAL AND THERE NEEDS TO BE A HUMAN TOUCH IN EVERYTHING THAT HR DOES

VIVEK PARANJPE

The change that we are talking about is indeed real. In the good old days, the career span had been up to 30 years or 35 years. I was reflecting upon the year 1990 when, in Hewlett Packard, we did a survey to figure out the career planning of the people. We said that within 30–35 years of a career, people may change about 10 roles or maybe a couple of careers, moving from finance to HR or vice versa, and maybe a couple of jobs.

But in today's world, careers are really ranging up to 50 years or 60 years. Today, the longevity of careers is going to make sure that people will work for 50–60 years and career definitions will be changed. If you look at the industrial era in the past, there were three stages of life and they were all pretty linear. First, you would study, then you would work for 30–35 years and then you retire. But today, the idea of retirement is gone. That means, there is a huge need for learning. And it has to be on time.

To showcase the longevity of employees, I will mention the example of Reliance Industries. People are physically fit and mentally fit at the age of 60 and could continue to work for another 20 years. The question that comes up is that 'do we let them continue in their same role for the next 10–15 years or do we retire them?' That becomes a big dilemma. And the dilemma is that because you do not retire them, the entire pipeline below gets choked up, leaving behind many restricted employees who are young and bright and who may quit you.

So in this situation, the solution is to retire them. And then, let's take them on contract as advisors, mentors, guides, coaches and so on. Engage them on critical new projects so that the pipeline below is not choked up. And at the same time, our work is done. The most important crucial element is that HR needs to have flexible HR policies, processes and programmes to accommodate these kinds of people. The HR processes are to be designed to take care of old people. So the concept of retirement is gone. It is a change of career and something which we have to respect. People can then remain and work till they can.

Each generation is different. My generation is very different from my father's generation. And my son's generation is very different from my generation and it's a reality of life. One has to accept that reality of life. And so, I think we, the HR community, have to create a flexible HR policy with flexible processes, flexible working conditions and flexible programmes to just adapt to the new generations' thought process. But above all, there is no substitute for human culture. I started my response with the art of conversation. There should be some 'human touch' in everything. Somewhere amongst the automated technology, we cannot allow that human touch to go away. But, the efficacy of the 'human touch' in the form of conversation is missing and technology did not tell you not to have the conversation. We use the pretext of technology, saying that technology is making things consistent, fast and efficient. That is fantastic. We should use it. But the human triggers have to be embedded within technology.

VALLI 3.20

HR'S ROLE AS A CATALYST IN THE TREMORS OF CHANGE

ASIM KUMAR BASU

When we see technological innovations, we only wonder about the speed and alacrity at which these are happening. In many cases, business corporations and organizations are caught unawares of such fast revolutions. All these force organizations to adopt changes, rather than allowing them to foresee the changes in advance and ensure workable and enduring solutions, including preparing the entire workforce to embrace the changes to succeed in the new realm of business reality. In most situations, we don't have ready-made answers for these rapid and quantum changes. But we are trying to be proactive to unearth some answers to this speed in the change of the overall business environment globally, affecting us in a way we never expected. As a result, we are falling behind in the attempt and preparedness in organizational development and its workforce to cope with the changing business demand. So from an HR perspective, I see some kind of tremors in the field of HR and workforce. It is becoming evident that there are several structural faults within the classical organization and the HR relations and functionality. To me, HR should act both as a catalyst and an analyst to first capture the future of corporations and the impending business environment, followed by arranging for things to sail through smoothly and by adjusting to changes with agility.

As an appropriate example, digitization has changed the face of HR management. The use of digital platforms has been a driving force of change across organizations. Transformation is happening at an accelerated speed but, unfortunately, many organizations acted too late to transform the workforce as per need. One can take note of digital disruption quite fast and can initiate actions in months but for many organizations and their people, it took years to fully embrace such fundamental changes due to the way they operate, making them fall behind in the competition. Change management is by far the most enduring bottleneck to digital transformation. While technology adoption continues to be at top of the mind in all digital things, I advocate that fundamental changes in leadership and talent attributes are far more critical to successfully embark on the digital journey.

To brief you about the background of the automobile industry, I would take the example of TATA Motors—one of the biggest organizations in the country. I refer to the Indian context—India's first five automobile companies are to its credit. TATA contributes slightly more than 7% of GDP. In the next seven or eight years, electric cars will be on Indian roads as commercialized vehicles for the use of commute. The next thing on the way is the driverless vehicle. These types of vehicles will be in the form of hybrid technology. That means these vehicles will be able to run on battery as well as on fossil fuel. There will also be some recharging stations for batteries and charging machines which will be able to charge car batteries in less than 10 minutes. So how is this innovation and technological change going to impact the employment scenario? This is going to create another 65 million jobs as per industry estimates.

The automobile industry has a big impact on the economy. HR practices are also bound to change with such unprecedented changes in the technological arena. The first setback is going to be the switching over from fuel-based vehicles to electric vehicles. This will call for new kinds of technical skills and knowledge for the workforce already employed in the industry. Training and developing the existing workforce in the automobile industry is going to be a herculean task, and some of this workforce might become redundant because of the lack of new skills. The HR fraternity cannot afford to lose sight of this vital and impending issue and needs to prepare in advance and address it appropriately. The Government of India is planning to protect them to some extent through a new mission. However, this change is not going to happen abruptly. All over the world, the present electric vehicles population is less than 1%. Only Norway has electric cars plying on its road.

Having said so, I must say that these kinds of technological innovations will have positive impacts as well. In fact, they will bring in more new opportunities. The primary thing the HR fraternity needs to do is to train and prepare the workforce much ahead of time to not only keep its employees ready but also to support the company to make it capable of withstanding all challenges and remaining in business successfully.

VALLI 3.21

GREAT PLACES TO WORK INSPIRE YOU AND GIVE YOU PEACE OF MIND

PREETI DAS

I am sure everyone agrees that companies that inspire you to work with peace of mind and the aspiration of long career growth are the best companies to work with.

The work arena, for the past two years, has seen a vast sea of changes. The salesforce in my world of work suddenly started to expand its horizons, becoming robust in its outlook. Also, it has become more effective, accountable and responsible for the company's achievement and advancement. I started looking at my salesforce and began following them. The trajectory that they carved has tremendous potential in my opinion and it made me take a look at various companies' trajectories.

What companies are doing is that they are looking at their workforce and their performance minutely. And with the innovation in digitization, many things are undergoing vast changes. Digital transformation is no longer a niche interest as it jumps out of the tech department and into the boardroom of leaders across industries, sectors and geographies. The current digital age is but a stepping stone in the evolution of the world, enabled by the exponential use of technology in the workplace.

The digital age is moving at such a fast pace that it is fundamentally transforming the way organizations operate. Be it in the private or the public sector, it is requiring them to develop new ways of thinking about service delivery that, in turn, influence the way operating models are designed. Hence, there are profound effects on the functions of HR departments in these organizations and their roles in identifying new approaches to managing the people.

Before diving into the implications of HR functions, it is important to identify selected organizational implications of the digital economy. The three main areas that HR needs to acquire or strengthen, which are directly related to the success of the digital transformation journey, are as follows:

- The restructuring of the organization to enable digital transformation.
- The alignment of thought regarding what digital means to the specific organization among the leadership team before initiating the transformation.
- The question of it how well it will fit into the overall business model.

This alignment will shape the digital operating model of the organization that is composed of aggregated future state digital capabilities (i.e., processes, people and technologies). It is HR's role to map the future required by the digital capabilities and locate where they should be executed in the organization. Digital capabilities revolve around a few main areas of an operating model.

This is the time for us to make a paradigm shift. I believe that our future holds four pillars of digital disruption. First, we cannot afford to sell our corporates so we will have to create customer experiences. Customers will buy experiences but not just a product. Second, there will be a continuous revamp of operational efficiency. Third, employees will be empowered by knowledge, which means that employees will take decisions. The manager will sit at the bottom and employees will sit at the top, forming an inverted pyramid. That will happen in the near future. And I think this will be happening in some parts of the world and its economies where employees are entrusted to work in the grey area. The last pillar is a business model transformation. The whole economy is going to change, and there will be a lot of customer-friendly products, advanced passenger cars, driverless cars, battery cars and so on. The economic and environmental change I mentioned earlier will be there. There will be a big structural change in the corporate world and HR is going to have more accountable responsibilities. They will have to switch over to the new role in the coming days.

HR people will work in totally different styles altogether. Skill is going to be more transient, and people will not be able to afford to depend on them to create career growth and development that are set apart for the long term. And there will be a requirement of hiring need-based talents as core teams will be shrinking further. I was talking to people from Snapdeal a year back, and they said they will not allow any workforce over 4,000 members. Then what do you have? You have a gig economy. So career paths will not be decided by the employees themselves. HR will do it differently.

Valli 3.22

People Will Look for Behaviours in the Leader Amidst Changes

SOURAV DASPATNAIK

While answering the question of what qualities a boss should possess, what we normally say is that he/she should be very much humane, he/she should be passionate, he/she should take care of us, he/she should give us opportunities to explore and he/she must support the workforce. And if asked about the traits desired within senior leadership, then everyone would prefer a positive behavioural outlook and patterns. It does not matter what degree one holds. Everything else may be disrupted but the quality, behaviour, innate talents and potential of managing HR need to remain within him/her.

Ultimately, HRM professionals are those upon whom business organizations' fates rest. If HRM professionals do not perform their role eloquently and with dedicated responsibility, the organization may not move on the right track. I am from the manufacturing industry but the roles and responsibilities of HR are of significance in all spheres. I know the psyche of people as I am an HR professional, and I exercise extreme caution while picking up employees and hiring them for a given period.

The younger generation is very intelligent and good decision-makers. The entire onus is on how a professional of HR will manage that and undertake risks, foreseen or unforeseen, and how he/she will handle that risky situation.

The quality of risk-taking by an HR professional will have an impact on the HR domain. I have seen this kind of situation in many industry sectors. These automotive industries are changing their strategies every second. They are no longer following traditional paths blindly. Electric cars may roll out on Indian roads next year. They already exist and are going to be commercialized next year. So leaders are going to rewrite the rules in the digital era. And keeping the basic tenets of management in place, HR functions like recruitment, selection and recruitment compensation management are all becoming more crucial in this digital era.

To mention the infrastructure space, I would say that this is the age of infrastructure development. Digital proficiency is the way of life nowadays and in India, it is treated as a blessing in innovation. But, in India, it is still in the nascent stage. Some revolutions have happened and the revolutions are mostly in the manufacturing sector, in the power sector and also in the transportation sector. With this digital proficiency, the main difference is that even the erstwhile 'safai karmachari' is in the same line of efficiency and proficiency. Right now, he/she knows the route he/she has to complete and he/she knows how much garbage has to be picked up along that route. He/she also knows how much remuneration he/she is going to get on a particular day. This type of consciousness is awakening and this is due to the digital era. Digitization has created a consciousness for workers, and these 'safai karmacharis', lowest in the pyramid, also know about their workload, their job profile and compensation management and they do their part of work more efficiently.

Also, netizens (people who use the Internet) like housewives, students, executives and other full-time or part-time workers are consciously aware of their work output, and they can calculate their earnings accordingly. This is due to digital proficiency. And that is why HR needs to be extremely agile to be able to deal with employees who are aware.

Valli 3.23

Self-Awareness—A Must for Understanding the Psyche of the Younger Digital Employees

V.C. Agrawal

I relate to one of my experiences as a coach in this context of rewriting the rules for the digital age. You see, what we do in coaching is that we coach while addressing issues of leadership styles. Employees normally strive for recognition of the situation. They also overlook their personal lives, their friends or society. The difference is that in terms of the family, if I am the father and I have two children and my wife at home and if there is a disconnect between me and my children when I go home after work, I will realize it there and then. But when I am working in the office, I am busy with so many things that I will not realize that there is a disconnect between me and the next generation of people in my office. These kinds of things are addressed in the coaching process.

I shared this experience with you to tell you that this is the case for digital-based employees. Many senior executives at the CEO level or CHRO level very often are not able to understand how wide the gap is between them and the younger, digital-based employees. We need to understand what the employees' requirements are and what their outputs are to the organization so that their issues are addressed.

So how to groom the leaders and managers in the organization to have an evolved mindset? My understanding of an evolved mindset is that which can understand the mindsets of the younger, digital employees and their needs. As I mentioned in the very beginning, you will not be able to understand the dynamics or psyche of these digital employees unless you are aware of it yourself.

The experience which I share as a coach is that understanding the needs of the millennial forms the first part of this task of rewriting rules. And before we try to understand their needs, we will have to become self-appraisers. Then only will it be possible to understand their needs. What I mean by the term self-appraiser is that we will have to become more emotionally intelligent to know the knowledge and skills of these younger, digital employees. I am speaking of the emotional intelligence that helps us to know others' needs. Unless we do that we will not be able to rewrite the rules in the organization. I tried to create a workaholic culture in my organization. The meaning of coaching workaholic culture, particularly at the senior level, is that employees should adopt the coaching style in their organization. Coaching work culture means that they will try to come closer to the employees and come closer to addressing their issues. Only then it will be possible to rewrite the rules in the organization to change the behavioural pattern to some extent, even if indirectly.

So here, the main focus lies on 'coaching workaholic culture' and how we impart this culture to our employees. This is done in the form of organizing workshops like management development programmes, training workshops, employee development programmes, symposiums and colloquiums for the employees' benefit. And this coaching and the coaching styles of workaholic culture involves encouraging senior leaders and employees' mentors to learn skills and talents from training workshops and take initiatives to mingle with their juniors and coach them. That really boosts the employees' morale and performance, enabling excellence.

CHAPTER 4

BEYOND CULTURE AND ENGAGEMENT: COMING OF THE SAPTARSHI

'Don't you know that a midnight hour comes when everyone has to take off his mask? Do you think life always lets itself be trifled with? Do you think you can sneak off a little before midnight to escape this?'

– Søren Kierkegaard

GARGI VACHAKNAVI

Gargi Vachaknavi, the daughter of sage Vachaknu, was an ancient Indian philosopher. She participated in a brahmayajna, a philosophic debate organized by King Janak of Videha, and challenged the sage Yagyavalka with perplexing questions on the issue of atma (soul). She is also said to have written many hymns in the Rig Veda.

From a young age, she evinced a keen interest in Vedic scriptures and became very proficient in the field of philosophy. She became highly knowledgeable in the Vedas and Upanishads in the Vedic times and held intellectual debates with other philosophers.

Gargi is among the prominent females who figure in the Upanishads. She was as knowledgeable in Vedas and Upanishads as men of the Vedic times and could very well contest the male philosophers in debates. She was a leading scholar who also made rich contributions to propagate education.

Once, King Janak of Videha held a Rajasuya yajna and invited all the learned sages, kings and princes of India to participate. The yajna lasted for many days. Janak, being a scholar, was impressed with the large gathering of learned sages. He thought of selecting the most accomplished scholar from the assembled group of elite scholars who had rich knowledge about Brahman. For this purpose, he evolved a plan and offered a prize. The galaxy of scholars, apart from others, included the renowned sage Yagyavalka and Gargi Vachaknavi. Yagyavalka, aware that he was the most spiritually knowledgeable among the assembled gathering, ordered his disciple Samsrava to take away the prize cow herd to his house. This infuriated the scholars as they felt that he was taking away the prize without contesting in a debate. Some of the local scholars did not volunteer to debate with him as they were not sure of their knowledge. However, eight renowned sages challenged him for a debate, including Gargi, the only lady in the assembled gathering of the learned.

These sages debated with him and asked questions on philosophical subjects to which Yagyavalka provided convincing replies and they lost the debate. It was then the turn of Gargi to take up the challenge. Gargi, as one of the disputants in the debate, questioned Yagyavalka on his claim of superiority among the scholars. She held repeated arguments with him. Gargi and Yagyavalka's exchange centred around the ultimate 'warp' of reality. Her initial dialogue with Yagyavalka tended to be too metaphysical, such as the unending status of the soul—moving away from practical situations. She then changed her approach and asked him pointed questions related to the environment existing in the world, the question of the very origin of all existence. Her question was specific when she asked him 'since this whole world is woven back and forth on water, on what then is water woven back and forth', a question that related to the commonly known cosmological metaphor that expressed the unity of the world and its essential interconnectedness. In the Brihadaranyaka Upanishad, the sequence of her posing a bevvy of questions to Yagyavalka together with his replies is narrated as follows.

> *'On air, Gargi.*
>
> *On what, then, is air woven back and forth?*
>
> *On the intermediate regions, Gargi.*
>
> *On what, then, are the worlds of the intermediate regions woven back and forth?*
>
> *On the worlds of the Gandharvas, Gargi.'*

She continued with an array of questions such as what was the universe of the suns, what were the moon, the stars, the gods—Indra and Prajapati. Gargi then pressed on with two more questions. She urged Yagyavalka to enlighten her on the weave of reality and asked:

> *'That, O Yagyavalka, which is above the sky, that which is beneath the earth, that which is between these two, sky and earth, that which people call the past and the present and the future—across what is it woven, warp and woof?'*
>
> *Yagyavalka answered, 'Space.'*

Gargi was not satisfied and then posed the next question:

> *'Across what then, pray, is space woven, warp and woof?*
>
> *Yagyavalka answered: Verily, O Gargi, if one performs sacrifices and worship and undergoes austerity in this world for many thousands of years but without knowing that Imperishable, limited indeed is that [work] of his. Across this Imperishable is the unseen, O Gargi, is space woven, warp and woof.'*

Then she asked a final question, on what was Brahman (world of the Imperishable)? Yagyavalka put an end to the debate by telling Gargi not to proceed further as otherwise, she would lose her mental balance. This riposte put an end to their further dialogue at the conference of the learned. However, at the end of the debate, she conceded to the superior knowledge of Yagyavalka by saying, 'Venerable Brahmins, you may consider it a great thing if you get off bowing before him. No one, I believe, will defeat him in any argument concerning Brahman.'

Her philosophical views also find mention in the Chandogya Upanishad. Gargi, as Brahmavadini, composed several hymns in the Rig Veda. Gargi was honoured as one of the Navaratnas (nine gems) in the court of King Janak.

(Chandogya Upanishad)

BY WHOM IMPELLED MOVES THE WORLD?

The evening prayers were just over. Now it was the question hour. The rishi was sitting calm like a flicker-less lamp. The young students came out with their questions. One of the students asked the rishi:

'Who makes my mind think?

Who fills my body with vitality?

Who causes my tongue to speak?

Who is that invisible one who sees through my eyes and hears through my ears?'

Indeed, this was a pretty formidable array of questions.

The rishi then looked at his disciples with all his love and said calmly:

'Dear boys, the power that inspires all these is one and is indivisible. It is behind and beyond all that functions visibly. It is the ear of the ear, the eye of the eye, the mind of the mind, the word of the words and the life of life. Him our eyes cannot see, nor words express; he cannot be grasped even by the mind. We cannot know, we cannot understand, because he is different from the known and he is different from the unknown. It is that which makes our tongue speak but cannot be spoken by the tongue; that which makes the mind think but cannot be thought by the mind; that which makes the eyes see but cannot be seen by the eyes; that which makes the ears hear but cannot be heard by the ears; that which makes us draw breath but cannot be drawn by our breath. This power is indeed the self and this self is not someone other than you. He who knows and realizes this truth enjoys immortality.'

After a pause, the rishi continued saying, 'If you think that you know the self then you really know not, because all you can see is his external form. Continue meditating on this self.'

'I do not think I know the self nor can I say I know him not,' thus the student submitted himself, seeking a positive solution to his problem.

'He who says "I know" knows it. He knows little. But the sincere seeker who begins by saying "I know not" knows the truth in course of time. It gradually illumines his mind. Once fully realized, the spirit is ever-present to him through all the states of consciousness. His soul grows from strength to strength and by the power of his realization of the immaculate presence he becomes immortal.'

Thus, the rishi replied to his seeking disciples. But when he looked at their faces, he could see that some of them had not grasped the full significance of all that he spoke to them just now. So he narrated a parable to illustrate the essence of his teaching.

Once upon a time, the gods defeated the demons in a certain battle. Though the victory was brought about by the power of Brahman, the gods boasted saying, 'Ours is the victory, and ours is the power and glory.' The Brahman saw their foolish pride and appeared before them. But the gods, blinded as they were by egoism and empty vanity, could not recognize him. They simply saw a wonderful being present before them. They became serious and wanted to know who that being was. They requested Agni, the god of fire, to investigate the matter.

As requested by the gods, the god of fire presented himself before that being and the mysterious being asked him, 'Who are you?' 'I am the god of fire,' said Agni. 'What power do you have?' asked the being again. 'I can burn all on Earth,' said Agni. 'Good, burn this.' Thus saying, the being placed a straw in front of Agni. The god of fire tried with all his might but failed. He ran back to the gods and confessed that he had failed.

Then the gods requested Vayu, the wind god, to approach the being and find out who it was. He went with all confidence but could not prove his might before the being.

The gods begged Indra, the most powerful among the gods, to find out who this mysterious being was. But when Indra approached the being, it disappeared instantly and instead, he saw the lovely goddess Uma, daughter of the Himalayas—the golden goddess. He asked her, 'Who was that being?'

Now the golden goddess replied, 'That was Brahman, from whom comes your power and glory. It was he who won the victory for you all, the victory over the demons.' Indra went to the other gods and told them the truth.

Then the gods realized their folly.

Having narrated the story of the glory of Brahman, the rishi summarized his teachings to the young students, 'The light of the Brahman flashes in lightning and in our eyes. It is the power of Brahman that makes the mind think, desire and will. This is the knowledge of the transcendental and immanent reality. Truth is the very body and abode of Brahman. All knowledge is its limbs. Meditation, control of the senses and passions and selfless service of all are its support. Those who realize the Brahman shall conquer all evil and attain the supreme state.'

The disciples were immensely pleased with the way of their guru's teachings and with joy they dispersed to their respective resting places to reflect upon what they had learnt.

(Kena Upanishad)

Editors' Treatise

Beyond Culture and Engagement: The Coming of the Saptarshi*

The workforce of the 21st century is global, highly connected, technology-savvy and demanding. Millennials are a major force but so are older workers, who remain engaged and valuable contributors. Critical new skills are scarce and their uneven distribution around the world is forcing companies to develop innovative new ways to find people, develop capabilities and share expertise.

The second most globally urgent issue is culture, which leads to 'retention and engagement'—a topic that often has no clear owner within HR or business.

---

* Saptarshi: In Hinduism, a Brahmarshi is a member of the highest class of rishis ('seers' or 'sages'), especially those credited with the composition of the hymns collected in the Rig Veda. A Brahmarshi is a sage who has attained enlightenment (moksha) and become a jivanmukta by completely understanding the meaning of Brahman and has attained the highest divine knowledge, infinite knowledge (omniscience) and self-knowledge called Brahmajnana. When a Brahmarshi dies, he attains paramukti and frees himself from samsara, the cycle of birth and death. Saptarshi, meaning 'seven sages', are extolled at many places in the Vedas and Hindu literature. The Vedic Samhitas never enumerate these rishis by name, though later Vedic texts such as the Brahmanas and Upanishads do so. There are seven stars. They bring down to the Earth the required knowledge and energies to strengthen the processes of transition (Pralaya). They are naturally the most evolved 'light beings' in the creation and the guarding of the divine laws. Their role is to bring with them knowledge, transition, knowledge creation and renewal, values and culture and carry through the Pralaya and establish the new yuga befitting the time. Saptarshis are the seven greatest sages of the Vedic realm. They have attained a semi-immortal status, that of an exceedingly long lifespan due to their yogic power and by the power of their penance. The seven holy sages were assigned to be present through the four great ages, to guide the human race. These seven sages worked closely with the Adi Yogi or Shiva to maintain the balance on Earth. They are the seven mind-born sons of Brahma, who live for a period of time known as a Manvantara. During this period of time, they serve as representatives of Brahma and at the end of a Manvantara, the universe gets destroyed and Saptarshis merge into the God and the task of filling and culturizing the Earth is given to newly appointed Saptarshis. (Collated from Wikipedia)

Our civilization developed via a strong culture founded on a strong set of values, over a long period. This has always been a guiding factor for leaders in all spheres of life and society itself. While talking about HR leaders, we must talk about HR leadership. In the past, leaders of countries, organizations, functions and even smaller units in society were guided by and benefitted from such values and culture.

Significantly, in the celestial song mentioned in chapter 12 of the *Srimad Bhagavad Gita,* translated by A.C. Bhaktivedanta Swami Prabhupada, Lord Krishna, while mentoring Arjun and resurrecting his valour, describes to Arjun all who are dear to Him. Pradeep Siddharth analyses eight shlokas from the *Srimad Bhagavad Gita* in *Sa Me Priyah: Hari Ko Kaun Dularo.*[34]

In the Ramayana, as well as the *Ramcharitmanas* by Tulsidas, we come across the concept of Ram, the king (leader), as 'maryada purushottam' or the embodiment of dharma (righteousness or ethical behaviour) and karma (work or action) towards his subjects.

The Ramayana reinforces the intent to learn from everyone, even the enemy. When Ram vanquished the demon king Raavan, he instructed Laxman, his brother, to learn all he could at the fallen king's feet.[35]

The Mahabharata mentions a similar incident. When Bhishma (the father figure of the Kaurava camp) was dying, Lord Krishna advised Yudhishtir (the king of the Pandavas) to go to the enemy camp and seek knowledge and wisdom. The entire *Santi Parva,* the eleventh book in the Mahabharata, is devoted to the advice given by Bhishma to Yudhishtir. Bhishma taught Yudhishtir about the duties of a king, how to establish a proper system of governance based on dharma and how to look after the prosperity and welfare of his subjects.[36]

The modern theory of leadership echoes a similar meaning—a leader exists to meet the needs of his/her followers. Indeed, Barrett's Theory of Leadership postulates that the highest level of leadership consciousness (level seven) is that of selfless service.[37] According to him, the distinguishing traits of level seven leadership are

- service to humanity and the planet,
- focus on ethics, future generations and social responsibility and
- a display of wisdom, compassion and humility.

The happiness of subjects or deep employee engagement, in the corporate context, is a recurrent theme in Indian teachings on leadership. As we have already pointed out above, the king (leader) has a duty towards his subjects who require care and not exploitation. When combined with spiritual instruction, it assumes the force of a sacred duty.

Dr. M.B. Athreya,[38] an Indian author, educationist and renowned management guru, has been observed to run enterprises, find prospects, address concerns and meet stakeholders' expectations. In the age-old Indian philosophical tradition, some business values are prerequisites for civilization. It also offers the following relatable values, which appear crucial for sustainable success.

DHARMA, ARTHA, KAMA AND MOKSHA

For individuals, leaders, institutions and businesses, Indian tradition commends these four objectives, in the following ethical order of priority.

- Dharma: Righteousness or the right path, which will uphold the familial, organizational and social fabric.
- Artha: The lawful and ethical pursuit, creation and acquisition of wealth.
- Kama: The fulfilment of all legitimate desires and enjoyment of all socially sanctioned pleasures.
- Moksha: The seeking of release, transcendence and liberation from mundane pursuits and the repetitive cycles of pleasure and pain.

As almost the entire adult population is drawn into the global workforce, businesses need to follow dharma in the creation and sharing of wealth. Dharma may be added as an important 'basic ethical ideal' to human dignity.

This sets a robust culture that makes people happy and engaged.

DEFINING THE SEVEN CHARACTERISTICS OF INDIAN LEADERSHIP DNA

Good HR leaders have to ascertain for themselves how they can create a better corporate culture through better communication, open and transparent leadership, sincere discussion and dialogue and good organizational practices. We have to look at how leaders treat individuals, how they communicate, how they motivate and inspire their followers, how they promote teamwork and encourage creativity and innovation. All these competencies and values of leadership ultimately become the foundation stone for building great cultures in the organization, creating an engaging environment.

However, there have been many authors and researchers who have elaborated the competencies found and required in modern-day leadership as well. Jim Collins[39] conducted very elaborate research with over 1,400 companies and leaders. While describing leadership, he confirmed that a successful leader is a level five leader, who is a paradoxical blend of deep personal humility and intense professional will. This applies equally to all leaders and particularly HR and people leaders.

In this section on culture and engagement, we will explore the most significant characteristic of a successful, winning and glorious leader. And what is better than to start from the fountainhead of all leadership—humility.

Humility is the foundation of all virtues as it gives rise to knowledge, realism, honesty, strength and dedication. Real character development begins with the humble recognition that we are not in charge. The humble individual progresses and is blessed because he/she willingly submits to higher powers and tries to live in harmony with natural laws and universal principles.

Humility is not merely the absence of pride but also a positive force that expresses itself in constructive action. This is the base and foundation of creating a robust culture, which is so very essential for a strong organization, society or state.

The humble person makes a realistic assessment of who he/she is and puts that dispassionate judgment into practice. He/She does not think himself/herself to be smaller or larger than he/she really is. In so doing, he/she avoids lofty pride as well as the depths of despair. Consequently, the humble person can attend to dharma without any pretensions or false notions.

Pride is the enemy of humility; courage is its handmaiden. It takes courage to do the right thing and to see things as they are and not as you would like them to be. If we have that courage, we become humble since we recognize empty pride for what it is. We develop a sense of perspective and realize that while our choices are based upon our principles, others may not remain steadfast when confronted by the temptation to do the wrong thing.

Henry Mintzberg once said that culture is the soul of the organization.[40] He refers to the structure as the skeleton, employees as the flesh and blood and culture as the soul that holds things together and gives it life force. Organizational culture holds tremendous significance for sustainable success and for achieving any enduring change in the work environment. This fact has also been established by many studies.

Every human being, despite how gifted and well-rounded they are, has some areas of relative deficit. There are Nobel laureates in physics who lack the skills and aptitude to be good farmers, and gifted physicians and lawyers who cannot change a light bulb. The uniqueness and the limitation of each individual provide the cement that binds our society through the building of a conducive culture.

The leader creates a draft while leading from the front and enabling easy travel towards the destination for the team. When the leader gets tired, obviously because of facing the wind, he/she drops back and lets another take his/her place until he/she is refreshed enough to again take the lead. Some behaviours of ducks when flying long distances can be related to major competencies on leadership, including self-discipline, strong and clear resolve, shared leadership, teamwork, sense of community, coexistence, humility and, above all, a sense of deep engagement arising out of honest ownership.

Organizational culture includes an organization's expectations, experiences and philosophy, as well as the values that guide employees' behaviour and future expectations. Culture is based on shared attitudes, beliefs, customs and written and unwritten rules that have been developed over time and are considered valid. Culture also includes the organization's vision, values, norms, systems, symbols, language, assumptions, beliefs and habits. Simply stated, organizational culture is the way things are done around the organization. While the above definitions of culture express how the construct plays out in the workplace, other definitions stress employee behavioural components and how organizational culture directly influences the behaviours of employees within an organization.

Thus, organizational culture is a set of shared assumptions that guides what happens in organizations by defining appropriate behaviour for various situations. Organizational culture affects the way people and groups interact with each other and with clients and with stakeholders. Also, organizational culture may influence how much employees identify with their organization and how deeply and truly they are engaged in the organization. In business terms, several other phrases are often used interchangeably for culture, creating a sense of engagement with the organization, its true purpose and the employees' own purpose that he/she would like to actualize.

Engagement is defined as the state of emotional and intellectual involvement in a group or organization—the extent to which an organization has captured the 'hearts and minds' of its people. It is, thus, the degree to which employees are pa sionate about their work and devote themselves to their work. Engaged employees go the extra mile to contribute to the success of their organization. In short, engagement means that employees work and express themselves in a physical, cognitive and emotional manner. Employee engagement is described in HR literature as the enthusiasm that employees feel concerning their work.

The best companies now know, without a doubt, where productivity—real and limitless productivity—comes from. It comes from stimulated, empowered, excited and rewarded teams of people. It comes from engaging every single mind in the organization, making everyone part of the action and allowing everyone to have a voice, a role, in the success of the enterprise. Doing so raises productivity not incrementally but by multiples.[41]

To conclude, engagement is a business concern. Research demonstrates that engaged employees create more value for the organization and achieve better results.

Engagement is about behaviour. It is based on people's desire to stay, be a member of the organization and make an extra effort and engage in behaviours that contribute to business success.

Engaged employees tend to speak positively about the organization. Engagement can be measured and improved and research demonstrates that organizations can improve engagement scores over time. In the mid-1990s, Hewitt Associates developed a model for the survey and assessment of best employers.[42] We participated and also benefitted from the model of engagement amongst the employees in our organization. The Hewitt model was developed on supporting business results.

Hewitt Associates define satisfaction as being the extent to which people approve of their employer. They also define commitment as the next stage above satisfaction—as the extent to which people want to contribute to business success. Only then does engagement appear, defined as the extent to which people act and intervene to improve business results. Hence, creating deep engagement becomes a very essential role of a leader, which establishes an emotional connect with the purpose of the organization.

We will focus on the lessons that were deemed important to instil in the hearts and minds of future rulers and leaders by ancient Indian sages. Given below are some examples of sutras drawn from the *Chanakyasutrani* of Chanakya.[43]

- *Sukhasya moolam dharma* (Chanakya sutra 1.1)

The essence of happiness is ethics. If you want to be happy and keep your subjects happy, you must be ethical in your dealings with them and make them also behave ethically.

- *Dharmasya moolam artha* (Chanakya sutra 1.2)

The essence of ethical behaviour is resources. Neither you nor your subjects will behave ethically unless you provide the resources to satisfy their basic needs. Therefore, you must strive to generate resources and share them equitably to create happiness for yourself and others.

- *Arthasya moolam rajyam* (Chanakya sutra 1.3)

The essence of (generating) resources is a kingdom. Resources can be controlled and surplus can be generated and used for the greater good through the administration of a kingdom. In the modern-day context, we can substitute the word kingdom with 'enterprise'.

- *Rajya moolam indriyajayam* (Chanakya sutra 1.4)

The essence of (administering) a kingdom is conquering (controlling) the senses. To rule kingdoms wisely, you need to control and discipline their senses. We can see the philosophical shift between the teaching of statecraft and the importance of ethics and self-development (and later, spiritual uplift) for a ruler (leader). This is a unique aspect of the Indian tradition.

- *Indriyajayasya moolam vinayah* (Chanakya sutra 1.5)

The essence of conquering the senses is moral (and ethical) discipline/ training. That comes from humility. If you indulge in sense gratification, you will not be able to develop a calm and dispassionate outlook which is a prerequisite for creating good cultures. You will also not have a balanced outlook because you will be constantly running after sense gratification. Hence, you must conquer and discipline the senses. The only way to do this is through training in morals and ethics and by cultivating a humble outlook.

- *Vinayasya moolam vruddhopaseva* (Chanakya sutra 1.6)

The essence of moral training is serving elders. You will only be able to cultivate a sense of morality and an attitude of humility if you learn from persons who are wiser than you. You must have the intention of serving them. Indeed, respect for elders is so firmly ingrained into the Indian way of life because it has been drummed into us for thousands of years by the gurus of ancient India.

However, why should we serve elders? This is because it teaches humility, which the sages considered an essential quality of citizens and society. Indeed, it is an essential quality of a modern leader as well. It leads to the acquisition of knowledge, both temporal and spiritual. In other sutras, students are advised to serve their learned elders to gain worldly knowledge.

Given below are two other significant sutras that bear testimony to the farseeing nature of the ancient sages and the universality of their teachings.

Daya dharmasya janambhoomih (Chanakya sutra 21.2)
Ethical behaviour springs from compassion/empathy.

Na asti ahankarasamah shatru (Chanakya sutra 21.6)
There exists no greater enemy than egotism.

We can only speculate whether stronger and better leaders would have emerged and our businesses would have been more successful and sustainable if modern management teaching had been based on the ancient methods of instruction followed in the gurukuls of yore.

The *Chanakyasutrani* guided citizens and kings to be successful in life. In addition to this, it recorded various values that we need to develop to run an enterprise in the competitive world.

According to Chanakya, kings and societies needed compassion and empathy, sense management, moral discipline and humility to create examples of good living and cultures. Similarly, to run an enterprise, we need to build a learning culture comprising the same values.

Further, Chanakya's learnings describe that leadership grows when we provide resources and demonstrate ethical behaviour. A kingdom led with these values will create happiness, satisfaction and joy.

Similarly, today's leader needs to use all possible resources to build a sustainable business. Further, he/she needs to practice ethical behaviour and create a sustainable world through an engaged workforce.

In *Manthan: Art and Science of Developing Leaders,* K.K. Sinha, Ajay Soni and Indranil Mitra further discuss this by saying that the first and foremost distinguishing feature was insubordination of the profit motive to cover the goal of development and nation-building with a strong sense of purpose.[44]

The basis of happiness is righteousness, to achieve which you need resources and organization. The early pioneers of Indian business realized this when confronted with the deplorable conditions in which India was left when it attained Independence—severe inequalities in income, low levels of employment, a weak industrial base and little or no infrastructure.

It seems as though the above sutras provided the philosophical underpinning for the early pioneers of Indian business and their early efforts to develop the Indian economy and society.

Common among these was the sense of doing something good for society. To explain this, let us refer to Indian philosophical tradition, which postulates that every individual lives under five types of debt—towards the gods, towards the Earth—including the plants and animals—towards the ancestors, towards other people in society and towards the spirits of those who lived before. Dharma enjoins us to live in such a manner so that these debts are liquidated. This has lessons for modern management.

In today's corporate context, if we give undue importance to material things like profit, our colleagues and employees will also restrict themselves to looking at material things. On the other hand, if we engage with them on the higher-order purpose of the organization, then probably they will look at enhancing and developing their abilities to fulfil that purpose. Hence, it is clear why the 'India way' stresses on being purposeful.[45]

KEY FEATURES OF BEING PURPOSEFUL

- Builds/Engages with the core purpose/vision of the organization
- Creates visions for his/her function/team
- Connects the employees to this core purpose and to the social setting of the organization
- Takes decisions (including tough ones) based on the organizational purpose/vision

BENEFITS OF BEING PURPOSEFUL

- Generates visionary leaders
- Gives long-term business sustainability
- Develops alignment between organization purpose and employee goals
- Assures higher discretionary efforts by employees

CREATING PURPOSEFULNESS

- Engage teams in discussing/creating vision/purpose
- Take business and people decisions considering the long-term organizational purpose rather than short-term gains
- Cascade the business strategy from the core purpose/vision
- Explore and enhance how your organizations and day-to-day actions connect to the greater purpose

PURPOSEFULNESS IN LIFE GENERATES HAPPINESS

'*Smile—you are in Sharjah*',[46] said a signboard installed on a main street in Sharjah called Al Arouba Street by His Highness the late Sheikh Khalid Bin Mohammed Al Qassimi, Ruler of Sharjah, back in 1971. His wish was to see a smile on the face of everyone who lived in or went to Sharjah. This has positioned Sharjah in the whole region as the smiling city and when His Highness Dr. Sheikh Sultan took over in 1973, he supported the idea by planting a bed of roses with the same catchline engraved on it, right next to the two largest bridges in the city.

I strongly believe that a smile is the most peaceful yet powerful language on Earth, which does not need any medium of translation to be conveyed.

Happiness is the enjoyment of life, also called 'subjective well-being' or 'life-satisfaction'. An enjoyable life is not always a good life but still something worth striving for. The United Arab Emirates has declared that they want to become the world's happiest country in 2021.

Research shows that laughter can help solve problems by making it easier to think, and the lighter mood leaves lots of room for that eureka moment.

The businesses and, more specifically, the people working in them can do a focussed chain of activities to create happier workplaces.

Here are the top tips for a happier office by Linda Chaccour, founder and happiness consultant of Emerge Coaching, Lebanon.[47]

Find meaning: To make work more enjoyable, regardless of your circumstances, seek and create meaning and pleasure in the workplace. Creating the right conditions at work lies within you—identify the tasks and activities that are meaningful to you and make you happy and focus on doing them first.

Acts of kindness: Offer a helping hand to coworkers and passers-by. Most of us assume that being kind and doing or saying nice things to others is for their benefit but research shows that acts of kindness are a powerful way to increase your own happiness.

Mindfulness: Mindfulness is the basic human ability to be fully present and aware of where we are and what we are doing and not be overly reactive or overwhelmed by what's going on around us.

Gratitude: Recent studies suggest that gratitude is linked to well-being and happiness. Grateful people are happier, healthier and optimistic and can cope positively with the changes, challenges and difficulties they experience in life.

In Bhutan, Gross National Happiness (GNH)[48] is a philosophy that guides the Government of Bhutan. It includes an index that is used to measure the collective happiness and well-being of the population. GNH is instituted as the goal of the Government of Bhutan in the constitution of the country. So the happiness of the people is the goal and purpose of the leaders and the government in all walks of work. The GNH index and its continuous improvement are more important than the GDP. Hence, countries have started giving priority to the gross happiness of the people—the citizens. This trend of prioritizing happiness seems to be spreading in the corporate world also, where human happiness seems to be favoured more than profits alone.

Deloitte[49] examined the need and importance of performance metrics within businesses and emerging practices and priorities such as flexibility among nations, which guides today's workforce. To help build a work environment in which passion and purpose among employees can flourish is a noble though tricky business.

Companies should redefine their engagement strategy and shift from strategies of 'holding people here' to 'attracting and engaging people' through measures that build commitment, align employee goals and experience with individual and corporate purpose and provide engaging work and a culture of development and growth.

Thus, business leaders and HR managers find themselves caught in an ever-intensifying competition for the 'right' talent. Keeping the Indian context and challenges in mind, we have identified the trends which will define the HR landscape in India.

Today's organizations operate in the era of social media. Every corporate decision is immediately publicly exposed and debated. Once-private issues are now posted online for every employee, and every potential employee, to read, and an organization's culture is increasingly visible for the world to see. Given the harsh spotlight of this new transparency, an organization's culture can become a key competitive advantage or its Achilles' heel. Culture and engagement are now business issues and not just topics for HR to debate. And there's no place for organizations to hide.

India's research[50] shows that in most companies, engagement is low. According to Gallup, only 9% of the Indian workforce was engaged while 31% was actively disengaged (survey data from 2011–2012). Upwards of half the workforce would not recommend their employer to their peers.

This is a new and systemic problem for organizations and is stemming from the fact that most organizations do a poor job of measuring their achievements or shortcomings concerning culture and engagement. Historically, companies have relied on annual engagement surveys, often costing heavily and taking months to deploy. And very few companies have a process or tools to measure culture and learn where it is strong, weak or inconsistent. At a time when corporate cultures are being continuously debated, shaped and redefined on social networks, the once a year survey is perilously obsolete.

Culture and engagement[51] are no longer less understood topics owned by HR. They are now imperative for every leader and every executive in the organization. What can HR do? Ultimately, the issues of culture and engagement are driven by leadership. Companies pushing aggressive growth plans, experiencing financial stress or going through layoffs or mergers often see a radical culture shift. While most leaders are measured based on business results, organizations must begin holding leaders accountable for building a strong and enduring culture, listening to feedback and engaging and retaining their teams. HR should, therefore, prepare leaders to build the cultures needed to ensure success.

In a digital world with increasing transparency and growing influences, millennial employees expect a productive, engaging and enjoyable work experience. Rather than focus narrowly on employee engagement and culture, organizations are developing an integrated focus on the entire employee experience, bringing together the workplace, HR and management practices that impact people on the job.

A new marketplace of pulse feedback tools, wellness and fitness apps and integrated employee self-service tools is helping HR departments understand and improve this experience. A productive, positive employee experience has emerged as a new contract between employer and employee. Just as marketing and product teams have moved beyond customer satisfaction to look at total customer experience, so does HR need to refocus its efforts on building programmes, strategies and teams that understand and continuously improve the entire employee experience.

Most companies have been delegating this issue of employee experience to an annual engagement survey. They have not assigned responsibility to any senior executive or team to design and deliver the employee experience. HR departments often find it difficult to obtain the resources needed to address an integrated set of priorities and companies often avoid updating their tools. To engage employees on an ongoing basis to help HR teams and line leaders understand more fully what the talent expects and values, many companies remain focused on 'point-in-time engagement' and have not yet pulled together the disciplines of performance management, goal setting, diversity, inclusion, wellness, workplace design and leadership into an integrated framework.

Companies may need a new approach that builds on the foundation of culture and engagement to focus on the employee experience holistically, considering all the contributors to worker satisfaction, engagement, wellness and alignment.

Culture serves to bind people[52] together and helps people communicate and collaborate. A new social contract is developing between companies and workers, driving major changes in the employer-employee relationship, ultimately changing the focus and emphasis on the relationship among people. The days when a majority of workers could expect to spend a career moving up the ladder at one company are over. Young people anticipate working for many employers and demand an enriching experience at every stage. This leads to expectations for rapid career growth, a compelling and flexible workplace, and a sense of mission and purpose at work.

Today, contingent, contract and part-time workers make up almost one-third of the workforce yet many companies' HR lack the HR practices, culture or leadership support to manage and engage this new workforce.

This is giving rise to a new organizational model, a network of teams, in which companies build and empower teams to work on specific business projects and challenges. Professionals come together to tackle projects, disbanding and moving on to new assignments once the project is complete. The nature of careers is also changing. Companies used to invest heavily in employees to keep them for decades and see them grow and contribute for the foreseeable future.

Today, because employees change jobs more rapidly, employers must provide development more quickly, move people more regularly, provide continuous cycles of promotion and give employees more tools to manage their careers.

HR leaders are beginning to see human capital strategies as one of their top priorities for growth. To meet their business goals, senior executives today are holding key positions in the HR function, which are accountable for developing creative new ways to acquire talent, build employee skills, develop leaders, engage employees at all levels and retain critical workers.

The Indian economy is poised for a growth cycle. A limiting factor will be the increasing scarcity of talent, which will only intensify the need for HR to ably lead the organization forward. HR teams that rise to the challenge will see their internal effectiveness, external market value and overall stature climb. To become an effective business partner, HR teams need to develop deeper business acumen, build analytical skills to underwrite their leadership, learn to operate as performance advisors and develop an understanding of the needs of the current workforce. This challenge presents itself at a time when shifting demographics, rapid technological advances, increasing globalization and the rise of new work arrangements are forcing HR to re-engineer many of their people strategies.

Global organizations today must navigate a new world of work[53]—one that requires a dramatic change in strategies for leadership, talent and HR. In this new world of work, the barriers between work and life have been all but eliminated. Employees are always on—hyper-connected to their jobs through all-pervasive mobile technology.

Networking tools like LinkedIn, Facebook and Glassdoor enable people to easily monitor the market for new job opportunities. Details about an organization's culture are available at the tap of a button, providing insights about companies to employees and potential employees alike. The balance of power in the employer-employee relationship has shifted, making today's employees more like customers or partners than subordinates.

Many of today's employees work in global teams that operate on a 24×7 basis. An increasing number of skilled workers in this new world work on a contingent, part-time or contract basis; so organizations must now work to integrate them into talent programmes. New cognitive technologies are displacing workers and re-engineering work, forcing companies to redesign jobs to incorporate new technology solutions.

Demographic changes[54] are also at play. Millennials, who now make up more than half the workforce, are taking centre stage. Their expectations are vastly different from those of previous generations. They expect accelerated responsibility and paths to leadership. They seek a greater purpose in their work, and they want greater flexibility in how that work is done.

For HR organizations, this new world requires bold and innovative thinking. It challenges our existing people practices, including how we evaluate and manage people, how we engage and develop teams and how we select leaders and how they operate. HR organizations now face increasing demands to measure and monitor the larger organizational culture, simplify the work environment and redesign work to help people adapt.

As these forces gather momentum, we see the future as a time for creativity, bold leadership and a fundamental reimagining of the practices HR leaders have been using for years.

Bolstered by the robust economic recovery and a stable central government,[55] India continues to be an attractive destination for global organizations. With a population base of more than one billion and over 61% belonging to the working age cohort, India is also home to the largest working population in the world. India today is one of the major talent hubs and finds itself on the cusp of the next wave of growth. Skill shortage, however, remains a key issue for businesses in India. This becomes a major challenge, given that ours is a fast-growing knowledge-based economy.

The secret is out. Many organizations used to think of performance management as a backwards-looking assessment programme owned by HR but no longer. Performance management is being reinvented for a new, forward-looking purpose—to serve as an efficient and focused business process that improves employee engagement and drives business results. Redesigned performance management processes may or may not include year-end ratings but, across the board, they tend to focus less on evaluation and more on agile goal setting, regular feedback, coaching and development. They shift the focus away from forced-distribution rankings toward helping managers coach people to succeed. By changing this one HR 'ingredient', it is possible to affect many others.

So far, however, the rising importance of revamping performance[56] management is just beginning to translate into a positive view of the process, indicating that organizations around the world—India included—feel that there is a very real and urgent need to change the way performance management is conducted. A lot of companies are discovering that their current performance discussions are focused primarily on an employee's pay level rather than on useful feedback, coaching and improvement needs. As a result, the employees rated low in the current forced bell curve rankings rarely get any constructive guidance to help improve.

Technology now makes transparent goal setting and agile performance management easier than ever. A host of new tools permits employees to share their goals, provide feedback and provide recognition online, even gamify the performance management process to make it more productive and useful.

Done poorly, performance management can not only waste valuable time but also harm engagement and retention. Done well, it can be one of the most inspiring and developmental events in an employee's career, driving performance improvements and organization-wide results. The days of traditional appraisals and forced rankings are coming to an end; performance management is now a tool for greater employee engagement, leading to the making of a very friendly but productive culture in the organization that ensures desired business results.

CEOs now expect human capital strategies to deliver a robust culture and deep employee engagement as one of their top priorities for growth. To meet their business goals, senior executives today are holding HR departments accountable for developing creative new ways to acquire talent, build employee skills, develop leaders, engage employees at all levels and retain critical workers.

The critical question is whether HR teams have the skills they need to rise to the challenge. Today's HR organization must be agile, business-oriented and data-driven to meet business needs and ensure attraction, retention and development of the right talent. These imperatives demand a massive upskilling of HR and create an unprecedented opportunity for HR to play an eminent role in business strategy.

At present, most CEOs and CHROs complain about the lack of the right talent skills within HR. What is behind this perceived lack of HR skills? HR needs to have the ability to rise to the occasion of massive change, be ever-accelerating and hence, take up the task of meeting the Protean challenge that they keep facing while the global economy, business, society, culture and individuals keep changing continuously, at high speed.

Given that many organizations do not invest enough resources in developing either the HR or the business skills of their HR teams in the right direction, it is no surprise that they are falling behind. This lack of new-age skills severely limits HR's ability to impact business strategy and advance business goals. But my HR would certainly need the robust and sharp Protean or Bahrupian strength, ability and confidence to adapt quickly to deliver the desired success.

Companies need to challenge themselves to develop programmes and professionals with the expectation to transform HR employees into skilled business consultants. Businesses report that their HR teams are 'not ready' or up to the job in critical areas including leadership, retention, global and analytics.

To achieve better business results, companies will need to reskill and invest in their HR and their talent capabilities. Thus, HR needs to be always change-ready to deliver in changing contexts, despite new turns in the game. The Bahrupia inside an HR professional is always awake and ever-ready with his/her robust and multi-capability teams to deliver their best always.

It is always true that culture and engagement are the responsibilities of the top leaders, who will have to decide on the vision, the mission, the values, the rules of culture and so on for the organization and ensure adherence and implementation. Much depends on the leader who has to set examples time and again for people to see as an example and emulate. The change and transition generally take time and have to be built into the organization by the leader, who has to demonstrate and set an inclusive work culture. If the leader does not adhere to the norms of culture, he/she cannot expect that everybody else in the organization will follow the norms. This does not happen. However, HR leads and the team also have an equally important responsibility in the organization—to ensure adherence to these values which are expected to set the culture in the organization. In fact, in today's time, we would like to emphasize that HR leads have a much more important role to play in setting up a culture and ensuring engagement in the organization. They have to act as the Saptarshi, who not only bring books of values and norms of behaviour into the new organization but also have a responsibility to stand perennially and continually in the visible sky so that they can ensure adherence and even guide renewals for improvement in the norms of culture and engagement in the organization.

A Saptarshi is a rishi or seer or sage, especially one credited with the composition of values and rules by the organization. HR professionals will have to take this extra responsibility of being a Saptarshi to position themselves to spread value-based knowledge, infinite knowledge and self-knowledge as per the organization's mandate and requirements. These sages of HR that act as Saptarshi, right from the beginning of the organization or Manvantara, stimulate and attain a continuous status due to their position and commitment. A Saptarshi works closely with the leaders in the organization to maintain a balance and live perennially, during which time they serve as the representatives of the organization's leadership.

So a Saptarshi responsible for ensuring and upholding values and developing a culture in the organization has a greater responsibility than merely being administrative support to the organization and its management.

HR, therefore, has to play the role of the Saptarshi from the mythology; a very important set of characters who appear along with their Manu, bringing an agreed set of core values, a mission and vision, and take up the responsibility of making these work and thrive in the organization.

Valli 4.01

HR Has to Move Organizations towards an Inclusive Work Culture Rather than Clannish Culture

DR. SAAGARIKA GHOSHAL

There is a cliché that change is the only constant. In HR, however, we have been changing more often. In most HR organizations, 'competencies' are attached to credibility. No matter how competent one is or how many degrees one holds, at the end of the day, we have to perform in the organization. 'Credibility', in today's world, depends on how well we are able to transform the organization to make it more profitable, sustainable and future-ready.

As HR leaders, it is very important to look at valid propositions in terms of competency frameworks. They will provide the basics or the base to move from one end to the other. But the fact remains that what we do in various organizations is very different. It depends on the intelligence or the 'competencies' of the team in HR or in the businesses to see how they are transforming the lives of every individual in the organization and how organizations are transformed and make a difference in the business.

This comes back in terms of the philosophy of credibility and values.

In terms of HR being the strategic business partner, an HR person is very much a part of the business and leads the business as much as the CEO does. The basic competency needed is to know the business thoroughly.

The value creation plan has helped us not only in terms of building the business more sustainably but in terms of building a culture of dependability and collaboration, harnessing mutual strength amongst the employees with less politics at the individual level. This is just a beginning and there are good signs. Intuitively, I can say it might work. It is a great idea to create value for an organization and also for individuals.

Good organizations realize that sustainability is the key and all good corporations who survive tomorrow will survive only on this. Various initiatives led by HR are focusing on building sustainable organizations. The organization needs to move to more inclusive work cultures. Technology is also changing at a fast pace, and we have Digital India which has put India on the global map. Technology is a great enabler that is changing our lives drastically. But we must not miss out on the human touch.

VALLI 4.02

NEED TO BUILD A CULTURE TO BE CHANGE READY FOR SURVIVAL TOMORROW

BALACHANDAR NATARAJAN

We have spent quite a long time defining the robust processes in the past. There is a need to go back to the basics to introspect and try and answer questions about the reasons why we do what we do and whether it is the engagement survey, the bell curve or the appraisal system. The HR manager needs the courage to ask these questions to make a difference to the organization or the institution he / she is a part of. The big change is that the HR leaders need to reinvent themselves to ask 'why' and to have the courage to take it forward from thereon.

At General Electric (GE), the organization structure changes every year, within one business or the other. For instance, if today their headquarter is in Tokyo, tomorrow it would be Singapore and the next day it would be in Paris. We need to build a culture of flexibility and adaptability in the organization to prepare for the future. To some extent, one can predict this by observing market trends. Good companies such as Unilever, GE, Microsoft or Asian Paints are organizations that have completely adapted to everyday change. One of the important responsibilities of an HR professional is to build an ability to adapt regularly within the culture. For this, we might have to shake the organizational culture and thereby, create new systems and new processes and move people from one functional area to another.

It's not education that gives us the wherewithal to be a leader or a manager. The skillset that one possesses is important. There is a shift from knowing to doing. Knowing can be bridged. For instance, a person can be taught to read a balance sheet in three months.

As a consultant, we would want an imaginative person or an engaged person. In the interview, we look for interesting people rather than only the skills. People are moving away from knowledge to skill since the knowledge gap can always be bridged.

Several companies have adopted programmes like 'earn while you learn' to continue education for their workmen and blue-collar workers. For instance, Ashok Leyland had three main tie-ups in Uttarakhand, including ones with the government and the NTTF Technical Training Centre, Pantnagar. These involved running a training programme for children who had passed their 12th standard exams till they got their diploma of four years. They had classroom education in the morning and work in the afternoon.

This helped them to build the skill set for the supervisory level by the time they finished their education. Such programmes help people of workmen level to move up to the managerial cadre. In Asian Paints, at one point in time, it was tough for a clerk to become a manager because of the type of people involved and the way the roles were defined. Managers were a lot of 30 or 40 people who came from the IIMs, year after year. The clerks would never be promoted. For instance, a sales executive would never become a sales manager running a branch, similar to the caste system. However, the same company has changed.

White-collar vs blue-collar is more about shop floor workers vs managerial staff. The concept was that the shop floor worker would continue to be a worker always because it was very difficult for him/her to transition to be a manager. Strict distinctions existed earlier, which are now giving way to a lot of fuzziness. People need to come out of the mindset where they slot employees into categories because a worker can be a supervisor and a supervisor can be a manager someday. The case in point is a barista who makes coffee in Café Coffee Day and yet grows—in seven or eight years—to run a city with fifty stores, handling the complete profit and loss, people management and environment. It is no rocket science, and there is no degree required to run so many stores. In the case of technology-driven businesses, though, some know-how would be required as compared to something like the hospitality industry.

I would like to quote an example from Café Coffee Day. When we hire people as baristas for the first time, they often come from interior villages and towns to work in this environment. There is a huge cultural shock for them. It is hard for them to even understand that when they can get a cup of coffee for five rupees in the village, why would people come to these outlets, sit for two hours and shell out ₹100 for a cup of coffee. These fellows might not have even worn slippers while walking in the village and here we expect them to wear shoes and uniforms. There is a huge shift in the quality of raw material we get and the way we transform them into rendering quality service demanded by the customers.

There is a huge transformation in terms of not just the knowledge of preparing coffee, which is rather easy to learn, but in terms of the delivery of excellent service day after day despite having tough situations on the home front. This shift takes time and we need to put them through multiple levels of training and development, coaching and mentoring before we transform them into a certified brewmaster whom we can trust with delivering superior service.

We talk about gamification these days to get people interested in learning. Some people want to learn and some are lazy about learning. People who want to learn would learn in whatever methods you offered them or even on their own on the Internet. There is another group of people who need to be goaded into the room to give inputs to them and that is tough. Such a group of people will always exist. Not all of us will want to do everything individually and voluntarily. There will be a set of people to whom we have to provide interesting inputs, delivered in a manner that is useful for them. They will have apathy towards learning and we need to take steps to get away from that apathy. If we measure the staff learning and staff people based on how well they do their jobs, they tend to automatically pick up skills we don't expect them to possess. We will have to go back and ask why people are not interested in learning something and go back to the basics of fixing that.

We are all learning skills. There is a huge shift towards self-learning. The environment around is such that a lot of self-learning is happening.

Valli 4.03

Potential Assessment and Continuous Rotation Is the Way

DR. RITU ANAND

The issue is not about managing performance but of differentiation or of differentiating payments. While we are not talking about compensation, we are silently implying it. The working generation is changing. Around 80%–85% of India and TCS, my company, is Gen Y. They don't want to be appraised in the way we have been doing so far. Terms such as management development are not going to be relevant for them. We need to change the ways we measure and reward people or else, very soon, they are not going to work.

Typically the manufacturing organizations, services and IT companies can boast about manufacturing and BPO processes that relate to back end processes. Assembly line operations such as number of calls, number matrix and predictive and prescriptive analytics are coming into the picture. Technology provides us with the analytics and matrix as a supervisor. And even if we don't do any appraisal, it shows the people who are high performers and are at the top end of the payment bracket. Nobody is interested in development in the traditional sense of the word. Facebook, Twitter, Instagram and WhatsApp are major sources of development in modern times. There are psychometric tests that indicate individuals' barriers and strengths. For development, they want short-term courses that they can do, maybe at midnight, because that is the time they are free. Employees are not interested if we are going to call up to fix a time and suggest ways for them to advance to the next level for promotion.

I get a lot of inspiration from stories of sportsmen. In a football team or cricket team or even in a basketball team, players are all working towards the achievement of a goal. After the match, there is instant feedback from the coach with a pat on the back for a job well done. That's it. If persistent results, with respects to runs, are not being achieved or goals are not being scored, that person is out of the team. That is instant and for everyone to see. There is transparency and there is continuous feedback as well.

Even though we are currently reading it everywhere, we should not jump into the fray and state that such an organization has dropped the bell curve or speak of the death of the bell curve because, ultimately, how do we pay to the jobholders differently? The companies that differentiate based on the matrix and prescriptions will succeed in retaining people while others will not. When a soldier standing at the Wagah border takes a bullet on the chest, he still puffs his chest and stands because he is motivated and inspired by the love for the country. In this case, the compensation does not play any role and nor does the appraisal. That kind of inspiration of countrymen we can never imagine among the corporate.

Culture and engagement are always very important. Continuous feedback, paying people at fixed and competitive rates to the market, keeping the variable component low and ensuring that larger mass gets the same and very few get high and low is what we need to do. This, coupled with potential assessment and continuous rotation, is the way to go in the future. Appraisals may be once a year or four times a year, depending upon the demographics of the company. In a stable organization, where the same people report to the same manager, one year may be regarded as enough. But if it is a dynamic, project-based organization then appraisal being done once a year is not enough.

VALLI 4.04

IN THE CONTEXT OF THE SO-CALLED VUCA WORLD, CULTURE AND ENGAGEMENT ARE RIPE FOR DISRUPTION

ASHWANI PRASHARA

In terms of redefining social contracts, restructuring the culture, employee engagement and so on, let us just reflect on the year that has gone by and the key events that have defined the year. We had BREXIT against the EU, the US had Donald Trump as its president and India demonetized its currency. So a lot of people say it is a VUCA world (VUCA = Volatility, Uncertainty, Complexity and Ambiguity). I would say that the world has been totally disrupted and in the disruptive world, organizations get disrupted too.

The first disruptive trend is technology. The tidal wave of technology is going to disrupt organizations and particularly the HR function in its wake. Of all the aspects of HR, culture and engagement will face the greatest disruption. Culture is the way you define how you work with each other. If expectations are not set, it would evolve very quickly. We are going to see a paradigm change in this area.

As far as engagement goes, thus far we have been used to having annual engagement surveys. Then, we tracked the engagement scores. How are we doing on the engagement front? What initiatives should we put in place to drive up the scores? Most interventions were driven top-down.

This will now see a paradigm change, and the pace and magnitude of these changes are only going to be even more pronounced going ahead. Engagement is no longer going to be an annual affair. It is going to be a daily affair at the very least, if not an hourly affair.

Imagine that in another 10 years from now, you have a mood meter of people coming into work. And you are able to gauge whether a person is coming into the office with a smile or a sad face. I think it is virtually going to be an hour-by-hour, minute-by-minute engagement strategy. The price of disengaged employees is more significant, and corporations will need to do significantly more on the engagement front. It is an exciting time and throughout this entire time, we are going to see disrupted HR functions. The function is going to be disrupted and technology will play a remarkable role in enabling us to delight the employee. But empathetic engagement—the need to connect with the heart—will continue to exist. If done well, tech designs can facilitate this 'high tech, high touch mantra'.

That is the meaning of disruption. Thanks to these megatrends and their impact, the HR function will look radically different in 2030.

Valli 4.05

It Is Extraordinarily Difficult for You to Build Culture Bottom-Up

K. Ramkumar

I see people in authority adopt doublespeak and that creates consistent confusion in the minds of people. In every organization and every institution, for the last 5,500 years of civilization, there have always been culture keepers. It is extraordinarily difficult for you to build a culture bottom-up.

So it is utopian that for centuries we have believed that somehow the powerless will drive while the powerful will listen, and cultures will be shaped bottom-up. I am not saying it is right; that is not my argument. The argument is that people in power employ an extraordinary degree of hypocrisy and doublespeak to make people who don't have power believe that they indeed can shape the culture, consequently, repeatedly disappointing them. They also negatively deal with every culture shaper who tries to do it, and as a revolutionary, either you kill him or you take him out of the system.

There is this odd person, an odd group, that once in a while finds ways to depose the culture keepers and acquire the right to redefine the culture. It does happen and it takes an extraordinary degree of courage. Take, for example, Irom Sharmila. You say she gave up fasting but you fast for those number of years and see what it means. So the equivalents to Irom Sharmila are there in every part of every institution—not only in the corporate world but everywhere. It is difficult. It is not easy. It is not process-driven.

The second point is that I find an extraordinary degree of disconnect when people speak of these two in the same breath. We talk about analytics and we talk about deep engagement. I find it extremely contradictory. You don't use numbers or research to find out how your wife and children feel or how your parents feel.

We keep ending the 'speaking' trend and personal connect and keep reflecting on WhatsApp. You cannot feel the pulse of the company by numbers. You feel the pulse of the company by going out, meeting people, talking to them and engaging them and touching them as human beings.

There is a lovely programme on CNN called Messy Truths. In Michigan, one of the pastors was asked why Hillary Clinton lost the election in such a bad manner. The pastor said that data doesn't vote. If you want votes, you don't do polls. You come and meet people and you ask for votes. They give you votes.

So he said, in the US, people thought that data votes. And eventually, data voted the other way round and not in favour of the people who thought of winning the votes. If the US elections do not prove that whatever claims researchers make about being able to predict human moods and behaviour simply by believing in data and, subsequently, wanting to run institutions based on only the data—sitting in offices like more and more HR people are doing these days—then I have serious questions about what will happen to new social contracts. My HR instinct is to be on the field 90% of the time—speaking to people, not answering emails.

The last point which I want to make is that most of the people coming into institutions now are from single-child households. We need to reimagine our workplaces accordingly. I don't think many of us are applying our minds for that. I believe it is a big challenge to be able to engage people, irrespective of which economic strata they come from. To put the child in a collectivity and expect the child to be able to display the behaviour the collectivity demands, we have to apply our minds to it. I don't think these problems can be solved by surveys and systems. I am a pro-technology guy but I don't believe in this move.

VALLI 4.06

LEADERS AND THEIR IMPACT ON CULTURE AND ENGAGEMENT WITH EMPLOYEES

SUDHANSHU TRIPATHI

Engagement, to me, is the total outcome of the employees' identification with the organization's purpose and being and his / her feeling that he / she has a role to play. And we can create all kinds of models around that. Employees feel engaged when they identify with their organizations' values and principles, not with what very nice-looking words and posters declare but with what they see being practised and lived on a day-to-day basis. Culture is multifaceted. Culture is a cause and culture is also an effect. I used to work in the largest corporate company in the country some time back, and I once had an opportunity to speak to the most powerful corporate lieutenant. He wanted me to work on culture and I said, 'But sir, culture is an output. How can I work on that?' He replied, 'There are a few things we need to do which will give us a kind of culture.'

Having said that, there are two dimensions of culture. Culture is impacted by the leader but culture is also what is called civilization. And it is not that a leader comes and changes the culture overnight. He / She also comes and internalizes the culture that exists. Any change that we want to bring in an organization requires a lot of clarity, effort, perseverance and time and has good chances of failure also. So in this complex kind of scenario, what are the few simple yet powerful things that can act as a guiding beacon?

I have some very clear-cut values and those values cannot be very fancy. They are values that resonate within an individual. To me, those values are words like trust, dignity, respect, transparency, accountability for everyone and preaching what you practice. These things are interpreted differently in different contexts but these are the common themes. I sit in an organization that is a diversified conglomerate but I believe in decentralizing power and authority.

Those who know where I work know us more by our companies and our leaders rather than our group and the leaders and we do this consciously. And to do that, we still need to have common threads around. We strongly believe that these common threads are found through these values. Somehow or the other, those values are the values that we hold dear. Those values are the values that we practice in all the methods we have to reach out to all those people.

So for us, cultural fit is an absolute must when we hire. For me, even the most successful, most capable, most intelligent person who is not culturally fit to be in the organization is not of much value because the disruptive power of our leader can be devastating to the organization.

These are the basic things I believe in and practise, and I believe that if these things are done, you will have not only a good culture but a culture with flexibility and good engagement, which is simple but powerful. And your engagement does not start by talking to employees but by letting the employee observe what you do daily.

VALLI 4.07

DEVELOPING A CULTURE WHICH CREATES PASSIONATE EMPLOYEES THROUGH MEANING AND EMPOWERMENT

RAJEEV DUBEY

In this age of disruption, while strategy, structure, processes and metrics are necessary, what will make the difference is how passionate employees are. And passion comes from two sources. One is meaning—the meaning that a person finds in his/her work. And the second one is empowerment. So I would like to make a case for creating a culture that provides meaning and empowerment to its employees, which in turn generates passion and unleashes potential.

It is much easier to engage employees when the situation is tough by involving them in searching for the solution. It is relatively more difficult to engage people when things are right and smooth. For example, I was running a company called Tata Metaliks for four years and it was a loss-making company when I took over. It was easy to create ownership because people were unhappy and dissatisfied with the existing state of affairs. We learnt to work together as there was a common vision and goal and people wanted things to change so that everyone could keep their jobs. Of course, that comes only with leadership that believes in people and their ability to do far more than they think they can.

When things are easy and there is no threat, it is relatively more difficult to engage the workforce. It requires much more effort and proactive behaviour to create the passion and desire for change. You need the skill to create a dream which paints a new and changed future. Passion is very important if you are to be a disruptive organization.

VALLI 4.08

HIGH ATTRITION IN IT MNCs—AN OPPORTUNITY, NOT THREAT

DR. A.K. BALYAN

My experience is largely from the decades spent in ONGC. In a Public Sector Undertaking (PSU), the overall work environment is different compared to companies in the private sector. However, each sector has its own characteristics and patterns of employee turnover. While the oil and gas sector has had different phases of high and low attrition in the last few decades, the IT and high-technology sectors generally have a high employee turnover. While the PSUs in IT/high technology may have higher attrition compared to PSUs in other sectors, they have tough competition in their sector. Still, they have a lower turnover rate compared to their private sector peers largely due to several caring employee welfare policies of the PSUs.

It is worthwhile to note that in a knowledge- and technology-driven PSU, the employee turnover may vary quite a lot in different functions within the same organization. The core functions/disciplines may face major issues in terms of retention. For example, in an upstream oil and gas company like ONGC—or, as we call it, exploration and production (E&P) company—some critical functions/areas are very vulnerable to attrition. While people do leave the world's leading companies also but attrition in critical areas impacts the growth and performance of the organization. An attrition rate of 3%–4% in the E&P sector of the oil industry is considered high. Attrition in ONGC, at one point in time, breached the 3% mark.

PSUs normally induct younger talent and invest considerable time, money and efforts to keep developing them, with the help of new technologies, processes and systems, particularly for critical functions and disciplines. It takes quite a few years of development efforts to transform a young engineer into a performing professional such as a reservoir engineer, expert drilling engineer, production engineer or geoscientist who can work independently and will be comfortable with newly emerging technologies. They assume the technical team leadership roles in the organization. If such trained experts leave the organization, it hurts the company. We do witness this kind of trend in the high technology area. Under such circumstances, the caring attitude of public sector work philosophy acts as a positive measure towards retaining people. However, one of the major aspects that influence attrition is the pursuit of enhanced personal capabilities via knowledge accumulation, growth and development. While compensation is also important, these issues perhaps influence people to look for other options.

It was amazing to learn from a senior HR executive from a leading international IT company that the company has over 18%–20% attrition rate. It was more amazing when the HR executive said that it is not a problem area for the company as it allows for the hiring of younger performing talent. The company was very selective in retaining the senior supervisory level where the core competence existed. At the working level, the company could afford to manage the high employee turnover, perhaps with lower compensation. The point the senior HR executive was making suggested that engagement and retention are not directly related. Their focus was on the engagement of a young workforce rather than on their retention. The young workforce was quicker to deliver results and had more contributions. The company also has a vibrant culture. The IT sector has a similar work style, qualifications and experience requirement of its workforce. The sector has developed policies and work processes that are least impacted by the attrition rate, unlike other industry sectors.

Another important factor is the culture of the organization. How people work, their interpersonal relationships, whether their views are respected and how much they were engaged and involved in decision-making impacts retention. ONGC may not have been able to match the compensation offered by the international E&P companies but it certainly offered unmatched freedom to work and experiment, development opportunities, involvement in decision-making and so on. We were confident that experts leaving ONGC would be able to recognize these advantages in due course of time and would like to come back to ONGC. We made some policy changes and advertised in newspapers that all the ONGCians who had left ONGC could have an opportunity for re-engagement at appropriate levels if they had added value, new knowledge and skills. We received more than 400 applications, many of them from people working in MNCs abroad. We shortlisted about 100 applications and after holding personal interactions, offered re-engagement to about 40 ex-employees. When asked why they wished to return, the majority of them accepted that money was not the only criterion. They were earning much more than what they were getting at ONGC but they had no involvement in the decision-making, no knowledge sharing, no opportunity to develop themselves apart from the risks of the job. In my opinion, two reasons forced them to decide to come back. One was the freedom to work, experiment and develop, and learn new things. The other was complete involvement and being an integral part of the decision-making in the organization.

Therefore, the PSUs are generally caring companies, and they have wonderful policies to provide to their personnel. These are fundamental aspects of the policy framework of the public sector work environment.

VALLI 4.09

ENGAGEMENT IMPLIES A CONNECT WITH PEOPLE

DR. KURIAKOSE MAMKOOTTAM

I have been an academician all my life, for almost 40 years. It's a pleasure to be amidst the HR practitioners. Though I am not a practitioner in the corporate sense, I do work with people.

From my perspective, the most important aspect of management, not only human resource management, is to attract, engage and retain people. This summarizes the job of a manager. Finding suitable people is very difficult, getting them to stay with the company is even more difficult and engaging them is perhaps the most difficult task.

This is not an HR-specific challenge but it is a challenge for the whole organization and managers across all levels. The complexity of the concerns has increased and that is why this topic is relevant in the current context. For the first time, four generations are working together—the veterans, the baby boomers, the baby busters, and Gen X and Y. This is an added complexity in an already complex work environment, in a country like India. We have a very high level of diversity which very few other nations or contexts have. We find multilingual, multicultural, multiregional and multi-ethnic complexity at the workplace. Creating a work culture within this diversity is a huge challenge.

The majority of the workforce today comprises people who are in their 30s, 40s or 50s. The proportion of employees belonging to Gen Y in the workforce today is relatively small. Therefore, the real challenge is to retain the older workforce. An added dimension, because of the changing demographics, is dealing with this diverse workforce. An important aspect that organizations have to address is that each of the generations has its own set of characteristics. There is a certain degree of differences in these generations in terms of lifestyle, attitude, perspective or work ethics. We need to find solutions if we are interested in the retention and engagement of the workforce.

The word 'engagement' is not new; it has been there since the industry started. Initially, the word 'motivation' was used. If we see the history of management studies from the 1900s and 1930s, the focus was to identify means to bring people to work for the organization. From there, we may have made certain academic distinctions between satisfaction and motivation and today, we are talking about talent management.

From an outsider perspective, there has always been a concern about how to get people to give their best. But the fact is that the workforce today is a very diverse workforce and their aspirations have changed. The word 'loyalty' is no longer in the people's dictionary. When we look at the demography of organizations, many organizations are ageing and there is very little innovation in the organization. We need to be concerned about imbibing a self-oriented sense of ownership. When we are concerned about engagement, we need to connect with people.

VALLI 4.10

WORKING WITH MILLENNIALS AND GEN Z—AN OPPORTUNITY FOR REVERSE MENTORING AND REVERSE LEARNINGS

P. DWARAKANATH

When we talk about employee engagement and retention, the context is important, and it has changed over the years. The political environment has also changed, and the world is like a global village with only political boundaries. The whole demographics have changed. And at the same time, technology has also changed.

While we are talking about retention and engagement, the culture of the organization is very important. It is no longer a choice but an imperative and a major business challenge. At SmithKline Beecham, regular engagement surveys were conducted globally to gauge the organizational and employee pulse. The survey had 20 questions that were responded to by employees across the organization. One of these questions asked was how proud the employees were to be associated with the company. Globally, the score for this question varied between 90 and 93. In Europe and the US, scoring wasn't usually as liberal as in Asia. However, the average score for this question used to be above 90. If the score dipped below 90, then the management used to be concerned that it might be a reflection of the organizational culture, concerning passion and commitment.

At SmithKline Beechem, to foster talent development, we believed in the philosophy of 'catch them young' or 'careers sans frontiers'. We used the '2+2+2 rule', which meant that if you wanted to become a leader, you would have to work in two countries, two markets and two businesses. This meant that leadership would not only be at the top but exist at all levels. The best way to predict the future is to create it rather than wait and watch till it has occurred.

Loyalty does not come with a 'cradle to grave' tenure in an organization but it should be judged based on an employee's contribution. I spent three decades working for one company in the private sector. However, because of the demand and supply scenario at present, it may not happen for others. We should not worry too much about how many years one works in one company but about what one contributes to the organization during their tenure.

Working with millennials and Gen Z can be a great asset to the leader. The organization and leaders should leverage reverse mentoring and reverse learning while engaging with the multigenerational workforce. This should be regarded as an opportunity rather than a threat or a challenge.

One of the best practices I found in SmithKline Beecham was that whenever a person we considered a good performer—both at the global level and in senior management—left the organization, we kept track of that person for the next few years. Research suggests that the first year after people leave is the most critical for them to adjust to the new environment. It is important to note that this was exercised both globally and in India, and it worked in many cases. People who left us came and joined back. Some of them did not join back but they acted as active goodwill ambassadors for the company. They usually gave the best feedback and talked highly about the organization. It is the style of leadership and the culture we develop that immensely boosts the engagement, motivation and management of organizational talent.

Valli 4.11

Manufacturing Industries Drive Employee Engagement and Passion, and Build a Culture of Pride

R.P. Singh

I have been working in the manufacturing sector for almost 40 years and my experience is also confined primarily to this sector. And from that perspective, I would like to suggest that in our organization, we do not have any problems with retention and the level of turnover is less than 1%. We do not encounter the kind of challenges that people find in the so-called new generation industry.

Today, we are talking about very innovative and non-repetitive jobs. But unfortunately, in the manufacturing sector, most of the jobs are repetitive. We are aware of our limitations. At the same time, we are also aware of the strong commitment and work culture that we have been able to nurture over time. A holistic approach towards employee well-being, driven by a strong leader and a collaborative internal trade union, is our strength.

We always go for the latest technology and train and retrain our employees to keep them abreast of technological advancements. However, there is no concept of lateral induction to meet advanced technological requirements. Employability is often quoted to be one of the greatest challenges for HR professionals looking for fresh hiring but not for us. This is because we believe in hiring novices and nurturing them through our in-house talent development ecosystem. This helps us in building and sustaining the culture unique to our organization that focuses on capability building, commitment building and culture building.

Therefore, we don't look for the most intelligent employees. Instead, we look for the ones who are most suited for those kinds of environments and the ones who would stick to such jobs as we can provide. We don't look for people from elite environments since, largely, we manufacture fertilizers and deal with farmers. We look for recruitment from tier two and tier three types of cities or villages. These factors have contributed to making us successful in retaining our employees.

While we don't need to bother about employee retention, we are concerned about employee engagement. With this aim, we try to imbibe and create pride and passion amongst the employees. At the time of recruitment itself, we tell the candidates that if they aspire to be a 'general manager' in five years timeframe, IFFCO would not be the right organization to work for. However, if they intend to work for the food security of the country, for rural development and the upliftment of the farmers, then this could be the right choice to work for. This might be the reason that very ambitious employees don't join our organization but the ones who do join us continue to work for long periods.

Our HR philosophy is that an individual is capable of giving his/her best when he/she is in a pleasant state of mind. This is where the holistic approach towards employee well-being helps. This approach contains a bouquet of interventions aimed at augmenting physical, mental, emotional and spiritual well-being. Some of the interventions even engage with family members of the employee.

Many organizations use individual performance-appraisal based monetary incentives to motivate people. IFFCO believes in group incentives under which underperformers also share the rewards as a part of the group. Based on suggestions from some corners, we introduced individual incentives but after two years, we realized that the individual incentive was doing more harm than good to organizational effectiveness. We, therefore, reverted to the group reward system.

We have never believed in the 'bell curve' or '360-degree feedback' or 'balanced scorecard'. We work as a family and care for the feelings of employees as family members. Employee initiatives leading to innovations are rewarded, and gains of such innovations are shared with them as a token of recognition. Any loss caused to the organization by an employee acting in good faith is not recovered from him/her and he/she is not penalized for the same as we sincerely believe that mistakes are a part of innovation/decision-making, and any action that hampers creativity must be avoided.

Valli 4.12

The Younger Generation Wants to Learn, to Demonstrate and Be Empowered

VEENA SWARUP

It is very important to develop our people. In today's scenario, as of August 2014, with volatile markets and uncertain businesses, talent management is most critical for the success of any organization. Jill Jusko, a senior editor who covers strategy and best practices in manufacturing workforce and operations leadership in her blogs, once wrote, 'Don't endanger the company's future success by failing to nourish the top talent. If you are not nurturing your high potential employees, then you are missing out on the opportunity to help boost the bottom-line.'

The main concern today is how we manage talent and keep them engaged. Is it by right hiring or the right placement or the right training and development? I have over three decades of experience in PSU. I worked for nearly 30 years with ONGC and then I moved to the EIL board. The working environment is the same in all public sector companies.

In EIL, nearly 2/3rds of our workforce strength are youngsters. We have the best domain specialists—engineers, in this case, being an engineering and consultancy company. We do hire the best through campus recruitment and all India tests. In EIL, as in any other public sector company, there are thousands of applications received for the written tests. We do want to create an environment and culture where they stay and work happily with EIL. We try our best to see that we stay connected with them and we keep them engaged. We endeavour to develop them during their journey within the organization.

Right from the start, when we get them on board, and during the one-year rigorous training we impart to them, they are taken through the entire gamut of the activities within the company. We chalk out a plan for them at various levels, orienting them for the organization.

The kind of training programmes and development programmes that are to be given to them are well-crafted. Today's younger generation wants to learn, demonstrate and be empowered. They are knowledgeable and want to be updated with state-of-the-art knowledge and whatever is the best in the world.

We have various development programmes at different levels for our employees. We groom and develop our people. When some of our best engineers leave the company to join elsewhere, it is a trademark in itself for us. We have been able to groom good people and our attrition rate fluctuates between 2.5% and 3% and our intake is around 100–150 per year.

Very often, when I address these youngsters during site visits, I enquire about their knowledge of the company's vision, goals and objectives—awareness about these is high amongst them. However, when I enquire about how many of them have ever mapped themselves as to where they stand in the big picture of the company, very few are aware. This younger lot is passionate about their work and has the best of knowledge. But what they sometimes lack is focus, which needs to be driven into them. As leaders, we need to drive their focus by providing them with the bigger picture. I have felt this to be important throughout my career. The moment they know where they stand in the total context and realize their position in the organization, they are rejuvenated, feel empowered and engaged and have a sense of ownership. This ownership and sense of belongingness help to retain talent better than any other motivational device.

VALLI 4.13

THE NEW GEN IS INFORMAL, FLEXIBLE AND FOCUSED

ANURANJITA KUMAR

Culture may be regarded as behaviour and norms regarding interaction with each other. Over time, various practices or behavioural tendencies contribute to an overarching culture. We often hear a statement when interacting with people or while hiring a person that the person is like a 'Citi banker' or from 'Levers'—a typical statement that brands the person. There is something in this talented individual that we relate to the particular brand. This resonates in the way we behave in a particular company or with particular sets of individuals.

Culture is not built overnight; it is built over decades or centuries. Citibank is a 200-year-old organization and we understand what Citibank culture means. Though sometimes, it may be difficult to pin down, we know it when we see it. Similarly, it would be true for many other companies.

Leadership has been ranked behind culture and engagement. Does leadership set the tone of culture or does culture breed leadership? Productivity and engagement reflect the financial impact of culture. We often talk in terms of the 'culture of engagement'. But it could also be a 'culture of disengagement'?

Culture may be negative or positive. It depends on the angle. There can be several surveys, involving engagement and satisfaction. Everything need not be benchmarked. Though I am not a great fan of these surveys, I feel that they need to be reviewed because of their resultant factors, such as financial impact or bad employee-related issues or employee attrition. The hiring rates depend upon the number of offers made, and there are enough matrices to determine success.

In the pre-2008 period, the culture of financial services as a sector was regarded as very dynamic and was perceived to be a sector that paid pretty well. A lot of people wanted to join it. Hiring talent was never a real issue because people like to work in a dynamic culture. In the financial crisis, the dynamic culture led to very risky behaviour which led to some severe financial losses across the board. This reflects the financial impact which negative culture can create, leading to disastrous consequences not just for the organization but for macroeconomics around us. Then, we decided to resurrect a responsible culture. This is the journey that we have started on that is yet to be completed.

Culture does not change overnight and is an evolution. Dramatically, the culture of a place would not change until there is some crisis. Cultural change is much bigger than the generational changes which are happening. With every generational change, working styles are changing, preferences about how we wish to work or about getting things done are changing. Citibank operates in 104 countries. This means that we deal with 104 countries of different cultures under the same umbrella, and we still bind together by the same glue. The culture is strong and holds the organization together. It does not change with generations overnight. Maybe in a few decades, it might be tweaked a little.

For instance, I was addressing management trainees who had joined Citibank recently and somebody raised a question about how fast he could become the CEO of the company. For a moment I reflected that when I was a management trainee, I would not have even asked the question because I would have assumed that this was very distant. But this is the Google era of instant gratification. The response needs to be handled tactfully. A new generation will not change the culture, though there will be a slow evolution of working style. Gen Y, for instance, is regarded as very informal and looking for flexible working times. There are policies and privileges to manage these aspirations and work styles but this does not mean that the work styles and culture of Citibank would change dramatically.

Valli 4.14

Need for Organizations to Act on Outputs from the Engagement Surveys

BISWAJIT ROY

As HR professionals, we often observe two sets of managers—one being an autocratic person while the other is not so autocratic. The people working under the not so autocratic person are happier, perform better and their delivery is much better.

Engagement surveys give us some matrices that provide us with an overall picture of the organization and its people. It is very important that once the results of the surveys are declared, some action is initiated wherever there are deficiencies. If we don't, then the instrument of the survey will not be effective and it won't give us the desired results.

The biggest problem arises when many organizations do engagement surveys but do not take any worthwhile action despite getting the results. Surveys don't reveal a clear picture because, essentially, they reflect the perception of the individuals to whom the instrument was administered. Nevertheless, it is better to have some information, despite all the associated fallacies and deficiencies that the survey instruments may have. It is better to have some yearly relevant information than not have any information.

If no action is initiated by the organization, people tend to lose faith in the survey instruments and the processes of the engagement surveys. Engagement surveys are not undertaken for fashion but for the cause of the organization to know exactly what they are headed towards.

Valli 4.15

Culture—Its Impact and Influence on the Organization and Its Balance Sheet

DR. J.K. MITRA

We tend to see culture and engagement as two separate things. The more apt word would be 'culture of engagement' because engagement is part of the culture element of an organization. Since the time of Hofstede's work on culture, we have seen that the culture of a company gets influenced by the culture of the country. India is a nation of many nations because of its cultural diversity. This is also applicable to our corporate situations. Indian practices are not so much in line with Asian corporate situations as they are with the global scenario.

When it is a small organization, it is a 'clan' kind of culture. We have numerous examples of organizations having a clan kind of culture and giving excellent returns. The problem takes place when it becomes depersonalized and shifts towards the market. Culture has a very important influence and it does impact the balance sheet of the organization.

Research on culture is problematic. The totality in which we want to describe it is beyond measurement. For instance, when we say Indian culture, it is very easy to say but very difficult to precisely define and differentiate it from the culture in Pakistan or Nepal or Bhutan. Although we all might have experienced it, since every unit is different, the cultural elements are different.

Cultures should not be perceived to be top-down, even though they may appear to be so. A leader personifies certain initiatives and that is why we consider culture to be top-down. But culture is evolving, and it is a gestalt phenomenon.

The types of people who are joining organizations today have grown up in an environment that is distinctly different from the environment of the earlier generations. For instance, there seems to be growing impatience, though this impatience need not necessarily be taken in a negative light. It may be impatience with corruption, impatience with things that are not working or are obsolete and impatience about not getting returns from investments in terms of time, energy and attention. This is certainly going to put forth a very important question about the ways to redesign HR practices. This element of impatience is not a corporate element but a national element. This impatience is the reason why we have seen changes in governance and government structure, nationally or regionally. Similarly, corporate environments will have to respond to these kinds of elements since the culture of an organization cannot be completely devoid of the culture of the country. Therefore, whatever is happening around us will have a direct impact on this element.

Employee engagement surveys don't reveal the true picture. However, they are very important because the surveys allow us to compare. Even if the scale is not correct, it is the same scale that we use across the organization and has been used in the industry over the years. So when we compare the 2015 results with 2014, however imperfect the survey instrument may be, we would still get some idea. We must not limit ourselves to the matrices which are typically used in these surveys. We must use many other kinds of behavioural details which may not have been captured by the survey. Engagement surveys were initiated because loyalty had to be discarded when organizations found that it is a double-edged sword; if we expect our employees to be loyal, then the organizations have to be loyal to them. But in difficult times, this becomes a liability. Therefore, loyalty has been replaced by the term engagement.

HR needs to essentially reconcile the inherent paradoxes. Any kind of survey or study that involves recording and documenting behaviours and critical incidences displayed by people is useful in understanding things taking place under the iceberg and is, therefore, very useful and should be continued.

VALLI 4.16

THERE IS A DIRECT CORRELATION BETWEEN CULTURE, ENGAGEMENT AND BALANCE SHEET

UMESH DHAL

There is a direct correlation between culture, engagement and balance sheet. Leadership drives and evolves the culture. Culture is the way an organization moves and helps to achieve a good balance sheet. Whatever we want to achieve in an organization, we have to imbibe that into the culture of the organization. This is reflected when we see things moving in the right direction and start getting the right results.

Every organization has its own culture. There are no organizations that are cultureless or are have a weak culture. We often talk about Japanese culture, Korean culture, American culture, British culture and Indian culture. The foreign companies or the MNCs, when they came to India, merged their culture with Indian culture. This is reflected in the results. Since the goal was clear, culture and engagement helped Lord Ram to make a bridge between India and Sri Lanka by using local resources—the Hanuman army—and achieve what he wanted to achieve. Therefore, real culture and real engagement can bring the desired results.

A conglomerate is not one organization but a group of organizations. In a conglomerate, the value system remains the same. But the culture can be different from organization to organization and from industry to industry within the conglomerate. For example, if one organization is into automobiles, it will have a certain kind of culture and if another organization is into software, it will have a different culture. But the fundamental ethics and value systems will remain the same. The local leadership in that particular organization/establishment will evolve the local culture.

Gen Y is more influenced by the West. This generation has to be handled carefully. We have to channelize their aspirations and energy for the right cause and overall goal of the organization. As a culture, we have to address this issue. We have to evolve certain changes, and we have to modify the culture. Values and fundamentals don't get modified but culture gets modified because it will influence our behaviour and also influence our path to achieve what we want to achieve.

Engagement surveys give us reference points or percentiles. A survey is an indicative tool that gives us some hints about our performance on various parameters and indicates various areas for further improvements. If we all look at our family systems, the values do not change when we nurture our children. Similarly, when there is a new on-board in the organization, we clearly define the value systems and the culture of the organization. Since they have high aspirations, they definitely try to bring about a modification of the culture.

Times have changed and the HR system has also changed. HR should shift from specific HR persons to all the managers. There are instances where the blend of foreign culture and Indian culture has tilted towards Indian culture. Initially, when foreigners come here, they try to enforce their culture slowly. But gradually, they realize that the intelligentsia of India has their own aspirations and their own imbibed culture. They allow us to have a good blend of both cultures. Then they start respecting our culture and we have to respect their culture. The essence is that we have to coexist.

VALLI 4.17

LEADERSHIP STYLES, CULTURAL CONTEXT, BUSINESS CONTEXT AND THEIR INTERPLAY

V. KRISHNAN

Culture, as a word, is used very extensively in the workplace. Culture in the organizational context refers to the way an individual feels at the workplace; the vibes a person gets while engaging at the workplace. Every organization has a cultural context that is relevant to the business and the strategic context. The cultural context is very deeply ingrained in the DNA of the organization. If the cultural context is in sync with what the organization is trying to achieve at the business level, then the culture is facilitative to business.

As HR professionals, the biggest challenge which we face when we are hiring somebody is to identify whether the individual will culturally fit into the organization, especially at leadership levels. People who fit into the culture of the organization are engaged employees as there is no dichotomy between their style and personality and that of the organization. Just as every person has a personality, similarly every organization has a personality. Therefore, certain people who will be extremely successful in one organization may not necessarily be successful in another organization. This is the reason why we sometimes find successful profiles from one organization not doing too well in another organization and, therefore, moving on soon.

If, for example, someone asks me about the culture at Dabur, the answer will be that it is very entrepreneurial. Dabur is an organization that has grown very fast. It is a public listed company and is highly delivery- and performance-oriented. Dabur provides a lot of freedom to its employees to work and challenge the status quo. Therefore, people coming from very systematized and structured organizations, with not much leeway to do things differently, may take time to adjust here.

As a practising HR manager, I have a very simple definition of an engaged employee. When packing up in the evening, if the person looks forward to the next day and when coming into the office in the morning, if the employee feels a spring in his/her step, then he/she is an engaged employee. When we really love our work, we see a lot of meaning in it and connect with the workplace and start enjoying our work. When we get the right person in the organization, who is a good culture fit, that employee will not be guided by just the KRAs or objectives. Such a person will do what is in the interest of the organization, beyond what is expected, and he/she will put in the extra discretionary effort to enhance the organization's performance.

Every organization has a cultural context that makes it successful. Hence, I am not a great believer in benchmarking cultures across organizations. It is important to understand what makes one organization successful and the ingredients of culture that facilitate success. The whole issue of benchmarking and trying to find out best practices should be done very carefully because what has made one organization successful in its given cultural context may not be replicable in another organization. Therefore, it is better to study and learn the elements of culture which worked for an organization and adapt them in the context of one's own organization if relevant.

Cultural context or DNA is generally uniform across the organization. However, across different functions, there could be subtle differences because of the leadership style of the people leading the function. There will be local climate differences across different functions depending on the function's deliverables and pressures in the overall business context. For instance, in an FMCG organization, in the typical sales function, the leadership style generally tends to be a bit directive and pace-setting at the frontline level. In the marketing context, we may find the leadership style to be more participative. So the different parts and functions of the organization may see different climates coexisting. The leadership style should be relevant to the deliverables of the function and the kind of people being led, in terms of their capability and maturity. Despite these different climates across functions and work groups, there will be common threads running across the organization via these same functions and work groups, defining the organization's cultural fabric. The simultaneous existence of different climates is possible but there will be strong common elements in the cultural fabric or thread.

VALLI 4.18

EMPLOYEE ENGAGEMENT HAS TURNED AROUND A LOSS-MAKING ORGANIZATION

LAKSHMINARAYANA K.

I would like to start with a small example of what employee experience is all about. A lady was shortlisted for the final panel interview. In the panel interview, she was asked what her dream was. She replied that her dream was the betterment of her parents' condition. She said that her parents had struggled to nurture, nurse and bring her up to the present level. She told the interviewer that she wished to take her parents to Singapore on a holiday trip. This point was noted down, a structured interview was taken and she was selected.

On the first day, when she had completed her formalities, she was handed over the appointment letter with another envelope containing air tickets for all three for a week's holiday at a luxurious resort in Singapore. This company still exists. Now is this the employee engagement that we are all talking about?

I would like to share what Mangalore Refinery and Petrochemicals Limited (MRPL), where I come from, believes regarding 'employee engagement'. We were the first private joint venture (JV) in the country, amongst the 250 odd public sector companies in the country contributing 20% of GDP to the country. In the PSUs, the HR revolution is not much talked about. In MRPL, the work culture was more respected as it was India's first private sector JV company, taken over by the Government of India. By this itself, you can imagine what sort of cultural values and ethics the company endorses and enjoys.

In less than a year, a loss-making company with a net worth of about ₹366 crores turned out to be a profit-making company with an annual profit of ₹266 crores. That means a net market growth of ₹500 odd crores. How was this possible in the short term, with the same workforce and with no additional equipment? It was possible because of the harnessing of human talent. And that is the real story behind employee engagement.

VALLI 4.19

THE SARAVANA BHAVAN MODEL WORKS WELL TO ENGAGE EMPLOYEES IN THE RETAIL SECTOR

VENKATARAMANA B.

I am the group president for HR at Landmark Group. We are a private limited company with about 20,000 employees in India.

About 85% of our employees work on the shop floor. It is not an easy job. They work standing for about nine hours a day; they work on weekends and public holidays and they get a minimum wage salary package.

When I had first joined the organization in 2009, I remember the attrition level was about 100%. This meant that we had a new employee for every position every year. This was not a good sign for the organization. However, today, I am happy that we have brought down the attrition rate to about 22% and I strongly believe that this has been due to our HR initiatives.

We analysed the pain points and grievances of our employees and built our HR initiatives upon the understanding of their needs. In the beginning, our store employees did not see retail as the best career option. It was not an aspirational profession, and they did not see growth in such a career. Hence, we created a career path, provided them with opportunities for higher education and brought respect and honour to their profession. At the end of the day, we created pride in their work, leading to loyalty. We created a unique work culture and built this culture on the values and ethos of life.

While we worked extensively to improve our frontline workplace, we also had to adopt a different approach for our corporate and regional offices. We work with many fashion designers in the office. We recruit about 80–90 design students from institutes like NIFT. Each year, they join us as designers, buyers, visual merchandisers and so on. They are a different breed altogether. We had to manage these extremes. We had to create a culture relatable to both our corporate employees as well as to our stores. Today, we have a huge workforce at our offices and are happy to see that we have good, fun-filled yet value-driven work culture. This has been the result of the pro-HR initiatives that were instituted in the organization.

While we brought in new initiatives, it was also important to transform how we worked as HR. I remember when I first joined the company, the attendance was taken in excel sheets, and we couldn't accurately confirm whether employees were attending to their duties. So as a first step, we introduced a biometric system and aligned our payroll to that. We also introduced a Human Resource Management System (HRMS) platform to make it easier to manage this. Today, we are in leapfrog mode where a lot of initiatives are technology-driven and we have even introduced bots to take care of such requirements. We have introduced e-learning and have followed this with gamification in many of our learning and development initiatives. We have moved ahead in terms of using technology and making everything more accessible to employees, allowing them time to excel at their roles. The work of HR has been twofold—to motivate employees and improve morale and, at the same time, to automate HR and make processes easier.

When speaking about HR and creating a good work culture, I often take the example of Saravana Bhavan in Chennai. They take care of their employees, provide them with accommodation and give them pocket money while also depositing salaries directly to their bank accounts. They are also allowed to go to their native place once a year. Statutory benefits like Employee State Insurance (ESI), Provident Fund (PF) and Employees' Provident Fund (EPF) are provided to them. These simple steps have ensured that the employees are very loyal to the company. The reason to bring up this Saravana model is to understand that different organizations require different HR practices. Saravana Bhavan does not even have an HR manager. Just by being empathetic to their employees, they are able to build loyalty. The same goes for many of our kirana stores. With simple yet effective initiatives, they build lifelong loyalty.

The same is true for any organization, big or small. Empathy, trust and listening to and understanding employees is a prerequisite to building a great work culture in any organization. If we take small steps to improve their lives, we will also improve our organizations.

CHAPTER 5

THE NEO HR: THE BAHRUPIAN CHALLENGE

'The irony of life is that those who wear masks often tell us more truths than those with open faces.'

– Marie Lu

ASHTAVAKRA

The sage Uddalak had a school where he taught the Vedas. Kahol was one of his best disciples. Pleased with him, Uddalak gave Sujata, his daughter, in marriage to him. When Sujata got pregnant, she desired her child to imbibe spirituality and intelligence. She started sitting in on the classes at the school, listening to the chanting of the Vedic mantras.

One day, Kahol was reciting the Vedas within the hearing distance of the child growing in the womb. The embryo heard the recitation of Kahol and whenever Kahol pronounced a syllable wrong, it squirmed in distress. Sujata informed Kahol that he had pronounced the syllable wrongly as indicated by the child in the womb. This happened on eight occasions. Kahol perceived this as arrogance on the part of the fetus and cursed it with eight deformities of the body. When the baby was born, it was crooked in eight places. He was named Ashtavakra, which means 'one having eight bends'.

One day, Kahol was persuaded by Sujata to go to the court of Janak to earn some money. In Janak's court, Kahol was challenged to a scriptural debate (shastrartha) by the philosopher called Vandi. Once the best philosophers were invited for shastrartha, in the presence of Rajarshi Janak, Vandi defeated Kahol and submerged the vanquished man in water.

Ashtavakra and Shvetaketu, the son of Uddalak, grew up together. Uddalak, Sujata and the disciples ensured that Ashtavakra was never informed of his real father. One day, however, Ashtavakra came to know the truth about his father from Sujata. He decided to confront Vandi and defeat him in a shastrartha.

Ashtavakra and Shvetaketu made their way to Janak's palace. Rajarshi Janak tested Ashtavakra and the latter answered with ease. Janak decided to let Ashtavakra face Vandi. Vandi and Ashtavakra began the debate and, eventually, Ashtavakra won. As per the condition of the contest, Vandi was to be drowned in water just as he usually did to his vanquished opponents but Ashtavakra forgave Vandi. In turn, Vandi let the earlier vanquished be released. Ashtavakra worshipped his father and was praised by all the freed sages. Kahol was extremely pleased with his son. He returned home with Ashtavakra and Shvetaketu. In the presence of Sujata, Kahol asked Ashtavakra to bathe in the Samanga River. When Ashtavakra entered the river, all his crooked limbs became straight. Ashtavakra gave god knowledge (gyan) to Rajarshi Janak.

Such was the Indian way of learning the best every time through churning and debates. Only the best excels and delivers the most desired results.

(Ashtavakra Geeta)

KACHA

Kacha was an ancient sage and the son of Brihaspati, the guru of the devas in Hindu mythology. The narrative of Kacha is mentioned in the Mahabharata, the Matsya Purana and the Agni Purana. He was known for learning the Mrityu Sanjivini Mantra (a hymn for reviving the dead). But Kacha failed to bring many dead devas back to life after earning the wrath and curse of Devayani, Shukracharya's daughter.

Kacha was sent by his father to learn and work on the secret of the Mrityu Sanjivini Mantra from Shukracharya, the guru of the asuras. The idea was to help the devas, who were about to lose the war, with the knowledge of this secret. Brihaspati advised him to impress Devayani, to impress Shukracharya, who was very fond of his daughter. Kacha followed his advice but unknown to him, Devayani fell in love with him.

In the meantime, the asuras came to learn Kacha's true identity and wanted to kill him as he could be dangerous if he learnt the mantra and left. Every time they killed Kacha, Shukracharya revived him with his art on the insistence of Devayani. The asuras eventually killed him and mixed his remains with alcohol and served it to Shukracharya. Shukracharya unknowingly consumed it, and when he tried to revive Kacha, he realized that Kacha was in his stomach and taking him out would endanger his own life. Shukracharya then taught Kacha the mantra and told him to come out. Kacha came out by tearing his guru's stomach open and brought his guru's life back with the help of the Sanjivini Mantra.

Kacha, having accomplished his mission, was about to start his journey back to Devaloka when Devayani expressed her love for him and asked him to marry her. Kacha told her that she was like a sister to him as she was the daughter of his guru—a guru being equivalent to a father according to Hindu dharma. This infuriated Devayani who was passionately in love with Kacha and she cursed him to not remember and thus never get to use the Mrityu Sanjivini Mantra at the time he would need it the most. In return, Kacha cursed her to never get a husband of strong character.

During a fierce battle between the devas and the asuras, Kacha decided to use the Mrityu Sanjivini Mantra to bring back all the dead devas to life. But Devayani's curse activated and caused him not to remember the mantra. This gave an upper hand to the asuras in the great battle between devas and asuras.

(The Mahabharata)

Editors' Treatise

The Neo HR: The Bahrupian Challenge

While talking of Human Resource Development today, we must look at the HR evolution very briefly to connect with the current time. We can start from the recorded history of the Chandragupta period—when the ruler received wisdom from Chanakya, his mentor. Chanakya created a great book of governance known as *Arthashastra*. There is, thus, a need to assess and walk through all the developments in HR through the ages.

Chanakya was very well-educated. He had a strong mind for facts and knew which developments in society could assimilate into the development of a robust civilization. He has been referred to as a great HR visionary.[57] As prime minister to Chandragupta Maurya, he started creating rules and regulations for the guidance of authorities at several levels for the smooth governance of the empire.

This laid the basic foundation of HRD, including its structure, talent development model and role in laying down culture in society and creating processes of engagement of people at work.

There have been several gurus or ministers in different empires in India, after the Maurya Empire, who have learned and developed rules and regulations to govern their empires and make them a happy place.

Touching upon the above as a part of history, we may analyse the changing face of work from there to the current time to tomorrow, when HR will emerge as one of the major sources of building a happy civil society.

I. THE CHANGING FACE OF WORK[58]

1. There have been three broad phases or 'revolutions' in the history of civilization:
    - Agricultural revolution: This involved a transition from nomadic tribal life to settled agricultural life. It took 5,000–10,000 years. A joint family system of coexistence was settled, and social bondage was developed.
    - Industrial revolution: Large scale production of goods and services and factories with an assembly-line system of production emerged.

People came and worked for survival. They stayed as there were fewer opportunities. Grandparents started getting abandoned and social and joint families started getting disintegrated.

- Technological revolution: A rapid acceleration of technological change came about, virtually changing the face of industrial society as we know it. A new generation emerged. Their parents took care of survival. This new generation wanted a certain standard of living and wanted good salaries, home EMIs, car EMIs, education loans and so on. In this generation, loyalty reduced—even though loyalty never existed in the first place and when it did, it was only as they did not have any options. But this generation got the option of better jobs.

2. This technological society heralded the rise of the 'knowledge worker', valued for the knowledge and skills he/she brings to a job. Knowledge management became increasingly important. This was because it was recognized that in the long run, tinkering with other factors of production like money and materials may bring about some gains for the company but these gains could be duplicated by other companies that had the necessary money and resources. The only way to achieve sustainable success is through the most valuable resource of all—the people of the organization.
3. Regarding the acceleration of change, consider the fact that even though there are over 5,000 years of recorded human civilization, most of the major technological innovations and changes have occurred within the last 300 years and nearly 80% of these changes have occurred within the last 100 years.

   After the 2008 downturn and recession, the information revolution died out. Today, information is freely available on YouTube and it is no longer a hidden thing. You can learn coding on YouTube and anything else you could want, from cooking to gardening, to music to subject knowledge and so on. Today, it is the social revolution or the digital revolution that is important. The new generation does not have the problem of survival. Their grandparents took care of that. They don't have to worry about the standard of living as their parents took care of that. The new generation is concerned about the quality of life.

   Quality of life means the quality of work and workplace, quality of jobs, quality of learning opportunities, quality of the environment, quality of roles and rewards and so on. No one asks anyone to bind themself with a contract. They will not want that. They want freedom. When employees don't have a mechanism for that, they always find themselves in trouble.
4. Another discernible trend in the workforce is that we find more and more women entering it. In the brave new world of the technological society, intellectual and emotional skills are becoming increasingly important, and

with the advent of a host of new gadgets to relieve the workload at home, women are entering the job market in increasingly large numbers. This is a welcome development that we should recognize and plan for.

With the Internet and computers and the changing composition of the workforce, the traditional concept of employees working in a centrally located office has also changed. Now, people can work from their homes or hotels also. As such, work premises have become fluid to some extent and are likely to become even more so in the future with the advent of satellite telephony, which makes it possible to communicate with anyone anywhere on the globe.

II. HR THEN AND NOW

The HR function itself has evolved from its beginnings as labour welfare and administration. In the old days, labour was regarded as just another factor of production. The primary task which the HR function had then was to ensure that labour was paid wages for the work they did and to see that there were no IR problems that could lead to a stoppage in production. It could best be described as a routine maintenance function.

The picture is quite different now. It is universally recognized that people are the most valuable asset of an organization and that it is only the people that can make a difference, not so much money or materials. The HR function now invests heavily in the training and development of employees for these reasons. Traditional IR has given way to collective bargaining and the partnership concept, where management and unions and associations are learning to work together to achieve the common goals of the organization.

HR, nowadays, places great emphasis on the software aspects of working in an organization, such as vision, mission and values. We recognize that it is important to create a shared vision, to have a mission statement and, above all, to have a set of core values. Indeed, the fundamental assumptions of HR today are radically different from what they were earlier. Earlier, HR people were only concerned with the work-life of an employee—output, productivity and so on. Nowadays, HR is concerned not only with the worker but the total person and recognizes that he/she is not just a mere cog in the production process but a complete individual.

III. ISSUES FOR SURVIVAL

The Learning Organization

What do organizations need to do to survive well into the new times? We have seen that one characteristic feature of this day and age is the rapid onslaught of change, fuelled partly by accelerating technological innovation and partly by human ingenuity, which gives rise to mergers, acquisitions, diversifications and so on. The answer is that organizations have to institutionalize the capacity to learn and to build into their system the ability to cope with change. It is important to recognise that creating a learning organization is a fundamental requirement for a company to be able to survive and grow in the long run.

Fair and Just Corporate Governance

The successful companies of the future will be those that are well-governed and those whose institutions, structures, systems and processes are such that the people working can give their best.

Corporate governance hustle has a 'hard' side and a 'soft' side. Both are interrelated and are equally important. The hard side refers to the architecture of the company, its hierarchy, levels, delegation and reporting relationships. The soft side refers to the culture of the company—the way of doing work, the vision and mission of the company and the extent to which these are shared and owned by its people and the value systems of and interpersonal relationships between the employees.

Maximizing Intellectual Capital

The people of an organization represent what is called its 'intellectual capital', which is the total of the knowledge, skills and competencies of its workforce and the degree to which they identify with the goals and objectives of the organization. The challenge for all of us today is to maximize the intellectual capital available to our respective organizations by increasing the competence of our people and by securing their commitment to meeting the organizational objectives. That is why companies nowadays need to place so much emphasis on training and development and that is why the 'soft' aspects have become so important today.

Strong Values

The most important thing that enables an organization to survive is a strong value system. It is not so much the nature of business or the profitability or capital assets; it is a strong sense of shared values among its people that makes an organization survive and ultimately flourish. Any organization that wants to survive well into the new millennium has to build a strong culture of shared values among its people.

The Human Touch

As pointed out earlier, an employee is not merely a worker that has to be compensated for his/her output. He/she is a total person with many roles, responsibilities and obligations. It is important to understand and appreciate this because you can only get the best out of an employee when you are sensitive to him/her as a total person and address his/her needs fairly and squarely.

The Living Company: The Organization as a Community of Human Beings

It is most important to recognize that an organization is not just an economic entity but also a community of human beings that depends on the efforts of its people for its very survival. These efforts have to be coordinated and in tune with one another if the organization is to achieve its goals.

Successful organizations in the new millennium will be those that can institutionalize a shared set of strong values into their culture and can develop their individual members successfully. The challenge for HR is to build companies like these.

Commitment to Values, People, Learning and Innovation

We have seen how a shared value system is of fundamental importance for ensuring the survival and growth of an organization in these uncertain times. Values and ethical rules help people see who they are and what they stand for. In other words, value classification leads to a developing sense of identity and generates a feeling of belonging, both of which are the most important things for ensuring survival and, ultimately, success.

It is equally important for the organization to be committed to learning. It has to provide opportunities for people to learn together so that learning capability is institutionalized in the structure and systems of the organization.

If learning capability is institutionalized, changes and innovations occur within the company. The organization not only encourages these innovations but adopts many of them. The innovators are the ones who will stay while the traditionalists will fall behind and eventually pass.

IV. ORGANIZATIONAL SPACE

Learning and innovation require organizational space along with freedom from control, direction and punishment for failure. At the same time, commitment to people requires trust. A culture of trust results in achieving levels of productivity that cannot be obtained by discipline and hierarchical control. Trust also allows for space and tolerance both within the hierarchy and towards the outside world.

V. PUTTING PEOPLE FIRST

Organizational Space

As already pointed out, people are the most important assets of any organization. A company can deliver only when its people deliver and people can deliver best when they have the freedom to work 'without fear or favour'. This requires organizational space or freedom from stifling control and the threat of punishment. The challenge for HR is to create this space and provide for every individual an atmosphere in which he/she can realize his/her talent and latent potential. Organizational space implies the freedom to question, experiment and challenge existing beliefs.

Tolerance Builds Strength

A prerequisite for organizational space is tolerance; we must be tolerant of activities in the margins and of the people who differ from us. We should always keep in mind that more important than intellectual tolerance is emotional tolerance—to be respectful towards people who see things differently from the way we do. The very foundation of a living company or a learning organization is tolerance. When we celebrate others' strengths in addition to our own, we are further enriched, and we also forge a deeper and more caring relationship with that person.

Code of Conduct and Ethics

It is useful to have a written code of conduct and ethics in an organization to serve as a reminder to its people to embrace the values of fairness and integrity in relationships and business dealings. Try as we might, it is not always easy to internalize and act according to these principles at all times. At least, when we do go astray, we can be reminded of our mistake and know that we have to correct ourselves. A written code also serves as a beacon or a guiding light, giving us ideas to aspire for.

HR Thought Leaders

We wish to refer to Dave Ulrich, the international HR guru. From the Michigan Business School, he has been researching and studying corporates and, particularly, HR functions over the last three and a half to four decades. We would like to refer to *Tomorrow's HR Management: 48 Thought Leaders Call for Change*,[59] a book he wrote with his colleagues, Michael Losey and Gerry Lake at the turn of the millennium. It forecasts changes in HR, in association with several other academicians, students of HR and HR professionals. The book talks about how HR practices, departments and professionals have become less clear at the turn of the millennium. HR issues were referred to as increasingly salient to business performance under several labels, suggesting core competencies, intellectual capital, organizational capability, high-performance work systems, process management, value-based management, empowerment, involvement, productivity, culture change and high-performing teams. Each of these labels or organizational initiatives rests on the assumption that HR practices impact executive thought and action along with the organization's performance. The book focuses on the issues and practices central to HR. Even though HR issues have been gaining prominence, traditional HR is under increasing pressure to rethink, redefine and reevaluate its roles. Some even refer to this as the demise of HR functions whereas others suggest outsourcing these and several others think of these as management roles. This was the time when several experiments were being undertaken to evolve outsourcing, shared services, strategic partnerships, line manager accountability and other forms of governance of HR departments. In 2000, HR started examining the current and future fate of business strategy, indicating what the business environment and strategy should be in the future. Questions like what is the capability available and what they ought to be and what the practices in HR are and what other practices could be developed to deal with the future strategy and capability required were being asked. Dave Ulrich emphasized that HR professionals must not look at only the present strategy, organization or practices.

The author referred to six broad areas of changes in HR, which include managing HR like a business, having HR professionals play new roles, respecting history and creating a future, building new infrastructure and globalizing and remembering the human in HR. While reading the book, one would feel that it describes the role of a Protean in HR, who will keep on adapting to new demands on HR and the organization to survive and deliver.

In 2005, we came across a paper presentation by Ulrich, at the SHRM Annual Conference,[60] where the theme was 'What Is the Next for Human Resources'. This was an elaborate paper analysing and presenting fundamental messages. He referred to the HR profession as being in a state of constant flux. This is not surprising as the whole world that we live in is in flux. While both theory and actions are going to be equally essential, HR has to be conscious of adding value to business and society. He mentioned that HR survives only because it adds value which is defined by the receiver more than the giver. We are generally very curious as to what factors or elements determine value. While HR practices revolve around people performance, information and workflows, HR will have to create practices to manage this flow. Ulrich also added another two elements, which are the HR department, which is capable of delivering value, and HR professionals who have to invest in themselves continuously to improve delivery. He also emphasized the HR value proposition.

After a decade and a half, Ulrich still brings out almost the same or similar element to determine the value needed to be delivered by HR against their value proposition. We all heard his presentation in May 2020, in the context of the Covid-19 crisis. While all disciplines continuously refer to the rapidly changing technology and its impact on countries, business, society and individuals, HR too is being asked to appreciate and anticipate the changing environmental conditions that will shape our future.

Ulrich believes that a crisis is a terrible thing to waste. He quotes Einstein by saying that 'in the midst of every crisis, lies a great opportunity'. HR is about the value created for others. Ulrich still believes that value is defined by the receiver more than the giver.

We would like to look at this from what Ulrich has brought out in the last 20 years, casting the HR value proposition onto the rapidly changing environment of today due to technological and digital changes. References are made to talent (competencies, workforce and people), leadership brand (new leaders and leadership pipeline), organization (capability, working place process) and HR effectiveness (upgrading HR competencies). There is hardly any element of change in HR when we refer to these repeatedly, decade after decade.

Is this what we call new or is it the proverbial old wine in a new bottle of digitized wine? Ultimately, whether we talk about assessments or actions from the menu card suggested by him, the issue of how HR always takes care of others remains. It also points out the softer element of how successful HR people can still be truthful to their profession, the people they organize and the society that they create. Today, the world is talking emphatically about happiness and not merely the so-called business excellence that delivers success.

The HR profession is at a crossroads or on the wrong road. Who is the custodian and developer of the HR profession today? The answer is disappointing. Universities, at one time, used to be the generators of new knowledge, articulators of values and builders of professions. Today, they are busy commercializing knowledge or generating scalable knowledge rather than creating knowledge, skill and values that guide the profession. Professional bodies are concerned with their own scalability and event management rather than building the profession. Consulting firms have mandated the creation and use that add to their top and bottom lines. Individual professionals are busy establishing themselves and sharing laurels. We need dedicated teams to be custodians of the profession. This is the time when the word 'human' has to be refocused on, redefined and redirected in the right ways to create peace, explore new possibilities and lead the world to be a place of joy for all those living. The HR profession is the right one to help everyone to contribute to this. We must not miss the opportunity by misusing our responsibility. We owe it to our profession. To this end, every human being can be considered an HR person, and those with a formal identity have an additional responsibility.

In 2018, Dr. T.V. Rao, an eminent HR guru from India who has been very relevant in the Indian context of business, raised a question about whom HR serves.

HR[61] must focus on review and reflection and result in a re-engineered and re-engaged HR function and make everyone his/her own HR manager.

HR has many stakeholders. Significant among them are the

- top management, representing business strategies and priorities,
- employees, so they stay motivated and competent and exhibit the right values and culture,
- HR function, so that it is occupied doing the right things and gets valued and
- external world (media, professional bodies and other agencies), for the dissemination of good practices and employer brand building.

Most HR professionals in the past have largely served the first and the last two stakeholders. HR has got a lot of visibility and significance among these three, as indicated by its positioning at the board level, media coverage and representation in professional bodies, along with significant growth in the profession itself.

Unfortunately, it is yet to establish itself as the most admired function among employees. It is yet to establish its credibility by serving the main stakeholders it is meant to serve, and that is 'employees'. Good CEOs are seen as 'HR-driven' or people-driven but not necessarily by their HR teams. HR generally gets entangled in its age-old Bahrupia image that effectively mesmerises all stakeholders—an image that adversely affects its credibility again.

HR has worked hard and made a significant impact in many cases on delivering short-term results. HR policies and priorities that have delivered short-term benefits in the recent past are concerned with retention management and attrition studies, recruitment, incentives, pay hikes and performance-linked pay, work conditions, employee engagement surveys, forced distribution and performance management and so on. In a few cases, upgrading of technology and use of HR analytics have also been undertaken. Some progressive organizations have worked on

- undertaking exercises to create a leadership pipeline through leadership development programmes,
- assesing and developing centres to identify high-potentials and future leaders,
- developing effective performance management programmes that have done away with forced distributions and that treat every employee as a potential contributor,
- ensuring 360-degree feedback to enhance self-awareness and prepare development plans to enhance their own managerial and leadership effectiveness and
- coaching and mentoring, through the organized development of coaching skills and creating a coaching culture.

Organization development and institution building concerns that focus on building lasting organizational culture, sustainability, intellectual capital and people capabilities for long-term sustainability have reduced. The focus has been more on adopting the trend of the day rather than building long-term culture and change. In their impatience to get short-term results, organizations have undertaken some of the above programmes as 'quick fix programmes' rather than long-term organization development interventions. High attrition in HR professionals in some organizations facilitated experimentation with many of the above. The multiplicity of consultants used and interventions undertaken diffused the focus from serving employees to self-serving HR.

Technology application and HR analytics have emerged as the new agenda but people are still learning. HR analytics has phenomenal potential but we are limiting the same to short-term concerns. For example, the application of HR analytics to predict attrition and retention are good initiatives. However, HR analytics is seen in some cases as merely a predictive tool of attrition and this restricts its use as an organization development tool that enables employees to self-manage motivation, engagement and happiness at the workplace. Technology should move from HR to the hands of employees and from HR managing people to self-management by employees. For HR to make a better impact, it should move and make a quantum leap to serve its main stakeholder—employees.

Dr. T.V. Rao suggests that administration or employee management should disappear from HRD radar. Culture building and value development should become the focus. Individuals should be helped to take more responsibility for their contributions and contribution management should replace performance management. Discussions on forced distribution should disappear and OD should return.

The new HR agenda must focus on review and reflection and result in a re-engineered and re-engaged HR function. HR should move away from serving the external world to servicing the internal world and focus on strategies that empower employees to engage and enhance their contributions. HR should enhance its in-house credibility, manage its attrition and enhance its engagement. Our approach to technology should change. Common sense cannot be replaced with systems and technology can only be an aid and not a substitute. The main agenda for HR now is to make everyone his/her own HR manager. If HR does not do it in a planned way, it will happen by default with little credit to HR!

Demographic upheavals[62] have made the workforce a mix of younger and older people. Millennials now make up more than half the workforce, and they bring high expectations for a rewarding and purposeful work experience with constant learning and development opportunities, and dynamic career progression. At the same time, baby boomers are working into their 70s and 80s and are being challenged to adapt to new roles as mentors, coaches and often subordinates to junior colleagues. The global nature of business has made the workforce more diverse, demanding a focus on inclusion and shared beliefs to tie people together.

As the workforce becomes both younger and older, and business challenges grow more global and diverse, fresh challenges in leadership development emerge. The 'new organization' is being led by a breed of younger, more globally diverse leaders. At companies where senior leaders are reluctant to yield their responsibilities, HR should develop solutions that promote development among upcoming leaders. The goal is to create a robust pipeline of new, more innovative leaders that take advantage of the strengths and skills of both younger and older leaders.

Companies must manage as many as five generations of workers, dispersed global teams and a heterogeneous mix of genders, races and cultures. They also have many types of workers in the mix, including full-time and part-time people, employees working at home and workers employed by contract agencies. There is intense competition for talented millennials, many of whom are less loyal to organizations than ever before.

In this digital age,[63] a principal characteristic of the new era is change that occurs at an accelerating rate, creating new rules for business and HR. Organizations face a radically shifting context for the workforce, the workplace and the world of work. This shift has changed the rules for nearly every organizational practice, from learning to management to the definition of work itself.

It is abundantly clear that technology is advancing at an unprecedented rate. Technologies such as artificial intelligence (AI), mobile platforms, sensors and social collaboration systems have revolutionized the way we live, work and communicate. This causes stress for individuals as well as societies; research shows that employees and organizations are more 'overwhelmed' than ever.

There is an exponential rate of technological change. More than 50 years after the formulation of Moore's law—which holds that computing power doubles in capability every 18 to 24 months—technology affects our lives more quickly and more pervasively than ever before.

Further, while individuals adapt to technology relatively rapidly, businesses and organizations move at a slower pace. The business practices of corporate planning, organizational structure, job design, goal-setting and management were largely developed in the first industrial age, and companies must constantly revise them to keep up. The gaps show the need for HR to adapt to technology and lifestyle changes.

Today, a new set of digital business and working skills is needed. Companies need to focus more heavily on career strategies, talent mobility and organizational ecosystems and networks to facilitate both individual and organizational reinvention. The problem is not simply one of 'reskilling' or planning new and better careers. Instead, organizations must look at leadership, structures, diversity, technology and the overall employee experience in new and exciting ways.

For HR, the implications of such changes can be profound.

Leadership development[64] continues to be a significant challenge for companies around the world as the transition to the new digital organization creates even larger leadership gaps. High-performing leaders today need different skills and expertise than in generations past, yet most organizations have not moved rapidly enough to develop digital leaders, promote young leaders and build new leadership models.

As digital disruption sweeps across every major industry, leadership capabilities cannot keep pace. Leadership today is less about the 'art' of leadership and more about the challenges leaders face. Above all, the dramatic transformation of business is driven largely by the switch to digital. Of course, technology is critically important but human capital remains indispensable.

A natural corollary of this is that leaders need interdisciplinary skills. However, the concept of 'leader as hero' no longer scales. Highly effective companies look at leadership as a team effort and recruit leaders who can work together, complement each other and function as a team.

When older business models no longer work, leaders need new capabilities.[65]

Most companies are digital 'immigrants', new to this world and built on older models such as control mechanisms and financial returns. Now, companies are scaling for different goals, such as innovation and moving at high speeds. These changes require not just new operating models but a different type of leadership to mobilize and execute these models. Because of these shifts, organizations need people who can lead teams and partner with broader ecosystems. This new type of HR leader must understand how to build and lead teams in all contexts, keep people connected and engaged and drive a culture of innovation, learning and continuous improvement. They must also be able to lead a workforce that now includes contractors, the contingent workforce and crowd talent.

Demographic changes are also influencing what is required for a leader to be successful. Millennials expect to be developed throughout their work-life via opportunities, mentoring and stretch assignments. Likewise, the most sophisticated organizations view leadership development as more than training. They combine organizational design, job design, mentoring and development programmes to create the leaders they need.

PREPARING FOR THE FUTURE

Organizations[66] are more boundaryless, agile, global, and transparent—and will be even more so in the future. Work and workers (yes, humans) will always be essential to organizations, but organizations themselves will be more diverse, and work will be organized, structured, and done in new ways, increasingly through arrangements outside of regular full-time employment.

It seems beyond debate: Technology is going to replace jobs, or, more precisely, the people holding those jobs. Few industries, if any, will be untouched.

Knowledge workers will not escape.

Agile is not just for technology anymore. It's been working its way into other areas and functions, from product development to manufacturing to marketing; and now it's transforming how organizations hire, develop, and manage their people.

The strategic underpinnings of most companies' workforce plans should change dramatically as a result of technological innovation. Digital transformation, the industrial internet, advanced analytics, artificial intelligence, robotics, machine learning, and a plethora of other innovations are fundamentally changing the nature of work.

In today's tightening labour market, Human Resources leaders must work relentlessly to develop and recruit people who advance digital transformation across their organizations.

Yet most have struggled to advance their own digital competencies.

The need for leadership development has never been more urgent. Companies of all sorts realize that to survive in today's volatile, uncertain, complex and ambiguous environment, (VUCA) they need new leadership skills and organizational capabilities to be developed by Human Resources.

Though most executives recognize the importance of breaking down silos to help people collaborate across boundaries, they struggle to make it happen.

Artificial intelligence is becoming good at many 'human' jobs—diagnosing disease, translating languages, providing customer service—and it's improving fast. This is raising reasonable fears that AI will ultimately replace human workers throughout the economy.

The vast majority of humans throughout history worked because they had to. Many found comfort, value and meaning in their efforts, but some defined work as a necessity to be avoided if possible. For centuries, elites in societies from Europe to Asia aspired to absolution from gainful employment.

All eyes are on the future of work and the impact that automation and machine learning will have on jobs. The blizzard of conferences, initiatives, articles, and reports on how to prepare for the changes technology will bring to our economy is important. But so is today—and it feels to us like the futurists are leaving behind what's happening now.

HR as a Business Partner

In the critical features and development that took place based on corporate research and experience, HR has been regarded as a business partner.

Business partnering[67] involves many challenges, issues and debates—from the model itself to titles, performance, relationships and the tensions that seem to go with the role.

Changing Context of Business Partnering

Organizations have been wrestling with how to make business partnering work since Dave Ulrich's book called *Human Resource Champions: The Next Agenda for Adding Value and Delivering Results*, came out in 1997. That's partly because of a lack of understanding of what it is and what it can deliver. Also, uncertainty over the approach, weak preparation and integration and implementation—along with shortcomings in HR's business partner capabilities—are major issues.

In Ulrich's model, which has been widely adopted, business partners represent one leg of a three-legged structure. The other two are a shared service centre for transactions and a specialist centre of excellence or expertise (CoE). It is designed to increase the effectiveness of HR and reduce costs.

The ultimate aim is to align people strategy much more closely with what the business needs.

Business Partnering—The Essentials

- It is designed to encourage line managers at different levels to take more responsibility for managing their people. They are, in effect, the 'fourth leg' of the Ulrich model.
- Shifting much of the traditional administration burden from HR to shared service centres frees HR to contribute higher-level thinking and advice, especially in the critical areas of talent, performance and change.
- HR functions should then comprise fewer, better deployed and more effective professionals, better able to contribute to business agendas.
- Technologies, outsourcing and data management serve as enablers.
- The benefits can be reduced costs, better HR ratios, improved HR effectiveness and more satisfaction with HR among leaders, managers and employees.

INDIA'S HUMAN RESOURCES IN THE 2030s

National HRD Network (NHRDN),[68] the renowned Indian professional body of HR leaders, has been analysing various surveys and research on HR functions and growth for the last 50 years or so. In 2020, NHRDN appropriately attempted to benefit HR and business support by giving a new perspective for the coming decade of 2030. They conducted a survey of a large number of professionals and businesses for this purpose and provided a way forward based on the findings, also emphasizing the required new competencies that the CHROs must possess to deliver success to their roles and their business. One should admire the professional contributors of NHRDN, including Mr Amitav Mukherji, Mr Darpan Singh, Mr Dhananjay Singh, Mr Gangapriya Chakraverti, Ms Keerthana Shashi Shekar, Mr Krish Shankar, Mr Shankhashuvra Misra and Mr Srinath Jagannathan, for creating these valuable findings for the HR function in India in 2030. It would be most relevant, in terms of discussing the neo HR, to bring these findings a decade forwards.

We all know the world around us is changing dramatically. These changes are across two key dimensions—technology and society—increasing the complexity of business. Technological changes on multiple fronts are enabling a host of new possibilities, changing business models and disrupting industries. At the same time, there are also big changes in society and people's attitudes and motivations. Some of these are also led by changing technology. While these are not sudden and very perceptible, over time they become significant. And at the heart of these changes are organizations and people—they create and lead this change just as they are impacted by it. The HR function, thus, is at this critical confluence of change and would have to play a pivotal role in harnessing and driving change.

The Big Trends around Us

Studies by the McKinsey Global Institute and the World Economic Forum identify technology changes and the likely impact they would have. As we look at the impact of these technologies and what it means for us, we see five major trends that would be relevant for us in India.

- The pervasiveness of AI and automation: Automation will have a big impact on organizations, as many routine jobs could be eliminated.
- Smart cities, smart homes and smart offices: Internet of Things (IoT) and AI will make our offices smarter, even if our homes and cities take more time to be smarter!
- The wearables revolution: The march of mobiles will continue, powered by mobile supercomputing, leading to the 'wearables revolution'.
- Clean energy/climate and environmental action: Sustainability and environmental protection will continue to become a big driver for change across organizations.
- Increase in inequality in India: The predictions are that future GDP growth over the next decade or so will be led by the quality of talent and not just by an increase in talent supply. Given that our education system might be radically changed and renewed, we will have many unemployable people, which could lead to increasing inequality and social tensions.

These five big trends will have a significant impact on organizations and will also impact our work and workplace in a big way. They will also increase our business complexity.

As we look at the above trends in technology and society, we can see two clear vectors. On one axis is the drive towards the increasing use of technology and automation and on the other hand, we see that individuals want opportunities to express their individuality far more. Successful automation needs a human-centred approach. While we believe that societal trends are not going to be dramatically different from our predictions above, we believe that the degree of automation and technological disruption is a much more unknown variable and will move in a continuum. We have to plan for scenarios with extreme and moderate technology impact.

Key Shifts in the HR Function in the Next Decade

Given the above context of change, the deliverables of the HR function will also have to change. Core elements of the HR function could be identified that need to change in the next decade.

To truly engage employees, organizations have to clearly articulate their purpose in meaningful terms for employees. At the same time, they need to provide opportunities for employees to discover their purpose and work on those. Having people with the right skills will be critical for the business, more so when there is so much flux in technology.

Organizations will have to leverage a variety of talent and embrace gig-working and flex arrangements at a larger scale. HR systems, processes and policies will have to be flexible for this.

Successful organizations will leverage the power of technology to help managers make the right people decisions by building the right analytics powered by AI. Performance management and talent management will be perfect areas for such objective and data-based decisions.

Successful organizations will move to a flexible job structure. Job crafting, by enriching roles to suit individuals, will need to be mainstream. Hence, more unique roles and a very flat and flexible structure will be the future for HR in India.

Focus on holistic well-being will be a key enabler of having a highly productive workforce. Given the increasing levels of stress, organizations will also have to enhance the psychological safety in their teams so that employees can be authentic. This will mean a greater focus on the elements of culture in the teams and promoting the enabling styles of managers.

All the above changes will mean that individual managers will have a greater role and autonomy in managing their teams. But for this to work well, two things need to be in place—greater training and mentoring of managers and a strong set of values and culture. This will also mean that the operational HR role will disappear. Organizations need to prepare for this by training and empowering their managers and reinforcing the right culture needed.

Dr. Sumantra Ghosal spoke of managing transformational change based on cases from Indian as well as global companies.[69] At times, there were various kinds of crises in the environment as well as in companies that owned businesses. He talked of causing radical performances by giving the result of business success and causing turnaround by revitalization as well as rationalization. He said that radical performance was possible in all companies in times of all types of crisis. He laid down that it was possible to achieve non-incremental improvements within a reasonably short period, even when the industry is shrinking, even when competitors are bigger and stronger and when charismatic leadership is not a prerequisite. The most interesting was his case that radical performance is possible even when the company is very successful.

While we are finding and talking of the above at the beginning of 2020, we generally could find the same combination of two features developing in HR at the fag end of the last century or millennium. In the 1990s and 2000s, it was already apparent that HR needed to gradually give up its operational role and focus more on its so-called strategic role primarily. And during the same period, greater emphasis was being laid on learning, relearning, mentoring and coaching. There was a similar emphasis on working on vision, mission and values for creating a strong culture to meet the emerging challenge of the so-called transforming HR.

Dr. Ghosal, in terms of rationalization, indicated a need to improve resource productivity, a sour element of business that needed portfolio choice, eliminating low-return activity, improving labour productivity and revenues and profits per employee, improving operating per employee items and improving capital productivity with ROCE. While talking of the sweeter elements in the name of revitalization, he indicated the creation and exploitation of new opportunities—such as new products and market, expanding share, building competencies, new capabilities and resources, learning, organizational capabilities, revitalizing the organization and learning, mentoring, etc., for people. What he spoke about 30 years back, based on real case studies, comprehensively covered the two things needed—and forecasted the findings of the 2020 report of NHRDN done by Deloitte—which were greater training and mentoring of managers and a strong set of values and culture.

We are also reminded here of Jack Welch, regarded as one of the magical CEOs, who took over GE in the year 1981 as CEO from Reginald Jones, at a time when GE worth was $40 billion and the company was considered very successful under the hands of Jones, who was rated as the CEO of the decade. Welch eventually handed over GE to Jeff Immelt, his successor, in 2001, after making it a $400 billion company. In the first decade of his performance and performance strategy, he was named by media as 'Neutron Jack'. He had a vision of being the most competitive enterprise and made a value statement which resulted from a series of brainstorming sessions by over 5,000 employees at Crotonville. He had laminated cards distributed to all GE employees as the company's value statement. He was passionately focused on the customer, leaving six-sigma quality, excellence and being intolerant to bureaucracy, acting in a boundaryless fashion, creating global intellectual capital, seeing changes as opportunities for growth, creating an environment of stretch and demonstrating 4Es of GE's leadership. He gave almost 4,000+ leaders of excellence to GE and other businesses in the US. He had created a culture under the great challenge of a bureaucratic organization by creating an environment in the company where people dared to try new things. All the leaders that he trained, including himself, wanted to put a small company spirit in a big company body and to build an organization out of an old-line industrial company that would be more high spirited, more adaptable and more agile than companies that are 150th of its size. He was the one responsible for changing the structure and the culture in the organization, which turned dreams into reality.

He introduced a radical delayering of the organization, killing bureaucracy and challenging, empowering and energizing teams. While he created a culture of performance and delivery in this decade, he substantially developed his team and people in the organization to be, what he called, 'a people factory'. He meant finding and building great people in GE, energizing and empowering the teams, demanding for people to innovate and being tolerant to mistakes and at the same time, keeping people first as his strategy and creating a system and culture optimum for rigorous performance. He would even review every employee in the management cadre, where he introduced his performance management system, unique to businesses of the past, with a vitality curve. People development and building leadership was his passion. He turned his organization into a leadership development centre, assigning high performers and a very able mentor from his business leadership team, thus making a multi-edged learning sword. He very emphatically introduced reverse mentoring in the organization, giving the senior leader a trained reverse mentor of around 30 years of age. He would spend thousands of hours training management trainees in Crotonville personally and simultaneously introduced techniques to replicate Crotonville, giving freedom to people below leadership cadres and creating openness everywhere. He empowered people at all levels to cross boundaries and exhibit processes of improving the business.

The only observation I would like to make here, for consideration of all HR professionals, is that nothing much changed over the last three to four decades in the business world, except acceleration of technology which created various business advantages and demanded new learnings, new skills for building capability in talent and the organization. The focus of HR has to be more on this for this decade if it wants to perform the role of a catalyst or transformer.

In summary, these shifts in the HR function will be necessary to respond to changes in the environment that we foresee in the next decade. These would have to be HR's focus for capability building and culture-building, taken together as the two magical building blocks of managing all future business challenges.

The HR Leader of 2030

As we look at the likely changes in the environment, a new genre of leadership is likely to emerge to manage the new 'entrepreneurial contract'—a networked and portfolio-oriented leader. As knowledge evolves, expertise and uncertainty will emerge as fluid, shifting patterns requiring constant reshaping of skill and competence. People who tap into diverse, eclectic knowledge networks will emerge as trusted leaders. Shareholders and consumers will trust leaders who have evolved a strong network of expert knowledge and enterprise. At the same time, leaders who curate startups, understand business-technology-consumer-society experiments and value creation through enterprise are likely to succeed.

The NHRDN survey outlines a few broad shifts that HR leaders need to make to be successful in the next decade, with the core being human-centred.

A deeper understanding of the drivers of business strategy will be essential. In an agile and fast-changing world, this grasp of the nuances of business will be even more important as the margin for error is small and decision-making delays will cost substantially.

HR is expected to become less siloed and newer practices need to be adopted based on emerging insights. Successful HR leaders will tap into eclectic expert knowledge across other disciplines and leverage that knowledge and network for more appropriate and sustainable decisions.

As HR moves forward from being an 'employee champion' to one that architects and facilitates a culture that enables employees to meet their purpose and feel included, it will become all the more complex with a very diverse, multifaceted workforce. Having an inclusive culture will become a business priority. Moreover, elements of culture that will differentiate a business will be critical deliverables from HR.

In the next decade, businesses will need to change course rapidly and ramp up new capabilities with speed. Leading change and transformation will be a big task and HR leaders need to come up with mechanisms to enable transformations faster and smoother.

A deeper appreciation of new technology, AI and its impact on work and on how it can be leveraged for people decisions will be critical for a successful CHRO. Also, he/she will also need to develop mastery over data analytics and its use in decision-making and at crafting an analytics architecture that enables managers to make great people decisions in the flow of work. At the same time, issues of bias and exclusion will have to be thought through carefully as we design these algorithms. Technology and data will be integral to decision-making at all levels and core to a competitive advantage.

At the heart of everything is the need to bring a greater human focus into our organizational processes and decisions, which will become even more critical given the steady march of technology and automation! People will look for more human-centric organizations. HR needs to lead this agenda and CHROs have to be role models of authenticity and human centredness.

IN CONCLUSION: PREPARING FOR THE FUTURE

We are on the threshold of a momentous decade. The big changes in the environment will call for some critical shifts in our HR actions. To prepare for the future, we need to start right away and shape our HR function appropriately and invest in building the right HR leaders for the future. Competencies, skills and behaviours need to be identified from time to time, which could form guideposts for the development journey of our HR talent.

HR becomes a Bahrupia, who needs to be ever-ready to identify a change in the profession and present effectively, creating the desired impact. He/She has to keep on learning from eclectic, expert knowledge from the past and present, and also from lively and appropriate assessments of the future. He/She has to act as a Protean, continuously developing the ability to change frequently and easily, fulfilling the requirements of the changing roles. HR has to be ready to do many different things as a versatile Bahrupia who scans the horizons of work and society to deliver the best. This is the neo HR that has to continuously emerge and re-emerge. This is the neo HR that is capable of harnessing uncertainties and demonstrating how to prosper in the unknowable new normal. This HR will have to keep learning continuously, not merely from the current experiences and the near past but substantially from ancient times to bring out robust tested learnings for tomorrow. That is why we have ventured to take our HR team down the lanes of the Upanishadic Vedanta, which gives a confirmed pathway with a clear purpose in mind for delivering happiness to humankind. Learned HR leaders also have rightly emphasized that even when there is great uncertainty in the future and that too on high-speed change mode, HR should still focus more on the process rather than solutions alone.

As mentioned earlier, Dr. Sumantra Ghosal, whom I, K.K. Sinha, adopted as one of my mentors, says that there is nothing called absolute truth in management theories or concepts. They keep changing. I am not a crystal ball gazer, nor do I want any madari as my mentor in life to harness the uncertainty for desired prosperity in the new normal. However, one thing is certain that HR, in these times of ever-accelerating and rapid changes, has to keep learning, develop strategies and systems and a strong value-based culture that can be implemented. HR has to deal with the challenges of the new normal promptly, like a new oracle, and lead the business to success by delivering the role of a partner and player. A Bahrupia does not remain in the stadium all the time but can rush to the arena and play, perform and deliver from any position as the need be. In the playground that he/she enters, as a very responsible player, he/she is ready to put on the boots of either the captain of the full-backs or the centre forward or the striker or the goalkeeper and meet the purpose of the game. He/She must be ready to take the required risk and protect the game of business going on. He/She has to be an archetypal Protean in play.

While he/she is taking substantial risks to protect the game of business, he/she will have to also keep in mind the risks of protecting his/her image, credibility and life as well, at times. He/she has to act as a hero on the stage and pick up any role as the situation demands and deliver through to bring success to the business at that point in time. He/She is a true archetypal Bahrupia, who can play a role or deliver dialogue as scripted by someone else but can also create his/her own script and survive through the process of delivery. At the same time, this archetypal hero has to always be mindful of the ethical and cultural standards within the organization and also outside. This is a Protean challenge. This is a Bahrupian challenge.

VALLI 5.01

HR—THE NEED TO KEEP THINGS SIMPLE

K. RAMKUMAR

The proposition that HR should reskill has been in existence for a long time. Thirty-one years ago, when I started my career, we were told that HR should reskill and be more business-friendly. Whenever we use trends and researches, we need to be careful. A reported preference survey is a dangerous survey since it is not reliable and valid and we need to take the results with a pinch of salt. We need to be very careful in terms of how we look at analytics. Analytics in itself is neither good nor bad.

HR divisions have a major contribution to the industries in India that have grown and scaled over the years to become competent. We need to keep the basics simple and don't need to over-theorize things and use complex terminologies like OD, engagement, etc. We should comprehend the fundamentals and for this, we should not look from the frame of HR only; instead, we need to see the broad perspective. If we only look from the HR perspective, then the perspective will be very narrow. Rather, we need to look from the frame of the economy and then look from the frame of business and then probably from the HR or marketing or finance perspective we can plug and play. Fundamentally, in a game of cricket or hockey, the field remains the same. And whatever position the captain of the team asks us to play in as per the needs of the team—one must contribute their best to it. We should not be identity struck and role struck since it restricts us from properly playing our game in the organization. One should avoid the marketing trap/HR trap and play the role in the organization as per the need of the team.

If we look at the bigger perspective, what is happening in the world today, the physical world is shrinking and the digital world expanding. However, the physical world will coexist with the digital world. Businesses would have to start thinking of ways to manage the transition. The customer processes are all moving towards the digital space. Therefore, while pizza may not be made in a digital world, it would still be ordered and tracked using digital technologies. For example, the concept of a bank branch has been replaced by the mobile and we need to find the means by which we can create conditions so that the thousands of people at the banks work towards this change. This requires programming skills, app skills and organization skills and not necessarily HR skills. We need to ensure that we think through it and can work with the business leaders to prepare our organizations to move towards these.

In the context of the broader economic frame, in India's demography, where nearly 70% of people are below age 30 and the growth rate is 6%, it is impossible to run an organization with an attrition rate of less than 15%. There is no point discussing this issue since if there are opportunities in the market, people will switch jobs because we cannot offer salary hikes too often or else the organization may become bankrupt. Economics suggests that in case the growth rate accelerates to 9%, the attrition rate may rise to 30% as can be seen in China, Indonesia, Brazil and Russia. All the fast-growing economies with young populations have witnessed this. If we are a fast-growing economy but a country with 50 years as the average age, the attrition rate is likely to be 3% or we have to be a 2% growing economy with a young population. We need to understand this economic data.

In many instances, even though a consulting firm may have suggested that companies should give the employees a 15% salary hike, the HR person needs to understand the cost economics of the business and then decide the percentage of salary hikes. These are the various perspective changes rather than skill changes that are needed to be implemented.

In the 4,500 years of the civilized world, every cycle of 40 or 50 years has created Gen Ys. At all times, young people are impatient. When we are with young people, we must realize that their needs are different and try to engage them accordingly. This has nothing to do with the 21st century. India is young today and we need to deal with a lot more people who are in the younger generation in modern times. However, this is not a new proposition and has been dealt with very well in the past and, similarly, would be done in the future as well.

It is a life stage issue that has been seen nearly 200 or more times in this world. If we find that the organization is of young people, then their needs are likely to be of one kind. But one must remember and be perceptive enough to acknowledge that as people age from a 25 or 27-year-old to a 32 or 35-year-old age bracket, their life stage requirements become different and their perspectives become different. The company policies and manner of engagement must suit this, rather than just getting swept away by the Gen Y argument. Also, we must realize that five years later, the organization would age further, so the policies would need to be further tweaked.

If such perceptiveness is there in the HR personnel, the board members of the organization would respect them more. Good HR does not imply that we give everything people demand but we should be able to convince people why we are not able to give something. People do understand the reasons and do not always quit the organization.

VALLI 5.02

CHALLENGE OF HUMAN RESOURCES INADEQUACY IS A CHALLENGE OF LEADERSHIP

PRABIR JHA

The danger with generalizations is that they appear simple but they can be very misleading. It is very important to be aware that when we discuss upskilling and reskilling HR, the danger is that it is mostly interpreted purely and squarely in terms of the HR function and is one of the biggest myths of corporations. The challenge of HR inadequacy is a challenge of leadership and a challenge for the organization as much as it's a challenge for HR, the function. These should not be seen as very asymmetrical issues. I believe that every organization, every country, every corporation, every age, every generation gets the HR it deserves.

There is a case to reinvent and reposition HR. We need to acquire certain newer skills and refocus our priorities. It all depends on our operating requirement, challenge and need. We have to make sure that as the world changes and as organizations change, HR in its entirety—that is, both the function and the leadership—would have to think of its role as an influencer of change by envisioning a newer environment and understanding what people are saying. While there will always be an issue of employee championship, the biggest role will be about enabling HR to be more effective. Talent analytics is important but there needs to be a larger outcome. We should not lose focus on the larger purpose, which is about growing successful businesses while helping people to continue to feel more fulfilled. This is the balance that HR would continue to bring even in turbulent and ambiguous environments.

In my current role, I help different business leaders run very different businesses. For instance, television, oil, life sciences, retail and so on are very different from each other. The kind of people who service these particular industries are also nuanced very differently because the consumer is different and the operating environment and the operating discipline is different. It is very important to fine-tune the nuances of HR to pick up on the differences in the tasks. I would like to reiterate that it is not an issue of fundamentals wavering but essentially an issue of influence.

The manner in which we sell a value proposition could be different because the generations are different or it could be because of other reasons. For instance, in our hydrocarbon business, we have people who are in the age bracket of 62–65 and they operate in a very command-and-control environment which, perhaps, is the need of that industry. But this is very different from the people who operate in the television industry. The beauty is in how we nuance HR. In Reliance, we are trying to move the HR people between sectors because we have the opportunity today.

I think it is working out fine since the cross-fertilization brings out new learning which comes because we move people across sectors. However, this is not an easy battle to fight since there is a lot more bias for the domain. Though fundamentally speaking, good HR is good HR anywhere, the challenge is to handhold and support. I have created a group focused only on creating an HR capability of a 1,000 people. We need to help them and handhold them into newer aspects of HR and hone the skills of industrial relations management.

All HR leaders have an issue with talent analytics. I have created a talent analytics group where we are trying to farm data and mine data but the larger issue is concerned with what we do with the data. HR has different levels and the need will change from position to position, level to level. The perspective of the HR head must necessarily be very different from that of the guy who is in the trenches but it does not, in any way, alter the significance, importance and criticality of that particular person because wars are not won by generals but by troops in the trenches. We need to make the people in HR come out of their cocoons and realize that they can definitely make a difference. It falls within the context of rotating people, exposing people, handholding people, standing by the people and getting the line manager to co-own the job of upskilling HR. The line managers must be willing to invest time and must help the HR person.

Valli 5.03

Performance, Care and Values Have to Be Equally Addressed for a Sustainably Winning Business

RAJEEV DUBEY

I believe that HR's major focus should be on unleashing human potential in pursuit of the organization's goals and purpose. In this era of technological disruption with AI, analytics, chatbots and so on, we must not forget that at the end of the day, the human being should be at the core. We must use whole-brain thinking to serve our core purpose. Whole-brain thinking combines the left brain of logic, intellect and rationality with the right brain of emotion, connection and empathy.

In the mad rush to employ technological solutions, we must not forget our original purpose of unleashing human potential through meaning and empowerment.

We must also remember that we are operating in a system where we have to show concern for the larger ecosystem and the community. The role of HR should not only be restricted to address requirements of white-collar or blue-collar employees but extend to meet those of the community as well.

In order to handle heterogeneity, I don't think we need to formulate different policies for different generations. We must listen to the voice of our people. In general, the command-and-control model is becoming less and less acceptable. People expect to be informed about why they are being asked to do something. They expect leaders to walk the talk. People are more conscious about integrity and the values of the organization for which they are working and want to be associated with socially responsible organizations. The younger generation is forcing organizations to recognize the importance of being socially responsible and becoming a more mindful organization.

Therefore, though we do not have different policies for different generations, we do have a policy that tries to be sensitive to the voice of people and which does not let us get away with the old style of leadership. Thus, we are becoming sensitive, listening more, trying to bring in greater integrity in our actions, being held more accountable, being required to speak the truth, to show compassion and have an attitude of sewa (service).

There was a time when good values and good business were thought to be antithetical to each other. Some 20 or 25 years ago, it was expected that we should not speak of sappy things like feelings or values because these were not associated with business. Thankfully, in the last 20 years or so, people have been saying that one cannot do good business unless one is driven by good values.

We must have sustainably outperforming businesses and, at the same time, we need to show extreme care for all stakeholders—whether it be customers, employees, shareholders or communities—and nurture and nourish the core values of the group. So performance, care and values—all three have to be addressed if we want to have sustainably outperforming businesses. This is the fundamental change that is evident in the last 20 years, partly attributable to the younger generation and the greater workforce diversity.

VALLI 5.04

SKILLING AND UPSKILLING IS A CONTINUOUS PROCESS

SHRIKANT GATHOO

According to my opinion, only two sectors exist—the professional sector and the unprofessional sector; or, professional organizations and unprofessional organizations. We are a business organization. Public sector companies like ours, in which almost 46% is owned by Foreign Institutional Investors (FIIs) and which are listed companies, are not different from any other company. We go and hire talent from the institutes, compete in the market and when we post results, we get evaluated in the stock markets exactly in the same way as any other company and there is no difference. However, the public sector context does give a certain specific slant to the entire discussion. But our basics are not different; they are the same. The fundamentals over the period have not changed. They were the same earlier and continue to be the same today. The context has changed and is the one that keeps changing as we move along.

There has been a shift in HR and the context has changed dramatically. Earlier we had human resources which were operationally reactive; for instance, in case of a showdown somewhere or a problem on the shop floor, trying to sort that out. From there, we have moved to being operationally proactive—wherein we really work to ensure that it does not happen again—and then to be strategically reactive and currently to be strategically proactive. There has been a shift in HR leadership and the context, the stage, has changed dramatically. Earlier, we had an operationally reactive HR; for instance, in case of a showdown somewhere or a problem on the shop floor, they would try to sort that out. From there, HR leads moved to being mostly operationally proactive, wherein HR worked to ensure that it does not happen again. Then HR became strategically reactive and currently, it is strategically proactive.

Many things have changed since 1979 when I started my career, some 35–36 years back.

The factors that used to impact locally are now impacting globally. But the level at which the performance is expected has changed.

One big thing we ought to recognize is that we were very different from the people who were working in our organizations when we started our career. Similarly, the people who join the company or the corporate world today are very different from what we are. We need to recognize that and factor that in to continue to remain relevant.

In my opinion, skilling and upskilling is a continuous process. In the current context of the country, we must keep in mind the fact that every fourth person joining the workforce today comes from India. We are one of the youngest countries in the world. All projections suggest that India is already being regarded as one of the fastest-growing world economies. This is one more dimension which we need to factor in. We need to understand that whatever worked in the past is relevant and that the fundamentals do not change.

VALLI 5.05

CREATING THE RIGHT ENVIRONMENT FOR PEOPLE TO GROW

YOGI SRIRAM

I am often invited to speak at various academic and industrial forums on a future-ready workforce. One question I'm always asked is what can we, as HR professionals, do to build a future-ready workforce? It is a very pertinent question for business in this day and age.

Reskilling in today's time and context is extremely important. It always was. But today, with the whirlwind speed at which skills are becoming obsolete, reskilling and upskilling are more important than ever. Omar Khayyam wrote, 'The moving finger writes, and having written moves on. Nor all thy piety nor all thy wit, can cancel half a line of it.' So what we have done yesterday is not so relevant now and competencies that were in demand until yesterday will need to be renewed.

Let me start with a few thoughts on why reskilling is important. It's not just the threat of technological obsolescence or an economic downturn. Reskilling is necessary even from a purely forward-thinking point of view. We often talk about engaging those around us. But do we understand what engages us and do we take time off to figure out what is it that really occupies us in terms of other faculties, besides the routine ones? HR folks thus need to first understand this for themselves. They should reflect on their own engagement levels. Are they busy firefighting, fending off negative feelings of facing the hubris of an arrogant boss or getting bogged down by the politics of the system?

TIME FOR HR TO STEP UP ITS GAME

I also think that there is a constant accusation about HR initiatives not being measured with enough rigour. So the ability to develop clear metrics and to be bold enough to stand up and say that please measure me and give me concrete feedback on our outputs is very important.

There is much ado about how HR should be connected to the business. There are two Centres of Excellence (CoEs) that must be 'joined at the hip' with business. One of them is learning and development, which tends to be conceptual and needs to be better connected. The other area is talent acquisition. People in talent acquisition must understand business and their strategic imperatives extremely well; otherwise, they are likely to stray away. This needs thorough preparation. General questions asked by HR cannot assess domain depth. The repercussions of poorly planned talent acquisition and development are severely adverse in the long term, affecting organizational effectiveness and leadership.

Therefore, 'talent' is extremely important. If we don't have the right leadership talent, the business will perform badly. If the business continues to perform badly, the business may have to be divested. The opposite is true if we have the right talent. We have the opportunity to start a new business or grow the existing business if we are confident of appointing and developing the right talent. In this context, the potential of the younger generation is critical to leverage. We have to take big bets on them. Especially in the Indian context, the learnability quotient of young Indians is very inspiring and they have a huge potential to impact the world they live in.

We must upskill ourselves on how to use technology irrespective of which life stage we are in. While intimate knowledge of business is very important, it is very important to understand the economic environment of business. The winds of change are already here in India. In the Indian context, whether it is the 'Make in India' policy or whether it is defence offsets, I think it is very important to understand government policies alongside business.

I feel very strongly that HR folks and line managers have a great role to play in creating an innovative culture, reducing a command-and-control culture and creating the right environment for people to grow.

HUMAN RESOURCES PARADIGMS ARE CHANGING

When we talk about whether any fundamentals have changed in terms of skilling, in my opinion, a skill that is practised and lived becomes a competency; if it is done over and over again, the skill holder becomes a benchmark in that competency. Domain knowledge and focussed specialized skills are important in every field. There has been a huge change in the skill requirements of HR folks. When I started my formal education in HR, we were taught about the provisions of the Factories Act of 1948, the statutory responsibility of a welfare officer, line and staff organizational principles, how many calories are required for a worker and so on. We have come a long way from there. Today, articles are comparing the competencies of a CHRO and a CEO. When I did my BA (Hons.) in Economics, terms such as 'demographic dividend' were not known. Today, the HR professional's lexicon is not complete without terms such as gig worker, working with a multigenerational workforce or dealing with FOMO (Fear of Missing Out).

Our performance appraisal systems and other HR systems in the past were based on the insights of experiments in social psychology by B.F. Skinner on (carrot and stick) classical and operant conditioning. B.F. Skinner proposed his theory on operant conditioning by conducting various experiments on animals. He used a special box known as the 'Skinner Box' for his experiment on rats. Eventually, the rat discovered a lever that, when pressed, triggered the release of food inside the box. Relating these theories to modern HR practices is not so common today because theories are dismissed as too professorial. Also, such associations tell us about how we can go wrong by basing our assumptions of what will motivate humans on experiments conducted on lesser forms of life. The kind of skill development efforts or competency development efforts required today has to be different as compared to earlier. Our skills and competencies have to be upgraded constantly during our entire career life cycle. HR does not belong to HR professionals alone. It belongs to those who are running the business. They too have to upgrade their skills and the CHRO can be the best champion to emphasize this. HR has a big role in constantly upgrading the HR skills of line managers. I feel that the insights into what gets millennials motivated today are extremely important and are quite different from what they were earlier. Today, in an IT company and IT Enabled Services (ITeS) company, up to 70% of the personnel cost is on account of billable hires. The manufacturing sector's personnel cost hovers at around 10%. People costs often shape the contours of the policy that is sculpted for people.

LEARNING IN THE NEW AGE

The word 'training' would paint a mental image of a classroom filled with a bunch of students with notepads, facing a board or projector screen, focused on one instructor who is the expert on the subject. The times, however, have changed. Reskilling today calls for personalized learning—involving content, methodology and media—suited to the specific needs and preferences of the learner. Today Learning Management Systems (LMS) are being replaced by Learning Experience Platforms (LXP). LXPs are recommendatory platforms that recommend content based on the learner's learning style. Similar to e-commerce platforms, they create deep engagement with the content. But how does an organization train its workforce for a future that is unknown? The solution lies not in creating 'efficient workers' but 'effective learners'. In other words, the members of the future workforce need to 'learn how to learn'. Cognitive flexibility in adapting to different pedagogy—be it videos, PPTs or instructor lead—is important.

There are two key aspects of future-proof learners. First is a high 'adaptability quotient' or the capacity to thrive in a changing world by objectively scanning the environment, identifying learning edges and picking up new skills quickly. Masako Wakamiya of Japan rose to fame at 82, in 2017, as an iPhone app developer. Sensing the importance of digital fluency, Wakamiya began teaching herself to code and upgrade her computer skills in the mid-1990s. The second aspect is learning transfer. A person with this ability—traditionally derided as a 'Jack of all trades'—can draw insights from a wide range of seemingly unrelated fields of study, break them down into their fundamentals and apply them to one's own area of work. Elon Musk, a billionaire technopreneur, is renowned for his ability to draw connections across disciplines, setting him apart from the rest.

RESKILLING FOR THE MULTIGEN WORKFORCE

There is a myth that only Generations Y and Z need to reskill since the older generations are already heading towards the sunset of their careers and age is a hindrance in picking up new skills. In my opinion, there is a big connection between the baby boomers and Gen Y. While we often talk about millennials or Gen Z in terms of people who are not loyal and who just flit around jobs like butterflies, I think they are people with purpose, with a serious mission, who need to be understood much better by using the lens of what we baby boomers stood for earlier.

Reskilling in today's context, especially when we think about millennials and Gen Y, is extremely important because creating a culture of innovation, role fungibility and entrepreneurship—with flatter hierarchies where people work together without sparring fiefdoms and silos—is very important. Integrating people into the organization and making them feel included is extremely important. When we hire people from another organization, amalgamating them into a new culture can be a challenge. In L&T, we have implemented a 'Technology Leadership Programme', which factors in deep domain skills required as strategic differentiators for a business. It is important to nurture technology leaders in specific domain areas and build the talent pipeline for achieving a strategic position of dominance.

Employee value propositions that build on a culture premium depend not just on compensation for retaining and attracting talent but on something that is much more intangible and difficult to copy. HR, along with the line manager, can play a huge role in building this culture premium. Controversial subjects, such as using forced choice and the bell curve, are important to discuss and conclude with conviction. In terms of using the bell curve, there are three or four companies that are currently in the news for citing various reasons as to why the bell curve should be not be followed. Bringing the conversation to the table and having great facilitation skills to come to a convincing conclusion is very important as an HR professional.

A MORE HUMANISTIC APPROACH TO HR

The study of psychology allows one to understand better employee behaviour and is useful while dealing with HR/IR (Industrial Relations) issues. While it can be directly applied by HR in its role as a business partner, it also provides senior management with a guide to the complexity of human behaviour when they engage with employees. So lastly, I want to talk about my favourite topic, which is social psychology. Unfortunately, most of the inputs in social psychology are from the random control trials conducted in the Western world. Research on these is less reported off late because Western societies are becoming more litigious. Therefore, the studies—whether they concern Zimbardo or Milgram or Hawthorne—are becoming less and less. Therefore, HR folks, along with line managers, should figure out how we can continue to learn from experiments in social psychology—within the boundaries of what local laws allow—to arrive at deep insights. Learnings gained through these experiments in social psychology, when relevant to the context, will enable HR to rediscover itself.

In some cases, HR has not yet shed the yoke of the 1980s, which were deeply influenced by industrial relations issues and preoccupied with protecting employers from the unsavoury side of the same. In such companies, HR remains a policing agency that enforces compliance and ensures checks.

CONCLUSION

None of this is possible if business does not support HR in supporting business. The symbiotic relationship between business and HR needs to evolve to suit the new era of social connectedness and discontinuities. The organization needs to work collaboratively to shift mindsets and enable the development of its people. Ultimately, an organization that fails to reskill its employees is like a combatant who brings a knife to a gunfight—disadvantaged and doomed. It is time to wake up and turn the tide.

VALLI 5.06

HR—MANAGING A MULTIGENERATIONAL WORKFORCE

DR. ASHA BHANDARKER

I have a little bit of information on some research that we have conducted in the Indian context. This is about something that has happened in the family. Son is Gen Z (about 21 years of age) and his mother is Gen X. Son comes to the mother and says, 'Mom, give me permission, I want to fix my eyebrows.' She is completely shocked by this. Of course, if you know about Gen X, you will know that many of us are doctors, lawyers, teachers or engineers. She says, 'Oh no, I cannot give you permission.' He urges, 'Why mom, why cannot you permit me? What do you people think about this? Why cannot it be? Why don't you permit me?'

She says, 'People will think you are a drifter! People will think you are shallow! People will think you are not serious.' So he says, 'Why should I think that people will not care about me?' Right, this type of person is going to be the typical type of person in your organization in a few years. What should be done with this type of person? In a way, maybe expression will be important. Self-identity is important. This context typifies what kinds of challenges, what kinds of gaps there are between various types of generations.

So what is the generation? The generation is defined as the date you have been born—your age or its essence. I was studying the concept of death and realized that this generation is different altogether. For example, those of us who have experienced the Emergency and the pre-liberalization era and, likewise, the post-liberalization era are one generation. People say generations are the same but generation gaps are different and it happens in every generation. That may be true but, qualitatively, the history is different and therefore perspectives and peoples' brains are very different.

Why should you care? One reason is that the percentage of such people in your company is going to be drastically large, and it has been seen in social groups that when you are in a minuscule minority, you tend to assimilate with the majority community. The moment the majority percentage is increased and exists in all kinds of social groups, people begin to assert their identities. So if this percentage is going to increase drastically, their demands are going to increase proportionally.

So to understand how to deal with them, we need to understand what their expectations from the workplace are. I will share with you the top five or six expectations from a study conducted by Dr. Pritam Singh, Management Guru, Padma Shri and former director of MDI, IIM Lucknow, along with me and one of my colleagues. What surprises me is the results I gleaned from this study on 2,158 engineers, MBAs and young executives, conducted about 7–8 years ago. They were freedom to take initiative, freedom to experiment, freedom to innovate and freedom to express. Further, the list included performance-based recognition and feedback, equity and fairness, trust and transparency, learning opportunity, personality development and work-life balance. If you see this entire cluster, what emerges is that the mindset of people is entrepreneurial. They have so much passion, so much energy and such dreams. And obviously, they are complete opposites of the previous generations and opposites of the kind of culture that exists in many organizations in India today. So this has an impact on the work cultures, leadership styles and HR practices and processes.

So how to handle or improve intergenerational relationships? If you boil it down further, it is a question of how to handle diversity. Diversity of thinking, mindsets and priorities of people from these different generations, operating in the same place and same organizations. Fundamentally, the conflict emerges because of the sense of threat. Seniors would be feeling more threatened by the younger people coming in—because of technology or because of skills they bring to the table and a lack of understanding between these different groups. And you may have seen, the less you know about groups and cohorts, the more you judge them and the more you reject them. On the other hand, we could also say diversity is the complementarity of skills. These complementary skills can be utilized only when we recognize and understand each other. So what to do?

First, try to help each to understand the other; each group needs to understand the other group. Bring more groups together in training contexts. Get into the act of mutual mentoring. We have heard about top-down mentoring and reverse mentoring but I am suggesting mutual mentoring, where each person cares for the other. Next, develop support groups. You should also have age-related requirement groups. That would help groups to become more confident and more comfortable fundamentally. I believe it is more about attitude. We have to develop greater tolerance, less judgmental orientation and more acceptance while focusing on merit and results.

The next question that arises is how to create an exciting, varied and innovative environment and work culture. My answer to this is that every company should become Google. Because if you talk to people, their ideal company to work for is Google. Why? Because Google allows experimenting, gives time off from work on projects and chances to express freely, sponsors small projects and engages in the organization building process. There is an example from India, from the IT space, in a company called Zensar, based in Pune. In terms of HR innovations, this is one of the companies which shot ahead in a big way. Almost 10 years ago, they were talking about how to engage people by building what is called a vision community. New entrants into the organization would be in groups where they would be mentored by seniors and, in the process, would go through all that I have talked about.

The vision community culminates in the voice of the community being put up to the board level for consideration. This is a form of engaging and empowering young millennials, which is part of the system. I think it is very powerful. It creates excitement and an innovative environment and does not come from a physical context. This physical context is good to have but it is not enough. We need to provide them with the space to unleash their passion.

The next question to ponder upon is how to manage millennials. As we discussed earlier, money is not a panacea any more. Money is taken for granted and, as far as the studies conducted by me indicate, never comes in the top or middle in the findings of the study. And it was a puzzle to me. If money could not attract them then what could be attractive as a company? Brand, youthfulness and vitality—these are attractive to them.

How to retain? Customize HR as per needs. As per the age groups, we can customize HR practices. And this is where I believe big data analysis is going to help us. This is in terms of understanding profiles and in terms of being able to respond in a timely way to the requirement of these groups.

VALLI 5.07

THE SUCCESSFUL CORPORATIONS OF TOMORROW WILL LEVERAGE THE BENEFITS OF WORKFORCE DIVERSITY FASTER AND BETTER

D.D. MISRA

The role of HR is indeed changing on account of demographic upheavals taking place all over the world. For India, demographic changes are likely to manifest themselves at the workplace in the form of a multigenerational workforce. Employing more and more women is not an option any more. It is a necessity. And those companies that don't like this are surely going to be left behind.

We may find that the greater the hiring of women in top management, the better is the financial performance of the company. For example, return on equity is higher by 35% and total returns to shareholders are to the extent of 3%. Research also suggests that women in board positions are more likely to achieve sustained growth. There are so many successful women bankers in the banking sector. And they maintain a competitive edge by utilizing all resources effectively at their command. This means resource utilization and optimization with their ascent. They are also able to bridge the huge gap in leadership talent and thus address the issue of scarcity. More and more women are coming to the top and this leadership scarcity will be reduced drastically. Women also bring in a diversity of talents and that improves the impact, or the bottom line, more decisively.

We also may examine that women leaders are more persuasive than their male counterparts. When feelings of rejection set in, women leaders learn from adversity quickly and carry on. This is an important gesture. This attitude is very important for success and growth. Women leaders also demonstrate more inclusive team building. Besides, women leaders are more likely to take more risks. Risk-taking is more important if risks have more chances of success.

In the growing economy, India is undergoing many demographic changes within the workforce and at a fast pace. This gives the opportunity to adopt an inclusive approach to successfully embracing workforce diversity. The successful corporations of tomorrow will be those that leverage the benefits of workforce diversity in a faster and better fashion.

Companies with diverse workforces are also able to attract the best talent because top talents are no longer represented by homogenous groups; instead, they are represented in the pluralistic terms of gender, generation, ethnicity, language and region. Thirdly, diversity leadership is also critical. The more diverse the boards are, the more they will come to the table with different kinds of ideas and opportunities about untapped markets and provide newer perspectives to new business issues.

Valli 5.08

HR—Focus on the Newer Generations Coming Up

MIHIR MALLICK

In today's world, rapid technological changes, cross-industry convergence and global competition are bringing in many challenges for us. The average life span of a company in today's time has reduced to 18–20 years. It is the responsibility of the HR fraternity to figure out how they should look at changing the HR processes.

First is the neo normal. Anything that has come as new to you, it should be taken as neo normal but cannot be taken as very absurd. The second is cultural innovation. How to know cultural innovations and where do we go with all this? And how do we take care of our millennials? I always wonder where these millennials come from. We build the environment and they are born and brought up in this culture. How is it that they come up with different sets of behaviours? How is it that they develop different sets of attitudes? Our deep-rooted psyche says anything new is abnormal. So 'new is normal' is the phenomenon we always talk about. This is something in which people and systems get habituated to everything new. That is why we call it new normal. If you look at the past revolutions that have happened, in the earlier days it was because manufacturing processes started using machines. Then in the second revolution, the efficiency of the machine was improved.

Third, we talk about the three Ws, also known as the Internet. This came from digitization. Now we talk about big data and IoT (Internet of Things) which will change our life. Our millennials and newborns will be affected by these, so more focus will be on big data. They will be socially connected and because of different media nowadays, things move so fast. I keep on getting so many

WhatsApp messages wherein we need to vote on certain issues which are of common concern to people and the messages support all these changes and the civil society.

Then, we should probably talk about organizational culture for which innovation is very important as we have seen the marriage of the telecom and finance industry. We have seen ATMs, Vodafone m-Pesa, Airtel money and so on. So it is a very good marriage that has happened between technology and finance. Similar things are going to happen again. In my opinion, creating an organizational culture and the home ground for the innovation to happen is an actual issue. Innovation per se is not an issue. Are we looking at providing that kind of breeding ground where the young ones come up with free thoughts? Or are we looking at having the kind of pace that can make them face failure?

Feel fast, feel steady and feel frequently is what gives wholistic learning. But are we giving them that much space here for overcoming failure? That is very important. Do we celebrate those failures? Then comes leadership of authenticity. Authentic leadership drives people to innovate and to conceive new ideas. Explore it and experiment it, fail faster, fail frequently and learn faster.

Then, we should talk about passion at work. In these cut-throat competition days, we are looking at the physical and mental fatigue of people. This brings in many challenges. The workforce becomes a part of a circle where slow and weak market competition can deteriorate the workforce's morale and resources. So we are looking at concepts that have come from a book called *Grit—The Power of Passion and Perseverance*, authored by Angela Duckworth. She is a professor of Psychology at the University of Pennsylvania. She describes grit as the ready-mix of passion and perseverance. It is not a normal passion but it is a consistency of service in a particular job over some time. That consistency is very important. So we look at consistency and we look at perseverance, which relates to tenacity. Grit stands for the growth mindset, intrinsic motivation, tenacity and resilience. These are a few important factors that will come into play when we talk about taking care of new demographics. Though we might call them Gen X or Gen Y or Gen Z, now it goes beyond that and we may call them by any name. But the point here is to ponder how to take care of those generations.

Valli 5.09

HR—Focus on the Needs of the Millennials: Learning and Their Growth

SAPTARSHI ROY

When we talk about challenges, it brings in new flavour and complexity in terms of managing the talent within the organization. Here lies the role of HR. They need to evolve in terms of how they deal with such new imperatives which have become very critical to the organization to actually take it forward. It is also necessary to engage this talent in terms of the growth of the organizations and meeting individual expectations, which are very diverse.

I would like to share the experiences of the organization in which I work—National Thermal Power Corporation Ltd (NTPC). I have worked in this organization for nearly 35 years. And like me, most of my colleagues have put in two and half decades of their work in this particular organization. If I look at the organization, the average executive engagement of employment within the organization is more than 25 years. It is a major power utility engaged in the generation of electricity, which is a requirement for every human being. Therefore its continuity, its sustainability and undisrupted supply is also a major factor in dealing with this industry.

If you look at the structure of the organization, we have three distinct generations of the workforce within the organization. Whatever name you may like to coin, I may say these three distinct generations of people come with different sets of patience under one roof. But the problem is, being in a typical public sector, the traditional concept of dealing with people-related issues have been largely driven by the one-size-fits-all approach. This is a challenge.

At the same time, for the people who are in the upper-age bracket, the pension is going to be a major concern. These are the kinds of diverse challenges which we have to deal with. So the one-size-fits-all approach needs to cater to different sections of workers who have different aspirations within the organization.

If we talk about the millennials, one of the major issues is their retention in the organization. A recent study was done by Deloitte, conducted on 60 millennials, and I was observing the findings from the Indian context. It was mentioned that given an option, 76% of the millennials of India would like to shift jobs within two years. So that is the kind of task we have in terms of retention, and organizations are struggling as to how best they can retain these talents within the organization. But, fortunately or unfortunately, that is not the case with the public sector. Normally, the attrition rate in organizations like NTPC is not even 1%. As I said, the executives in this organization have been working here for more than 25 years. It is not that if they are not satisfied and their expectations are not met, they will exit the organization. They will continue to be in the organization. At the same time, they pose new challenges for the organization with regards to how best we can utilize them productively so that they can serve the purpose of the organization. That is the new imperative which might be missing and might be beyond the comprehension of many of the new technology organizations.

We had this problem as we started this concept of providing an urban facility in projects and stations. Typically, our operations are mostly in remote locations, near coal-bedded stations. Coal is not available in cities but in remote locations. So retaining these people at those remote locations is a major challenge because most of them today come from the country's premier educational institutions (engineering and business). After having an excellent training programme, during which they are exposed to different talents and skills for different facets of business operations, they are placed into our project locations—typically, green fields where urban facilities are not available. They expect to have access to the internet, be able to visit malls frequently and lead a quality life—things which, at those locations, prove to be a big challenge. So in terms of upgrading the physical facility, we have started an initiative to do whatever is possible. But soon we realized that we cannot create cities out of the remote corners. So any amount of efforts that have truly gone towards upgrading the physical facilities falls short of their requirements and expectations. Then what is the next thing that needs to be done?

Another major challenge we faced is that soon after these young entrants joined and worked for a few years, they got married. Their partners were educated and working somewhere. Opportunities for them would largely exist in the cities and we don't offer such kinds of opportunities for the employment of their spouses in our remote locations. So the next round of pressures normally built up was the seeking of transfers to specific cities, based on postings. We have very limited opportunities where we can accommodate. These are the kinds of expectations our new millennials have, who are younger employees. Then dissatisfaction starts. They start comparing. In their case, the equity is not being meted out and so on. So one of the methods is work-life balance. We don't have adequate opportunities available to offer employment to their spouses. As a public sector organization, we are bound by rules and regulations. We just cannot recruit at our whims and fancies. Therefore, we started new processes, wherein we experimented with the idea of keeping critical operating personnel because our power stations need to be operated $24 \times 7 \times 365$. We developed a scheme wherein they work for two and a half months in the project and then go for 15 days leave, fully paid for by the company. This new experimentation has yielded a tremendous amount of response from all these people. This is something that we had not attempted earlier.

Perhaps, we had a lot of scepticism and apprehension before we began this new system. But over some time, we found that these are some of the means by which we can at least mitigate certain requirements—like work-life balance—of the people who are joining our workforce at a younger age. I think they see some kind of reason and value in that. That has been one of the major satisfying factors—dealing with their expectations in such kinds of remote locations.

So these are some of the live experiments which we have been practising. We are still evolving some processes because this experimentation or initiative is not enough. We need to look into many more such innovative means by which we can largely meet their expectations. One of the needs which we will certainly be able to fulfil is their appetite and urge for learning and development and career and growth opportunities. That is something which we can offer. As an organization, we are trying to address these particular issues and place solutions before them to show some kind of value proposition in their association with our organization for a longer period.

CHAPTER 6

CONCLUSION: THE NEXT MANU

'I have no name,' she purred. 'I am whoever the keepers of my fate tell me to be.' He grasped her by her wrist, running a thumb along the sensitive skin underneath. 'Then let me call you mine for a dance or two.' 'Thus has been my destiny' she said.

– Sarah J. Maas

SATYAKAMA JABALA

Satyakama Jabala is a boy whose mother is a single parent. As an adolescent, he is very inquisitive about atma, God, the universe, people, societal laws and so on. He wants to find answers to all his questions and wishes to find a guru.

Eager for knowledge, Satyakama goes to the famous sage Gautama, requesting the sage to adopt him as his disciple.

The sage asks him,

'My dear child, who is your father and what family do you come from?'

'O Guru, I do not know.'

'Go and ask your mother,' advises sage Gautama.

Satyakama returns to his mother and enquires about his father. Jabala, his mother, tells him, 'Go and tell the sage that your mother went to many places and served many men in her youth and does not know who your father is. And your mother's name is Jabala, so your name is Satyakama Jabala.'

Satyakama goes back to sage Gautama and shares that he is of uncertain parentage as his mother does not know who his father is.

'My mother asked me to tell you that her name is Jabala and my name is Satyakama—I know nothing more about my family,' Satyakama explains without fear.

'So I am Satyakama Jabala.'

Gautama is pleased that the boy's mother has taught her son to tell the truth.

'Only one from the best of families could give this explanation so sincerely,' he said. 'I will gladly accept you as my student.'

(Chandogya Upanishad)

RAIKVA—THE CART DRIVER

Long ago there lived a king called Janashruti. He was knowledgeable, pious and charitable, and he cooked food for all in his kingdom. He believed that he was the greatest patron and that there was no one else like him. He used to measure his merit by the quantity of gifts and money he distributed. He had also mastered the languages of birds and beasts.

One night, he lay on the upper storey of his palace, enjoying the beauty of the evening twilight. He observed two swans flying past, continuously conversing with each other. One of them said, 'Don't you see the bright band of light that emerges from King Janashruti? Beware, lest you cross the flaming light of his fame and get yourself burnt. You must know that today there is none as famous as he for abundant charity.' Swift came a reaction from the other swan. 'Goodness gracious! You speak as if this Janashruti was greater than Raikva the cart-puller! The king is but mad for name and fame. It is these that drive him to action. Even with all his charity, he is ever restless. He hankers after praise.' The first swan was taken aback and asked, 'Who is this Raikva who is just a cart-puller yet is greater than the great Janashruti?'

The king overheard the two swans as they flew out of sight and night closed in on the city. But the king was restless. Raikva's name began to haunt him. 'I must find this man little known to fame but one who is at peace with himself and with the world,' he said with determination.

Janashruti then dispatched a servant to find the great soul. It was not an easy task but with a lot of difficulties, the servant found Raikva who sat scratching himself under a cart. The servant asked him whether he was Raikva. 'Yes, I am,' was the quiet and dignified reply. The servant went back to the palace and reported to Janashruti.

Janashruti made elaborate preparations and went to Raikva with 600 cows, a chain of gold and a mule-driven carriage. He offered them all at the feet of Raikva and said, 'Sir, please accept all this and teach me spiritual knowledge.' Raikva snapped back, 'Take back the chain and the carriage and the cows! Knowledge of the self is not for sale!' Janashruti went back and returned after a while. This time, he brought with him a 1,000 cows, a chain of gold, a mule-driven carriage and his daughter to be offered as Raikva's wife. He offered all this and prayed that he would be taught the higher truths of existence. Raikva was not moved by the gifts. But he was moved by Janashruti's persistence and sincerity. One who has these two virtues is eminently suited to be a perfect disciple.

Raikva said, 'In this creation, there are many elements which are worshipped as gods. There is the wind that sweeps everything. The fire burns up whatever comes in contact with it. There is also the vital breath that activates a living being. But all these are moved by the Spirit within. This Spirit is not created by anyone. It exists by itself. And yet, it creates and sustains the creation. Thus, the entire creation is a complex instrument that is carrying out its work at the behest of the Spirit.'

'O, king! Have neither pride nor vanity for the charity that you dispense. Go thou, great king, to thy palace. Give but not with pride. Give generously but not with egotism. Give freely but not with an eye to fame. Give, not as something that is yours, but as something given to you by the Spirit for giving to others. He who sees this truth becomes a seer and to him, nothing is wanting and he becomes the enjoyer of things.'

The king was extremely satisfied with these words of wisdom from Raikva. While departing, he gave a 1,000 milch cattle, numerous gold coins and chariots and his daughter in marriage to Raikva. Raikva did not reject these this time.

Thenceforth, the village came to be known as Raikvaparna—named after the philosopher of the cart.

(*Chandogya Upanishad*)
https: / / upanishads.org.in / stories / raikva-the-cart-driver

CONCLUSION: THE NEXT MANU*

From crystal balls to Nostradamus, we love to hear what the future has in store for us—both as an individual or as mankind. Everyone hates surprises if it does not come with the word 'party' or 'gift'.... I'm sure businesses hate surprises too, especially the nasty ones.

Let us consider a scenario. You are at the crossroads of your life. You have to make certain choices, like marriage, that have a lasting impact on your life. You wish you had a crystal ball that could accurately predict how it is going to be. If not, you wish you could at least make an 'informed decision'. For an individual, information is scarce and most of us are not trained in decision-making. Corporates have an advantage on both counts.

---

* Manu: The father of humans. It is a term with various meanings in Hinduism. In early texts, it refers to as an archetypal man or the first man (progenitor of human and humanity). It could be in a typical sense that the word Manu is used for an HR leader as a good metaphor at times. He represents all humanity and human beings—human resource. In several texts, Manu is the name of 14 mystical rulers on Earth or alternatively, the head of mythical dynasties to begin with each cyclical Kalpa (aeon) when the universe is born anew (after the Pralaya/deluge). According to the Puranas, each Kalpa consists of 14 Manvantars and each Manvantar is headed by a different Manu. The current universe is asserted to be ruled by the seventh Manu, the Vaivasvata. This Manu keeps changing his presentation, recognition, allies and genesis like the typical Bahrupias. He was warned of the flood by the Matsya Avatar of Vishnu and built a boat that carried the Vedas and the species of life. Manu's family and the Saptarshi, the seven sages, were taken to safety, guided by Manu with the help of the fish. The metaphor of Manu is referred to by us as an HR lead, as a protector and father of HR, father of all the rules and regulations written or developed by Manu to sustain dharma. When the deluge comes at the time of the seventh Manu's exit, there would come a totally new, transformed universe and progeny, along with the next Manu. This next Manu, who will be the eighth Manu, will play a multidirectional role of the wise man, the progenitor, the protector, the learned, the mentor and the guru who will bring life and order to the next universe after the deluge. This Manu shall be needed to play all roles assigned or created every time. [https://en.wikipedia.org/wiki/Manu_(Hinduism)]

Informed decision-making involves two main components—information and decision. Information is wealth. Whoever said this was futuristic. Then again, he/she might not have imagined the volume of information we get.

Everyone wants to know about the future. Perhaps it is very interesting, giving knowledge and strength to build one up for the coming times, its comforts, its powers and its opportunity of learning and growth. Everybody wants to know the future but at the same time, people are also afraid of the future. If you really want to handle the future, you have to build up your strength. That is required to meet the challenges of the future.

It is like the oracle of the past. As per Greek mythology, people would walk up to the temple of the oracle and ask questions and receive replies regarding their future.

One cannot know how far oracles are effective even now, but some people have certainly been working as futurists or crystal ball gazers, like Nostradamus and others. In the previous century, we had people like Alvin Toffler, who wrote *Future Shock* in the 1970s, *The Third Wave* in the 1980s or the *Power Shift: Knowledge, Wealth and Violence at the Edge of the 21st Century* in the 1990s, outlining the rapidly changing future. All his other books continued to identify emerging strategic changes, exploring the social, economic and political implications of technological developments on society.

Future Shock[70] by Alvin Toffler, gives startling insights into the working of organizations in the future (which is today). The book is widely regarded as a masterpiece of futurology. The author had foreseen that the two strengths of an organization, permanence and hierarchy (which the author calls bureaucracy), would be doomed and replaced by 'adhocracy'. This came true. The author had foreseen the following scenarios that later took place in the 1990s and the early 2000s):

- There would be a fair amount of mergers and acquisitions taking place that would continuously overhaul an organization, something the author termed as 'organizational upheaval'. The phenomena would threaten its permanence.
- The work would mostly be done by project teams, which would be promptly discarded after the job was completed. This would make the organization highly unstable.
- With the exponential increase in production, the production time would be reduced, making the downtime very costly and requiring a faster flow of information for faster executive decisions. This would result in the bypassing of the hierarchy—the 'hands' would take the decisions and not the managers.

Some predictions made in the book have, more or less, been coming true and organizations that have survived have made certain changes—such as flat structures, faster information flows and development of task teams—as foreseen by the book.

The Third Wave[71] by Toffler gives a seminal, eye-opening account of futurology and is intended to whet the appetites of people from history, philosophy, sociology and management studies who were planning to be an active part of businesses and other fluid environments.

Toffler came out next with his *Power Shift*. Power is related to knowledge and the role it plays in our lives. Without knowledge, we cannot win a battle—whether it be in war or market competition. Knowledge is the key to success. Toffler gives many examples of how knowledge has changed lives in *Power Shift*. With knowledge, we can gain power which can shift hands.

Before our digital age, manufacturers were in control. One example Toffler writes about is the Gillette razor company and the power it had. Gillette had complete control over its product in the beginning. Gillette controlled how many razors went to each store and how many different styles/brands a store would display. The store owner had no control. Manufacturers kept their competition running because of the information they had. They knew how to accumulate knowledge about their consumers. From this knowledge, power was born. The invention of barcodes shifted power from the manufacturer to the retailer. Barcodes revealed a lot of information about the consumer to the retailer. The invention of computers for barcodes further shifted the power from the manufacturer to the retailer. Today, the same manufacturers beg for space in stores. Store owners know what the customer wants from the information they collect through the barcode system. This is a good example of how power can shift because of technology. Once regarded as purely administrative tools, networked information systems are increasingly seen as strategic weapons, helping companies protect established markets and attack new ones.

A network's main function is to share information. Corporations are leading towards an electronic interaction network. This interaction allows the buyer to place an order with the seller and have the transaction take place immediately. This leads to intimacy with customers and suppliers. Information sharing potentially leads to blurring boundaries of information. The information can be used as a weapon for the 'go-betweens' and intermediaries. Toffler forecasted that technology would prove that extra intelligence does lead to a better life. The invention of the computer has proven this fact. Before long, the power of computers will leap forward because of parallel processing, artificial intelligence and other stunning innovations. Speech recognition and automatic translation will, no doubt, come to be widely used, along with high definition visuals, displays and a concert-class sound. The same networks will routinely carry voice, data, images and information in other forms. Upgrading information leads to intelligence.

Microprocessors revolutionized the mainframe computer. In recent times, the next step has been the introduction of 'hypermedia', databases capable of storing not only text but also graphics, music, speech and other sounds. More importantly, hypermedia combines databases and programs to give the user far greater flexibility than earlier forms of data.

When we talk of the current times of business and enterprise, their performance depends substantially on our knowledge of the future and also how we can manage the knowledge or information while dealing with the challenges of the coming time.

We are reminded of Gillette or Kodak, and so many other companies, who had control over the future of their business and their own organization's performance. Somehow, they either did not use the opportunity and information or could not take steps to handle the future and make it brighter.

In the business segment, there have been several crystal ball gazers and consultants who can survey, analyse and forecast, sharing the wisdom of the future so that one can take on the challenges of the coming times and still survive and remain successful. This type of assessment of the future enables enterprises and organizations to harness uncertainty and gives them a clue regarding how to prosper in unknowable times, the new normal times, which demands continuous learning. This requires the ability of a very versatile player and a very competent performer who can rise to every challenging occasion and deliver their best, beating new challenges like a forceful Bahrupia and prompter preparing and developing their team members.

TALENT TODAY AND TOMORROW

Leaders (particularly the HR leaders) must recognize potentials and extend a hand as a mentor to the talent. We must take good care of our people who have to be trained, and skill development has to be undertaken regularly.

The onus is on the management and HR leaders of the teams to instil a sense of purpose in them and make them perform. The purpose-driven organizations, which are the winners, are the ones where though the skills may not be at a premium, the complementarity of the purpose exists. It would remain a challenge for the HR leaders and the business leaders to ensure that we create purpose in the organizations to bring people together to deliver the best.

The growth from manager to being a leader requires continuous interventions. There has been a globalization of talent. As has happened with businesses, the same thing has happened with the talent. The businesses have moved from being local to global; much before that happened, the employees moved from being local to global. They have been the ones who have moved preparatory to change in business occasions like the change-ready Bahrupias.

The global war for talent suggests that the future has a very strange way of becoming the present suddenly. If we sit back to relax, we are in for a rude shock because the norm for talent is constant disruption. We need to work in global teams that involve modular work dealing with hands-off points between different countries or project work, based on continuous service. We are going to see a lot of changes in computing capacity, data analytics and complex domain learning where an individual will not only learn from one's own domain but would need to learn from different domains and different technologies. There will be no comparisons. If HR draws a skill map of the organization today, they need to anticipate the changes that are likely to happen in the next 3, 7 or 10 years within the organization.

The gap between the global and local is increasing rather than decreasing. There is a chronological age and a psychological age for an HR leadership position. The crisis in HR leadership today is not the absence of leadership but more in terms of whether our HR leaders can stretch to the kind of demands of variety that the context places. Performance is not static and it changes colours and shapes or designs like a kaleidoscopic Bahrupia.

It is a cultural concept that defines whether we are willing to differentiate among employees in terms of rewarding performance. If we declare some employees as critical resources, we might lose them to the market. But as long as the system is transparent and meritocracy exists, we should have the guts to declare and differentiate performance, long-term incentive and variable pay. The purpose is growth, profitability and profit. We need to reinvest for stakeholders and convince them.

However, if we intend to need workforce capability creation at the front-line levels, HR can and should take the lead in terms of co-creation. Hence, the key requirement of new-age learning is creating an ecosystem where HR professionals go through crucibles of experiences, ideally through different business cycles, and are guided by seniors to reflect on such experiences and convert them into insights. This has to be a deliberate process.

Capability building across experience with mentoring and coaching also needs to be nurtured. An important aspect of today's recruitment is to ensure the right balance between generalist and specialist workers in a company. Potential companies are more likely to be distinguished by a diverse array of T-shaped employee skills that aim towards the integration of generalists and experts. While the top line represents the generalist with good basic knowledge and understanding of operations, the vertical line reflects the skilled professionals—supposedly the domain specialists. While adapting to new technologies is certainly crucial, having motivated and talented employees is an absolute must.

The workforce today is not only multigenerational but is highly diverse. There is gender diversity and also socio-economic diversity that we see at the workplace. Things that we, the baby boomer generation, took for granted are not even understood as basic requirements by the workforce that comes in today. And similarly, things considered as very important by Gen Y were perhaps not even on the horizon or on our radar at any point in time. At some level, workforce capability is very strongly linked to enterprise capability. The strategy in our case regarding whether to buy or build talent is borrowed from biotechnology; the idea is to create for every new skill, a nucleus which we may buy and then let the cells proliferate by building along that nucleus.

The way forward is coaching and development and to position a performance management system to bring about the desired change. HR has to work and invest more for such talent development.

We need to increase the pitch and frequency of dialoguing the quality of discussion with the manager, the kind of preparedness of the manager and the time the manager spends with the subordinate for the review of performance.

Teams should not go into HR degrees but they should specialize in something which makes them feel important and adds value and then that becomes the fulcrum and the basis for us to have a conversation with the other person. Why are we spending all our lives trying to tell the operations guys how to engage? They will know how to engage because they will give value to the employee.

Indian organizations jumped onto this bell curve bandwagon in 2000, not fully realizing what its consequences could be. And the worry is that a lot of us started focusing on doing away with the bell curve. The performance management system is always a business process and not an HR process. This is something that needs to be reviewed. We tend to focus disproportionately on rewards as tools for managing performance. Rating is largely a process of distribution of rewards. Doing away with the bell curve is not synonymous with doing away with the performance management system since the bell curve is just a small part of performance management.

It seems, at times, that we are now ready for deglobalization. All that was built in the last 30 years in terms of integrating the world will have to be dismantled. We don't know whether HR will be needed at all or whether HR will be meaningful at all in the days to come, fundamentally because of the way technology is replacing people. We have to make HR leads ever-ready.

ORGANIZATION OF THE FUTURE

There is a deluge of information but a lack of knowledge. This is the paradox of the technology invasion. Hence, the role of HR should keep changing always. Learning is not a very easy habit. So are we truly learning and are we in HR trying to reinvent our way of looking at disjointed experiences? Today's digital medium is such a means and mechanism for us that it keeps the entire distributed workforce together.

HR leaders need to convert the potential talent into actual talent that is industry-ready. One of the most fundamental changes we have seen is in the role of HR functions itself, from the one which was defined by Edwin Flippo to Dave Ulrich. Personnel management in the 1970s was a line management responsibility and the role of the personnel manager was to aid, advise and assist the line manager in procurement, development, maintenance, compensation and separation. There are four quadrants in which he talks about HR as a strategic partner, with a metaphor added about employee champions that has completely confused the HR managers. One of the tasks of HR is to effectively leverage this huge potential. We have a huge surplus.

The role of HR is changing. One of the key things is the rate of change happening in the industry. The dynamism in the industry is changing the way HR has to act. Earlier, the change could take place gradually. One prominent change that has taken place now is that HR has to react very fast to situations. In fact, HR has to predict what is really going to happen. If any organization has to survive in these turbulent times, their HR must be able to predict the future in a better way than their competitors and that is where HR needs to play a Bahrupian role. It has to be in our DNA to be at the forefront. Technology cannot be a bane. It is always a boon. Technology has enabled HR. It removes the middlemen.

In 1974 when we (Dr. T.V. Rao) started the first HR development department, it was started with a certain philosophy. One would like to underline that HR is a philosophy. The HR philosophy is that every individual dedicates a major part of his/her life to the service of an organization. Over a period, across the last few decades, a lot of change has taken place. HR has become strong as a department but philosophy has been left behind or sidelined. The human part of HR has been sidelined. They have done a lot of good work for the corporation, won the credibility of the CEOs or group-chairman and have become business heads in some of the companies. The basic competency that is missing in the HR professionals is the ability to work for the larger goal of creating 'happiness at the workplace'. They have also talked about HR values. This is very important. At the same time, they have also talked of the HR function as business strategic partners. We forget the first two but look at the third one and that becomes very important for us. So the change is there. We suggest delinking performance appraisals from rewards. Because the moment we link them with rewards, a vicious circle gets created, focussing on rewards rather than development. HR would not be completely sidelined but will have to be lean and smart.

HR is becoming like a mobile device—introduced for the sake of communication and now, a mobile device can do everything.

When we talk of digital today, it has to be very contextual.

While technology will grow, HR has no reason to worry. Anything that is an operation under the HR system will be done by software programs. The HR professional must constantly reskill themselves to move from the operational space to the actual human development space.

There are two applications of augmented intelligence. One within HR, where HR activities would be augmented by artificial intelligence and that would include things like predictive analysis. The second is the use of AI in the changing business scenario, where AI would be used to benefit the business. For doing that, we have to make sure that the HR professionals understand business. For this effective running of the business, we must train people and make them accept and embrace technology—whether it is augmented intelligence or machine learning—rather than find ways and means of convincing people that this is nothing to be afraid of. The only part that we could add is that whatever augmented intelligence we use, at the end of the day, we do not see H in HR disappearing. Technology does not mean that we convert everything into non-human activity. The touch and feel must remain. In fact, with the use of technology, there will be more emphasis on skills like empathy and relationships.

We could hire people for defined agilities to make a difference by changing things and also develop innovative practices to bring about digital savviness. They could do a lot of reverse mentoring to our leaders and help them become digitally savvy.

Technology should become only a means to enhance organizational effectiveness and make the right business decisions but the human touch shall and must always remain.

The potential of digital technology is immense. The core value will assume paramount importance in terms of creating a broad governance framework in this set of organizations. Conventionally, in a typical organization, we consider that communication is one of the strongest backbones for developing commitment and culture. Another thing is the excitement of learning. We are using technology to learn our new skills and develop competence and new skill sets wherein the people can learn 24×7. And they need not go to a predefined place to learn. So these are the kinds of changes and excitement which are going to be part of the future.

Technology is to be harnessed carefully and in the right way. In addition to the emergence of the digital era, two more strong variables will be affecting the future of the workplace, people processes and overall transformation of the HR function. The first variable is the impact of globalization, which has brought a strong global connect, intense competition and also global turbulence. The second variable is the demographic shift of the workforce towards millennials, which we are all experiencing already. Digitalization will also have a huge potential to transform learning and development offerings through e-learning modules and e-games, leading to higher involvement, internalization and flexibility in the capability development process. De-learning, relearning or reskilling would all become relatively more effective and relevant through digitalization.

We will train our HR persons. They will become subject matter experts so that if people have any difficulties, they can approach one of our internal HR persons. Of course, in all these, we should not lose sight of continuing to provide the 'human touch'—the glue that connects people to people, organization and society at large.

While we need to embrace technological change, which includes artificial intelligence, robotics, etc., we cannot get carried away with technology and forget the human being, who is behind it all.

Things are changing and even getting disrupted but we have changed ourselves and that is why we have survived. We need loyal employees. We need people who can move to our organization to be successful. All the companies that have built core employees are the survivors. Everywhere at the bottom, we will find that if a company has a very strong employee base they survive much longer than others that have no such base.

We are today at the microcosm of the environment and should be ready with anchors, mentors or counsellors to meet the challenges of real disruption. The paradigm shift in performance achievement is about you—it is about your own matrices, your own performance and how you are going to move in that direction.

There is no substitute for human culture. We should start our response with the art of conversation. The efficacy of 'human touch' in the form of conversation has been missing and technology did not tell us not to have the conversation. But we have used the pretext of technology as an excuse to avoid it, saying that technology makes things consistent, fast and efficient—which is fantastic. We should use it. But the human triggers have to be embedded.

Companies that inspire us to work with peace of mind and aspiration of long career growth are companies to work with. We have a gig economy. So the career paths will not be decided by employees themselves. HR will do it differently.

Whatever change may occur due to technology or in skills, everyone will prefer behavioural outlook and patterns in the leader. This quality of risk-taking by an HR professional will have an impact on the HR domain. We may see this kind of situation in many industry sectors. These automotive industries are changing their strategies every second. They are no longer following traditional paths blindly.

Unless we are aware of ourselves, are a self-appraiser and emotionally intelligent, we will not be able to understand the dynamics or the psyche of the younger digital employees. Coaching work culture means they will try to come closer to the employees and come closer to address their issues. And then only will it be possible to rewrite the rules in the organization to change the behavioural pattern to some extent indirectly.

The change which comes or, rather, is brought in periodically is a change with aspirational agenda or even anticipatory ones. These types of changes are not very volatile and the management, particularly the leader and the HR, would be aware and can prepare intelligently in advance ways to deal with the change successfully.

However, a change that comes in totality in the form of a transformation will emerge more as VUCA trends—volatile, uncertain, complex and ambiguous/unknown. This has the potential to come as a deluge, the Pralaya that we are talking about, bringing a total change of time—a time when the yuga, the trend of time, also transforms itself. The next yuga always demands such kinds of challenges in transformation which has to deal with both the rationalization (the sour) of the existing learnings and also the revitalization (the sweet) at the same time.[72] Some changes which are categorized as revitalization may not be as painful as rationalization, where the organization changes its business, its products, its manpower optimization, its manpower productivity, the norms and so on which is certainly very painful and may emerge to throw up a challenge like a deluge, a Pralaya, by a change of time to the new yuga.

CULTURE AND ENGAGEMENT

Some organizations are implementing a 'value creation plan'. Instead of doing KRAs, rewards and recognitions around it, they say that they are creating value for organizations and individuals for a horizon of three years. There are benchmarks wherein they reward and recognize people. Since it is a value-creation plan, they also recognize and allow failures. There is no punishment for failures and they try to make sure that the same failures are not repeated in future as a team in the organization. As a nation and as an organization, HR has to move towards more inclusive work cultures rather than class cultures. India is amidst growth expectation. A lot of things are on the positive side, such as a young population. Technology is also changing at a faster pace and we have Digital India, which has put India on the global map. Technology is a great enabler that is changing our lives drastically. But we must not miss the human touch.

There is a need to build a culture to be change-ready for survival tomorrow. We have spent quite a long time defining the robust processes in the past. There is a need to go back to the basics to introspect and try and answer questions about the reasons why we do what we do, whether it is the engagement survey, the bell curve or the appraisal system. It's not the education that gives us the wherewithal to be a leader or a manager. The skill set that one possesses is important. There is a shift from knowing to doing. Knowing can be bridged. As an HR consultant, we would want an imaginative guy or an engaged guy. In the interview, we look for interesting people rather than only the skills. People are moving away from knowledge to skill since the knowledge gap can always be bridged. We all are learning skills. There is a huge shift towards self-learning. The environment around is such that a lot of self-learning is happening.

There is a need to keep the variable component low, and coupled with potential assessment and continuous rotation, it is the way to go in the future. The issue is not about managing performance but of differentiation or of differentiating payments. While we are not talking about compensation, we are intending and implying silently about compensation. The working generation is changing. Around 80%–85% of India is Gen Y. They don't want to be appraised in the way we have been doing so far. Terms such as management development are not going to be relevant for them. HR, therefore, needs to change the way they measure and reward people or else it is not going to work. Culture and engagement are always very important. Continuous feedback, paying people at fixed and competitive rates to the market, keeping the variable component low and ensuring that the larger mass gets the same and very few get high and low is what we need to do. Appraisals might be once a year or four times a year; it depends on the demographics of the company. In a stable organization, where the same people report to the same manager, one year may be regarded as enough. But if it is a dynamic, project-based organization then appraisal being done once a year is not enough.

In the context of the so-called VUCA world, culture and engagement are ripe for disruption. In terms of redefining the social contracts, restructuring the culture, employee engagement and so on, before we go there, there is a need to just reflect on the year that has gone by and the key events that have defined the year. We had BREXIT against the EU and India demonetized its currency. So it is a VUCA world and in the disruptive world, organizations get disrupted too. The first disruptive trend is technology. The tidal wave of technology is going to disrupt organizations and particularly the HR function in its wake. Of all the aspects of HR, culture and engagement will face the greatest disruption. Culture is the way you define how you work with each other. If expectations are not set, it would evolve very quickly. We are going to see a paradigm change in this area. Engagement is no longer going to be an annual affair. It is going to be a daily affair at the very least, if not an hourly affair. Imagine that in another 10 years from now, you have a mood meter of people coming into work. And you are able to gauge whether a person is coming into the office with a smile or a sad face. I think it is virtually going to be an hour-by-hour, minute-by-minute engagement strategy. The price of disengaged employees is more significant, and corporations will need to do significantly more on the engagement front. It is an exciting time and this entire time we are going to see disrupted HR functions. The function is going to be disrupted and technology will play a remarkable role by enabling us to delight the employee. But empathetic engagement—the need to connect with the heart—will continue to exist. If done well, tech designs can facilitate this 'high-tech, high-touch mantra'. That is the meaning of disruption. Thanks to these megatrends and their impact, the HR function post the surprising and disruptive changes will look radically different in 2030.

We see an extraordinary degree of disconnect when people speak of analytics and engagement in the same breath, which is extremely contradictory. Most of the people coming into institutions now are from a single-child household and many of us in HR are applying our minds as it is a big challenge to be able to engage them, irrespective of which economic strata they come from.

Culture is impacted by the leader and employees feel engaged when they identify with the values and principles of their leader. Cultural fit is an absolute must when we hire. Even the most successful, most capable, most intelligent person who is not culturally fit to be in the organization is not of much value because the disruptive power of our leader can be devastating to the organization.

There is a need to develop a culture that creates passionate employees through meaning and empowerment. In this age of disruption, while strategy, structure, processes and metrics are necessary, what will make the difference is how passionate employees are. And passion comes from two sources. One is meaning—the meaning that a person finds in his/her work. And the second one is empowerment. So we would like to make a case for creating a culture that provides meaning and empowerment to its employees, which in turn generates passion and unleashes potential.

IT MNCs may not be bothered by even 20% attrition as this is taken almost like an opportunity and not a threat. Engagement and retention are not directly related. Their focus is on the engagement of a young workforce rather than on their retention. The sector developed policies and work processes that are least impacted by the attrition rate, unlike other industry sectors.

When we are concerned about engagement, we need to connect with people. Four generations are working together—the veterans, the baby boomers, the baby busters and Gen X and Y. This is an added complexity in an already complex work environment, especially in a country like India. We have a very high level of diversity, which very few other nations or contexts have. We find multilingual, multicultural, multiregional and multi-ethnic complexity at the workplace. Creating a work culture within this diversity is a huge challenge. The word 'engagement' is not new; it has been there since the industry started. From an outsider perspective, there has always been a concern about how to get people to give their best. When we are concerned about engagement, it's most important to connect with people.

Loyalty does not come with a 'cradle to grave' tenure in an organization but it should be judged based on an employee's contribution. The organization and leaders should leverage reverse mentoring and reverse learning while engaging with the multigenerational workforce. This should be regarded as an opportunity rather than a threat or a challenge. It is the style of leadership and the culture we develop that immensely boosts the engagement, motivation and management of organizational talent.

In the manufacturing industry, the culture of the organization is the key and we have to work more for employee engagement while trying to imbibe and create pride and passion. Many companies believe in hiring novices and nurturing them through an in-house talent development ecosystem. This helps them in building and sustaining the culture unique to their organization that focuses on capability building, commitment building and culture building. Therefore, these organizations don't look for the most intelligent employees. Instead, they look for the ones that are most suited for those kinds of environments and the ones who would stick to such jobs as they can provide. These factors have contributed to making them successful in retaining their employees. Some organizations in manufacturing never believed in the 'bell curve' or '360-degree feedback' or 'balanced scorecard'. We work as a family and care for the feelings of employees as family member. Employee initiatives leading to innovations are rewarded and gains of such innovations are shared with them as a token of recognition. These companies sincerely believe that mistakes are a part of innovation and decision-making, and any action that hampers creativity must be avoided.

Today's younger generation wants to learn, demonstrate and be empowered and not endanger the company's future success by failing to nourish the top talent. They are knowledgeable and want to be updated with state of art knowledge and with whatever is the best in the world. The moment they know where they stand in the total context and realize their position in the organization, they are rejuvenated, feel empowered and engaged, and have a sense of ownership. This ownership and sense of belongingness help to retain talent better than any other motivational device. The new generation is regarded as very informal and looking for flexible working time. If we do not nurture our high-potential employees, then we miss out on the opportunity to help boost the bottom-line. The main concern today is how we manage the talent and keep them engaged—by right hiring or the right placement or the right training and development.

Leadership has been ranked behind culture and engagement. Does leadership set the tone of culture or does culture breed leadership? Productivity and engagement reflect the financial impact of culture. We often talk in terms of the 'culture of engagement'. But it could also be a 'culture of disengagement'? Culture does not change overnight and is an evolution. Dramatically, the culture of a place would not change until there is some crisis. Cultural change is much bigger than the generational changes that are happening. With every generational change, working styles are changing and preferences about how we wish to work or about how we get things done are changing.

Culture has a very important influence on the organization and its balance sheet. Engagement surveys should be continued as they give a useful understanding of things taking place under the iceberg.

Times have changed and the HR system has also changed. HR should shift from specific HR persons to all the managers. There are instances where the blend of foreign culture and Indian culture has tilted towards Indian culture. They start respecting our culture and we have to respect their culture. The essence is that we have to coexist.

The cultural context needs to be in sync with the business context to be facilitative to business, which can be influenced by the leadership style. The cultural context is very deeply ingrained in the DNA of the organization. If the cultural context is in sync with what the organization is trying to achieve at the business level, then the culture is facilitative to business. The leadership style should be relevant to the deliverables of the function and the kind of people one is leading, in terms of their capability and maturity. Despite these different climates across functions and work groups, there will be common threads running across the organization via these same functions and work groups, defining the organization's cultural fabric.

Under these circumstances, HR has to emerge as Saptarshi in this context, showing the path and laying norms, rules and values to build a strong and stable culture that supports engagement within the organization.

THE NEO HR

The proposition that HR should reskill has been in existence for a long time. HR needs to keep the basics simple and not over-theorize things, using complex terminologies like OD, engagement and so on. If we look at the bigger perspective, the physical world is shrinking and the digital world is expanding. However, the physical world will coexist with the digital world. Businesses will have to start thinking of ways to manage the transition. If such perceptiveness is there in the HR personnel, the board members of the organization will respect them. Being practical and finding real ways to intervene and deliver appropriate results is better than merely studying research papers and then planning to incorporate them. Most of the time, HR deals with impromptu resolutions of the challenges that appear before the organizations. They know that there cannot be any ready-made and so-called tested solutions that fit all such occasions.

Any challenge of HR inadequacy is a challenge of leadership and a challenge for the organization. These should not be seen as very asymmetrical issues. Every organization, every country, every corporation, every age, every generation and every challenge gets the HR it deserves. There is a need to reinvent and reposition HR. We need to acquire certain newer skills and refocus our priorities. It all depends on our operating requirement, challenge and need. As the world changes and as organizations change, HR professionals—both in the function and the leadership—would have to think of their roles as influencers of change and challenges by envisioning newer environments and carving out newer resolutions that are the new best fits for the organization, its situation and its requirement for survival.

All HR leaders have an issue with talent analytics. We need to create a talent analytics team where we can farm and mine data but the larger issue is concerned with what we do with the data. HR leads at different levels, situations and challenges may need to change from position to position, level to level. What is most needed in the HR lead is a sense of judgment, a presence of mind and values of courage, empathy and relationships. We need to make the people in HR come out of their cocoons, irrespective of the intensity of any paid one that may be there, and realize that they can make a difference by getting resolutions and delivering success by playing a mix of roles most required for completing the act, scene and the story—like the Bahrupia who enables happiness to all the customers of the organization.

Performance, care and values have to be equally addressed by the smart Bahrupias for a sustainably winning business. HR's major focus should be on unleashing human potential in pursuit of the organization's goals and purpose; not always as the Bahrupias, in acting or performing roles on stage, but also as enablers, as prompters from the prompters' pit, unleashing the rich human potential in the organization. In this era of technological disruption with AI, analytics, chatbots and so on, we must not forget that the human being should be at the core at the end of the day.

Skilling and upskilling is a continuous process. There has been a shift in HR leadership and the context, the stage, has changed dramatically. Earlier we had an operationally reactive HR; for instance, in case of a showdown somewhere or a problem on the shop floor, they would try to sort that out. From there, HR leads moved to being mostly operationally proactive, wherein HR worked to ensure that it does not happen again. Then HR became strategically reactive and currently, strategically proactive.

HR needs to create the right environment for people to grow. The symbiotic relationship between business and HR needs to evolve to suit the new era of social connectedness and discontinuities. The organization needs to work collaboratively to shift mindsets and enable the development of its people. Ultimately, an organization that fails to reskill its employees is like a combatant who brings a knife to a gunfight—disadvantaged and doomed. It is time to wake up and turn the tide.

In the changing expectations amongst generations, HR needs to customize as per needs and as per age groups. HR leads must develop continuously with regards to the questions of how to handle or improve intergenerational relationships and how to handle diversity as well. HR leads must also similarly know what is attractive as a company, its brand, youthfulness, vitality and so on.

The successful corporations of tomorrow will leverage the benefits of workforce diversity faster and better. The role of HR is indeed changing on account of the demographic upheavals taking place all over the world. For India, demographic changes are likely to manifest themselves at the workplace in the form of a multigenerational workforce.

HR has to continuously figure out how they should be changing the HR processes that take care of the new generations coming up. HR has, therefore, got to keep learning and stay updated, creating a virtual learning organization that keeps building up its capability on a continued basis.

HR needs to focus and address the needs of learning and development and career growth opportunities for which the millennials have a greater appetite and urge. When we talk about challenges, it brings in new flavour and complexity in terms of managing the talent within the organization. Here lies the role of HR. They need to evolve in terms of how they deal with such new imperatives which have become very critical to the organization to actually take it forward.

We recently heard Mukesh Ambani address the keys to his success. He was narrating a couple of qualities and values that he said his father had taught him, describing this as boundaries of work that create value in the organization and retain it, creating a successful organization for the future. One which he emphasized very much was the value of courage. He said that the entrepreneur should have wisdom and exercise it and must have courage—courage to the extent that even fear would be scared of him/her. He talked of empathy, faith in technology and talent and also a heart-to-heart relationship with people. We think that nothing more is needed for a leader or an entrepreneur to deliver continuous growth and success if all these things are practised sincerely and consistently.

In so far as courage is concerned, he wanted courage not only in the entrepreneur–leader but in every person in the organization who deals with the future of the business or a part thereof, so that they could face dangerous events without withdrawing. Courage is a moment when a person only has one thought—'go for it'. We have to depend not only on our ability to forecast future opportunities and threats but also have strong values of courage, empathy and relationships. Understanding the pillars of honour, courage and commitment existing in a motto or tag line is not enough—they must be embedded in the fabric of the organization and this is an expectation that is demonstrated through the attitudes and behaviour of employees. Leaders must live and breathe their leadership and the institution's values and their subordinates must have incentives to accept them.

One would have noticed that recently in an online chat, Dave Ulrich talked about boundaries of work in values to deal with the new normal. He spoke of situations where there is great uncertainty not only regarding solutions but also regarding processes. Upon hearing this, I also recalled that Swami Vivekananda, while delivering a talk on work and its secret in Los Angeles, California, in the 1900s, said that one of the greatest lessons he had learnt in his life was to pay as much attention to the means of work as to its end. He was a great man from whom learning flowed and his own life was a practical demonstration of his great principle. Swami Vivekananda talked about learning great lessons from that one principle and the fact that it appeared to him that all the secrets of success are there to pay as much attention to the means as to the end. Our great defect in life is that we are so much drawn to the ideal and the goal is so much more enchanting, so much more alluring, that we lose sight of the details of the process altogether. But whenever failure comes, if we analyse it critically, in 99% of cases we shall find that it was because we did not pay attention to the means and the processes that Dave Ulrich mentioned, almost 100 years after Swami Vivekananda.

With the means, the end is assured and it must come. We forget that it is the cause that produces the effect. The effect cannot come by itself and unless the causes are exact for you, the effect will not be produced. Once the ideal is chosen and the means determined, we may let go of the ideal because we are sure it will be there when the means are perfected. If we take care of the cause, the effect will take care of itself.

In the case of Maruti Suzuki India Limited's strike, which turned into terrible violence in Manesar, there were several occasions when HR personnel were exposed to extreme danger. Awanish Kumar Dev, GM (HR), was on duty the evening the violent rampage took place in Plant Manesar, and he burnt to death. It was shocking news for the entire country and HR people particularly. Not that such incidents had not happened before with HR people or officers but this was a very violent and painful incident that demoralized the HR personnel completely. There were several meetings, gatherings and conventions to protest against this incident but time goes on. There have been many cases in our life as well where we have had to undergo acute violence, including the use of firearms and other forms of physical violence like rods and sticks. The HR professionals who come out of the best institutions, qualified to take up a career in HR, are least bothered about such life-threatening or violent incidents in their career time. What role does HR need to play in such incidents? Is there any special training or education given to them when it is known that they will certainly be exposed to such violence? Perhaps not. It is all their personal learning or experiences that teach them to protect themselves and protect the interest of the business and the employees and other members involved in such incidents of terrible violence.

K.K. Sinha writes:

I certainly would like to narrate the incident of Bahrupias in their jatra performance in Dumka, almost 40 years after my initial memory as a child in primary school. This is an incident that arose out of a jatra, or an act, performed by Bahrupias in Dumka in the year 1967 or 1968. It was played out by Santhalis and some Bengalis from the neighbouring rural areas, who had come to the small town to earn some money and also to satisfy their urge for performance and creativity. There was a political disturbance at that time, which had its reasons or root in some political issue of power in Bihar. I was a postgraduate student and living in a hostel at Patna University. As per the government's order, students living in hostels were asked to evacuate their hostel rooms overnight and go away to any place they felt to be secure.

We picked up our bags, leaving everything else in the room, and rushed to the Patna railway station, not knowing which way we should go. Ultimately, I took the next train going to Jasidih and reached Dumka by the next morning—my Nani's place. This was my visit after almost two decades. I had my cousins and friends there, who had grown up. It was a good time, staying there for almost three to four months, but I wasted substantial time which could have been used for studies and preparing for the coming exams. While in Dumka, we reminisced about many old incidents, and I was curious to watch some of the Bahrupia plays or jatras, which were a common feature there. While we did see one or two from the epics, the Upanishads, there was hardly any improvement in the script or the dress and costuming or music and even presentation. We used to be amused, watching them once again after a gap of time. One day, we heard that the troupe from the rural area was visiting to perform jatra on 'Santhal Hool', the play that was always so popular amongst the youngsters. We were prepared to spend some time watching it when it was played by the villagers.

The Santhal Hool was, accordingly, played by the Bahrupias and with a lot of fervour. During the Santhal Hool, there was so much excitement in the people—not merely the performers but the audience too, every year, every time. When the Santhal Hool was staged that year, there was a huge crowd that assembled such that the police had to actively maintain order and peace. The play started and the crowd cheered occasionally. When the two brothers (Sidhu and Kahnu Murmu) were being hanged publicly by the British, there was a lot of excitement among the people who suddenly started shouting slogans. The crowd went out of control, followed by some rampage and also a mild lathi-charge by the police.

We recall that the two brothers in the story were hanged. They were arrested by the police, along with a few other crew members, and taken to the police station. Later, we heard that they were even assaulted in the police station and we were told that they were released by the police on some bonds of peace. That was also the usual story of the Bahrupias, who were exposed to violence and even death at times.

This was an incident and story of Bahrupias depicting a very emotional case of engagement, involving not just the Bahrupian performers but also the viewers.

The engagement of employees is the responsibility of the manager but it primarily falls under the guidelines and support of HR. Business leaders have always agreed to the engagement provided to their employees. Performance is not only because of the leadership but primarily because of the level of engagement sustained in the organization. Motivated and committed employees, therefore, are found to be resolving problems and persisting until they find creative solutions to the problem. Having a sense of a mission and a social goal for the organization helps employees to see the purpose of the work and, therefore, the goals beyond their immediate self-interest and beyond the achievement of the firm and its owner.

We remember a couple of metaphors or stories of a stonecutter or a truck driver. It is said that there were thousands of stonecutters at a project site where work was going on. The cutters were busy chiselling and cutting pieces of marble stones collected in a big volume to carve out stone pillars, arches, doors and so on for a temple. One passerby was curious to see this work that people were engaged in, day-in and day-out, intensely working to create a piece of art with every moment of their labour. The passerby asked one of the stonecutters curiously, 'What are you doing?' The stonecutter, visibly annoyed, responded, 'Don't you see, I am cutting the damn stone and that too continuously every day.' The passerby was taken aback but the curiosity did not die. Moving forward, after 20 or 30 stonecutters, he asked one person again, 'What are you doing?' This stonecutter wiped his sweating face and looked up with a smile, giving an amazing answer, 'Sir, I am building the best Ram temple in Ayodhya, the grandest of all structures of this kind made in the world.' This showed the deep engagement within the stonecutter, who felt a big purpose in the assignment he was discharging.

The success of the project, therefore, depends substantially on the engagement level of the employees. The magic is in identifying the right people and hiring them, developing them internally and improving their morale, unleashing them to perform and giving them a strong, grand purpose of work. This is what is needed from HR or the leaders or managers who want the desired results. There is always a need to instil a sense of mission, using management practices that can help produce an engagement and motivation that allows the organization to be efficient and innovative.

Peter Capelli,[73] when he came for research on 'India Way', found that there were sophisticated HR practices and extensive programmes that were common in India as a means to reach the labour market with planning and performance management.

Their research of Indian companies found that hardware and, later, software companies in India nurtured basic DNA by having long-term business approaches to the principles of managing employees. These companies or leaders found the magic formula of driving employees first, over the customer—who was being treated as second. Managers were being made accountable for the employees and their performance, both quality-wise and productivity-wise. There was good networking permitted to employees, who could express themselves, their challenges, their suggestions and their proposals for new initiatives.

They found in their research that 68% to 70% of the HR executives reported that they were closely associated with creating a strategy with the other top leaders in their companies. In an interview with Mukesh Ambani of Reliance Industries, he observed that the strength of India is really in the depth of talent that we have. A large number of organizations and their leaders, like Mahindra & Mahindra or the Tatas and Tata Consultancy, had similar views and a conviction of driving this as a trump card in the organization through their teams, managers and executives.

It was also found that after hiring the right employee, the Indian companies spent heavily on learning and training. Most of the companies that hired trainees, technical or non-technical, spent a lot of time and money—going up to six months or one year—to ensure that the deliverables were as per the desires of the planned schemes. Hence, most of them had a very sophisticated executive development programme, which they also called an academy organization. This was the situation in not only manufacturing, software or hardware organizations but also in service industries like banking. Everyone understood that unless people in the organizations are mobilized and energized on a sustained basis, in support of business priorities and purpose, success can be elusive. More than 65% of the Indian HR teams or heads in interviews said that their function had the same level of respect in the company as all other functions. In fact, one of the CEOs of a leading manufacturing organization even articulated that the CEOs of companies should be HR Managers today. A very powerful statement and conviction. Capelli thought of employees as family, creating commitment and culture in the organization continuously and creating a culture of learning and development all the time. The stress on personal relationships creates problems in assessing talent as well. One of the CEOs expressed that their biggest weakness was that they were unable to reach scientific and reasonable assessments of white-collared productivity. Many of the organizations also felt that performance evaluations or assessment always remained a tricky issue, causing a lot of gaps in relationships and challenging the deliveries or results. In most of the companies studied, strategy was based on internal competencies that ultimately came from the actions and efforts of the employee. The fact that the Indian CEOs give so much attention to employee issues, therefore, is not just because they want to be generous to the employee but primarily to ensure results and drive the competitiveness of their business. When it comes to judging people, their capabilities and their expectations, we tend to be very poor judges. Sometimes, the danger in our business or industry is that people are not performance-oriented enough. When our personal relationships get mixed in, we tend to take a softer approach which may adversely affect the results. Hence, companies need to be striking a very good balance in the holistic engagement of employees to sustain results and performance.

We have seen views and expertise from mostly the HR professionals in business, in addition to a few from the academic and consultancy area. Seeing these, some consensus emerges around several themes, like HR is under scrutiny, HR needs change, changing HR will represent important challenges and demanding new competencies and if HR does not meet the challenges of change, it will be at risk of being disbanded. All these discussions in our Round Tables suggest the unpredictability of change and will increase over time. These further suggest that whatever will happen, will happen faster than anticipated.

Turning worker knowledge into productivity and leveraging intellectual capital will become the workforce challenges of the future. Change redefines success and simply understanding its pace emerging in the future and the unpredictability of it does not mean that the companies have learnt to manage 'change'. HR professionals cannot assume that they will design a perfect programme by managing change. They will have to continuously build up their learning ability and their analytic ability to forecast the future and deliver programmes that give the desired result. We can see in the HR industry and businesses of today what the future is likely to be. Furthermore, HR will have to understand that change within business or outside would also mean change within HR or its outside.

HR, we noticed while identifying or defining its list of roles, gets substantially entangled in several metaphors for its professionals and substantially enjoys defining, redefining and using as well as popularizing these metaphors for the pride that they expect from other people in the business or outside. HR professionals may be called leaders or leader-builders, architects, stewards, partners or even players. Learning and image-building would be very important because they shape behaviour. HR professionals internally appreciate that they would love to shed and do away with many of the images they have been building. This, they know, only complicates the understanding of their future identity and, in all probability, multiple roles will be played by HR professionals depending on business context and the performance of the HR professionals. Knowing alternative metaphors may increase debate and discussions. They do not generally improve the role and the value of their deliverables; rather, they complicate the process of delivery and the risk involved. They may assume that they are doable, if not deliverable, but they learn secretly that they enjoy changing their role to adapt to new situations. They enjoy generating a different face covered by different varieties and colours of masks, creating a magical impression amongst the team business and giving them substantial pseudo satisfaction in getting entangled with this kind of halo that is continuously being created by themselves or their business leaders.

In the least, some of the HR work existing or being created can be done differently and with different kinds of masks, material and colours. If we meet the HR professionals from the previous decade, the expectations, skills and outcomes will be different, but the DNA that delivers results concurrent with the business world may be the same. The main advantage that the changing masks and colours and expressions give to the HR professionals is that it creates a sense of surprise and charisma in the rest of the team business. While giving an advantage in achieving the result substantially, it also will keep giving an advantage in the impression or the so-called professionalism that can be demonstrated in the rest of the team business continuously. But one very hard fact which must be learnt and understood by the entire business world is that in this process of managing a change with different kinds of postures and masks and appearances, the HR professional gets pressurized by the business, the work, opportunity or demand, the leadership, expectation and the complexities that they have to respond to in the shortest possible time to protect the business and continue the delivery as expected. This is quite a challenge.

We may be reminded again of what Mukesh Ambani said while articulating four values, with courage and fearlessness being the most significant for success.

I recall that in the early 1970s, while posted in the Hindustan Steel Limited (HSL) washery at Santhaldih, there had not been a single week when there was no bomb explosion somewhere in our Santhaldih township. This was also the prominent period of the United Front government in West Bengal.

I also remember this particular rainy night, while driving on our way back from Dhanbad to Santaldih after a union-management meeting in Central Coal Washery Organization (CCWO), Dhanbad headquarters, we found a narrow road blocked by some fallen branches of a tree after crossing the Panchet dam. As we came closer, assuming that the branches must have fallen due to the strong monsoon winds, a bomb landed on the car's windscreen, blowing it to splinters and injuring the driver and the United Trade Union Congress (UTUC) senior leader in the front seats. In the quickest response, we all jumped out of the car and ran through the water-filled paddy field, in the total darkness of the monsoon night. I don't recall the time or distance we ran, ultimately finding some lantern-lit hutments, whose inhabitants sheltered us for the night and came back to see us off in the morning only to witness that everything of the car, except the body shell, was gone! With the help of the Damodar Valley Corporation, we returned to our washery that day. Everybody was very anxious but I felt very light and it stayed with me for the rest of my service time as the burden of fear which I had carried so far on myself had suddenly disappeared completely. It was like the epiphany Gandhi had that night in Pietermaritzburg, in South Africa, after getting thrown off from the train. This precious epiphany I got that monsoon night on the Santhaldih road, fortunately, stayed with me for the rest of my life and enabled me to act in all kinds of roles in HR like a fearless and confident Bahrupia and also to face a variety of challenging situations in the future. I have, perhaps, not perfected and am still learning through this process for the rest of my Bahrupian future.

INVENTING THE NEW HR

As Yogi Berra once said, 'The future is not what it used to be before.'

Predicting the future is not easy. It is not about a hunch or intuition or a sudden burst of insight. Much of the forecast is based on extrapolation and some speculation with doses of experience. The famous poet T.S. Eliot said:

'Time present and time past
Are both perhaps present in time future,
And time future contained in time past.'

The new is the past in the present. Therefore, the future will be a bit about the past in the present. There are already tectonic shifts that are happening. There is a lot that the pandemic of 2020 has given us to witness, respond, come to terms with and thus thrive upon. We can create the future we wish to and the future equally will create the present then, for us. In a sense, there will be universes of HR that will emerge. The one that we have seen in the past will be unchanged—the human side of HR that leans heavily on empathy, kindness and care, enabling a culture. The other universe will be the one that will be reliant on current and emergent technologies. In a way, an HR professional will straddle multiple universes. They will be expected to integrate these universes and bring meaning and value to the organization and the people therein.

In each of these universes, there will be a multitude of roles that one will assume. So an HR professional will have to straddle these universes and maintain the ability to respond to the CEO and the board. In as much as the stakeholders are concerned, there will be no perceptible change. Yet, there will be a major shift in the role.

The Emergent Roles

Post the pandemic, the emerging roles of HR have changed. Jeanne C. Meister and Robert H. Brown, in their *Harvard Business Review*, spoke of the 21 HR jobs of the future. The Cognizant Center for Future of Work and Future

Workplace jointly embarked on a nine-month initiative to determine exactly what the future of HR will look like. They outlined, amongst others, the following roles—director of well-being, work-from-home facilitator, human bias officer, HR data detective, human-machine teaming manager, future of work leader, distraction prevention coach and many more. All point to one thing. Discontinuous change brings with it roles that need to be performed.

In all these tumultuous changes, the continuous roles will not change. A good example is people and organization purpose alignment. This aspect of the role has assumed greater importance in recent times. The employee value proposition for the organization while bringing in talent is changing. The millennials seek a purpose in what they do. This was expected of an HR professional, who is almost a chief purpose officer beyond the chief people officer! The purpose needs to be individualized and the collective needs to feel it with as much intensity as the CEO. We have not reached this point yet but the demands and expectations of this role have not gone away.

Korn Ferry, in its paper on the 'Five Forces Impacting Organizational Design', speaks of global virtual mobility and this means greater opportunities for employees in a cost-effective way for employers. The models of working, such as onsite, remote, hybrid and outsourced, will change the way work is rendered. There will be new demands in managing various models of talent, such as employees, contractors, gig workers and part-time employees. In this role, the emergent policies that will uniquely play to each of the talent pools will determine the culture of an organization. In short, the role gets more complex. That too in virtual environments and a distributed workforce.

The Skills of Today for Tomorrow

There has been a huge disruption in the world. The HR professional of the future lives in a world that will continue. It will bring in huge ambiguities along with a long list of things that will be expected of them. To start with, the person needs a strong grounding in technology and the process of helping the accelerated adoption of technology in the organization, including HR. Building talent experience throughout the employee life cycle is a nuanced skill. The World Economic Forum, in its list of top 10 skills we would need in 2025, outlined analytical thinking and innovation as the top skill. It was followed by active learning and learning strategies. Complex problem solving came in as the next important skill. Critical thinking and analysis were next. Technology use figured high up in the list. Analytical skills and the ability to tell a story are key skills today. The ability to execute flawlessly is an evergreen skill. What is different is how we have this executed in a distributed workforce. All these skills are in the realm of thinking and doing.

The world cannot get enough emotional intelligence skills and HR needs to lead from the front. It is even more important in today's virtual world as it is a lot more difficult in this environment. Influencing skills remain as important today as they will be for tomorrow. The difference is the ability to influence culture in a distributed workforce of permanent employees, gig workers, contractors and part-time employees, each with their own asks. Building trust and integrity into the fabric is even more important for tomorrow given the virtualization of talent, business delivery and vendors. HR leaders need to build their skills in creative ways to upskill their employees. The recruiter is the new talent development contributor for his/her ability to show up gaps in available skills. The ability to collaborate internally to secure talent will be the edge.

The Differentiators

Organizations that focus on connect, development and care will stand out. Employee experience is a big differentiator. Technology positively influences employee experience if managed well. If we can look at our employees as 'customers' and deliver services no different than what one would extend to an external customer, that can set the tone for a great experience. Open communication and the ability for anyone to speak up and have the leadership in an organization respond with alacrity is a differentiator. In Covid-19 times, the organizations that are getting high marks are the ones working harder on their resilience and empathy. The ability to communicate with honesty, even with difficult messages, and yet keep the spirits high is endearing. The empathy that seemed a nebulous concept has been experienced in its reach and depth. This lends to an organization's culture and creates a strong employee value proposition, building a strong brand in the marketplace. All of this while facing the changes owed to automation, digitalization and adoption of artificial intelligence. According to the 2020 Deloitte Global Human Capital Trends Report, '[i]ntegrating well-being into the design of work itself can strengthen the link between worker well-being and organizational outcomes, supporting well-being not just for individuals but for teams and for the organization at large.' Another differentiator is the opportunity to focus on equality and equity and being more inclusive—something that is so important to our younger generation.

Organizations need to focus on including their people on the continuum of decision-making. Incorporating their representatives can make a big difference. Some organizations have a 'millennial officer' on their leadership team. The future of work is as much about developing employees and making them ready for the future at any time, anywhere and with any learning programme possible—and, of course, on any device. The opportunity to work on any job will mean a strong emphasis on internal mobility.

The Changing Landscape for HR

In a recent LinkedIn recruitment survey of companies in the Asia-Pacific region, it could be understood that companies are more likely to hire less and build and borrow more. The emphasis on 'borrow' adds a new layer of complexity. Internal mobility as a key talent identification process will see greater advancement. Recruiters will play a big role in unlocking the potential of staff within an organization. This will lead to more employees seeking opportunities within instead of looking outside for a change in their job. Virtual recruiting is a given and so is relying on AI for screening and shortlisting. However, we would like to be careful about a cookie-cutter approach, with defined algorithms, as that in itself can be misleading. Fighting in the market for talent is a strategy as old as the Himalayas. Working in times that disrupt normal channels will be the order of the day. By 2027, India is set to have the world's largest workforce, with more than one billion people of working age. At the same time, there will be ongoing disruption to the types of work they will do and the skills they need to do those jobs. The World Economic Forum has already estimated that more than half of the workers in India would need reskilling by 2022. This calls for rapid work to be done in the area of learning and development.

In a recent PwC-NHRDN survey, it was seen that the pandemic of 2020 has caused a change in the way many things are being viewed. For instance:

- 59% of the survey respondents anticipate the biggest shifts in their operating model and organization structure in future.
- 25% of the workforce is expected to see a permanent shift and move to a work-from-anywhere model.
- 16% of the existing work is expected to be automated going forwards.
- 9% are looking at hiring freelancers with relevant skills.

HR roles will be interesting and ever-changing, much like the Bahrupia. In future, there will roles that were done in the past, that were asked in the past, partly done today and will be done in the future. There will be totally new roles. HR will have the opportunity to define and manage the digital and physical, rational and emotional and will integrate the world of humans with machines. There will be the need to have people working at level three in building experiences that integrate the digital machines with the people, making the experience wholesome. In short, the new roles will revolve around the integration of the physical and exponential robotic future.

The Threats (Read Opportunities Therein)

Managing the interface between humans and machines will be a threat. Machines will start to become more intelligent than people. Will machines outsmart men? A lot of questions come to the fore. What is respect, autonomy and being human? What will the loss of personal touch mean? Will this be a replacement for high touch, and will this create a loss of a sense of belonging? There will be challenges in managing the areas of organization design, capability building and culture. Building and sustaining culture in a moving and distributed population will be a challenge. Working in a multigenerational workforce has to be managed carefully. The way the millennials have taken to learning with digital is something that is to be replicated across generations. With the proliferation of technology and with a different model of working with gig, part-time and contract workers, there is a bigger threat of personal identifiable information being hacked or affected, the prevention of which is sacred in HR. Post pandemic, what employees will remember is not just the safety measures that each organization took, but whether they 'felt safe'. In each one of these cases, we need to see the opportunities therein and address them suitably.

A COMPASS FOR HR

Given that the future is not getting any easier and we have to create the future and navigate the rapids, it may be an opportunity to look at a way to address these challenges and, perhaps, to create an ABC of handling these changes.

At every opportunity, commit to challenge the norms of the current and prepare to face the world of tomorrow. We can never predict the future. We can only prepare for it today. The rate of change has never seen such speed. As said by Charles Darwin, '[i]n the long history of humankind those who learned to collaborate and improvise most effectively have prevailed'. It is the survival of the fittest and those adaptable to change. One needs to commit wholeheartedly to the actions that change brings in.

Develop a team that can manage today and handle the future. Development is a long journey. One has to build reliable people who can move to a position of credibility. The far end of credibility is trust. In an ever-changing world, one has to develop a diverse team; one that can play different roles. Much like what happens in a theatre, with actors playing different roles with a commitment beyond compare.

Care is a rare commodity and in short supply. In a world that has changed so fast and so soon, the one thing that stands out as a bedrock of engagement is the deep-rooted faith in care. Care will find its way into areas of policy at one end and connectedness with employees at the other. Care to communicate beyond the strategies and care to communicate the soul through the stories of the everyday employee. HR is not known to be on the front foot on matters relating to communication. The new world needs it. There is a need for HR to communicate the story of how several parts come together. A good place to start.

CONCLUSION

HR has for long remained a first level street-player, as a Bahrupia. Enacting different roles, playing them well but, for most parts, remaining at level one—a stage where they follow processes, carry out transactions expertly, align themselves with the policy framework and remain doers. Perhaps, a Bahrupia may do so to earn a livelihood. They move to level two when they manage their stakeholders, understand them, set expectations and deliver on the promise. At level two, the Bahrupia knows his audience and plays the role such that each one in the audience can resonate with their acting. In the new age of HR, the Bahrupia needs to elevate their role to an art form, to level three. This elevated form at level three is displayed when the audience (read stakeholders) are fully absorbed in the role of the actor. This is when the audience goes beyond identifying themselves with the role and feels that they are playing that role!

Moving to the deeper questions of immersion of the stakeholders into what is being played out, learning new skills needed—given that the audience keeps changing—and readying themselves ahead of time for it is what helps them reach level three. The immersion of the stakeholders in the new world is the ultimate value of HR. The 'how' is the digital and robotics world, the 'what' is the world of feelings and emotions; the world of the fusion of the 'what' and the 'how' into the 'when'—the time when the two universes come together—raises the discourse on how best to thrive in the new world. Much like the evolution of the Bahrupia, who elevates the performance to an art form. Therein lies the future of HR.

As HR professionals, we may still feel we are incomplete and the journey is still going on. We are reminded of the half-golden mongoose of the Mahabharata, who kept hopping from yajna to yajna with the insatiable desire to find that something more—something more pious than Yudhisthir's post-victory maha yajna, something that could change the other half of his body into gold as well and complete this ever-incomplete journey.

We have acted like a typical Bahrupia who has been dealing with all varieties of personalities and its varieties of roles, whether of a hero or supporter or a villain or even a lady.

This is a compound of several personalities—meaning, amongst other things, a pattern, a model or a type. It is thus referred to as the beginning or origin of the pattern, model or type and Bahrupias or HR professionals present or deliver with the holistic approach and readiness which can help in winning a universal acceptance in the play. This is because people can largely relate to and identify with the characters and the situation, both socially and culturally. When such archetypes are deployed contextually, one can be assured of realism in the work. These archetypal Proteans can also allow the stakeholders in business or spectators in the game or the play to connect their roles with the characters. This experience can help the stakeholders to see parts of themselves that they had not considered before, as can be seen in the simile of a football ground or game. This HR of ours is a hero, the mentor, the sidekick, the scapegoat, the villain and so on. At times, the hero experiences a downfall as a result of poor performance which is not appropriate to the requirement of the act. It may be that in many plays, the main character experiences a downfall as a result of poor performance. This might bring about an opportunity for redemption later in the story or the play or it could be the ending of the story. Some of the HR heroes may be unable to bounce back after experiencing the fall but they demonstrate every moment of victory and have a high degree of performance for every word and every moment of the play. They may be like the Maruti Dev, whom it is difficult for one to forget though one may have seen several such archetypal HR leaders in their career in the past. They make society more aware of its positive and negative aspects, similar to the way that a court jester could tell the truth about a royal leader when no one else could. These archetypes bring an aspect of realism to the play that helps the story jump off the page to the reader's heart.

He/She, at times, appears to me as Manu, which has various meanings in Hinduism.

In early texts, it refers to an archetypal man or a woman or to the first man who is the progenitor of humanity—the Manu, the eighth of the fourteen of the current yuga (aeon). This Manu has a multifaceted Bahrupian role, even in that of the prompter behind the scenes who always remains ready to lend a hand or to protect against any kind of deluge or Pralaya, should there be an ill act or occasion in the path of the business of reincarnation. This Manu enters the scene ready to deliver the required transformation through the deluge, the cataclysm or the Pralaya—collecting pairs of species and, most importantly, the Saptarshi—in the wake of the new yuga's requirement of establishing a Dwapar, a better time that is due and most desired for the future of HR.

'No man, for any considerable period, can wear one face to himself and another to the multitude, without finally getting bewildered as to which may be the true.'

– Nathaniel Hawthorne

References

1. Joseph, Tony. 'The First Urbanites: The Harappans.' In *Early Indians: The Story of Our Ancestors and Where We Came From*. New Delhi: Juggernaut Books, 2018.
2. Get Better Together. 'IKIGAI—10 Rules for a LONG & HAPPY Life.' September 15, 2019. https://www.youtube.com/watch?v=ezO3M8W5g6s&feature=youtu.be.
3. Parthasarathy, A. *Vedanta Treatise: The Eternities*. Mumbai: A. Parthasarathy, 2004.
4. Davos Business Summit (2002). Agenda: Leadership in Fragile Times.
5. Sinha, K.K., Ajay Soni, and Indranil Mitra. *Manthan: Art & Science of Developing Leaders*. New Delhi: Bloomsbury Publishing India Pvt. Ltd, 2017.
6. Ulrich, Dave, Michael R. Losey, and Gerry Lake. *Tomorrow's HR Management: 48 Thought Leaders Call for Change*. New York: John Wiley & Sons, 1997. Christensen, Ralph. 'Where is HR?' *Human Resource Management* 36, no. 1 (Spring 1997): 81–84.
7. Ulrich Dave, Michael R. Losey, and Gerry Lake. *Tomorrow's HR Management: 48 Thought Leaders Call for Change*. New York: John Wiley & Sons, 1997.
8. Ulrich, Dave, and Wayne Brockbank. *HR: The Value Proposition*. Boston, MA: Harvard Business Review Press, 2005.
9. Rao, T.V. *Future of HRD*. New Delhi: Macmillan India Ltd, 2003.
10. Sinha, K.K., and Himanshi Tiwari, eds. *Return of the Surya: The Ever-Rising and Transforming Human Resource*. New Delhi: Bloomsbury Publishing India Pvt. Ltd, 2019.
11. Rangarajan, L.N. (1992). *The Arthashastra*. New Delhi: Penguin Books.
12. Sihag, B. (2004). 'Kautilya on the scope and methodology of accounting, organizational design and role of ethics in ancient India.' *The Accounting Historians Journal*, 31(2): 125–148.
13. Kokane, Tushar, and Santosh Bagwe. *Chanakya—A Visionary Human Resource Manager.* Chennai: Notion Press, 2019.
14. BIMTECH and NHRDN HR Round Table in association with S.V. Nathan, Chief Talent Officer, Deloitte India. Theme: Forces of Global Change: Reinventing HR. Subtheme: Changes in Digital Technology: Evolving New Organization. With support from Deloitte Global Human Capital Trends Report, 2016.

15. BIMTECH and NHRDN HR Round Table in association with S.V. Nathan, Chief Talent Officer, Deloitte India. Theme: Rewriting the Rules for the Digital Age: Reinventing HR. Subtheme: Finding the Organization of the Future. With support from Deloitte Global Human Capital Trends Report, 2017.
16. BIMTECH and NHRDN HR Round Table in association with S.V. Nathan, Chief Talent Officer, Deloitte India. Theme: Rewriting the Rules for the Digital Age: Reinventing HR. Subtheme: Careers and Learning: Real time, All the Time. With support from Deloitte Global Human Capital Trends Report, 2017.
17. Ghosal, Sumantra, Gita Piramal, and Christopher A. Bartlett. *Managing Radical Change: What Indian Companies Must Do to Become World-Class*. New Delhi: Viking, 2000.
18. Colvin, Geoff. *Talent Is Overrated: What Really Separates World-Class Performers from Everybody Else*. New York: Portfolio, 2008.
19. Pandit Ravi Shankar, an Indian sitarist and a composer of Hindustani classical music.
20. Capelli, Peter, Harbir Singh, Jitendra Singh, and Michael Useem. *The India Way: How India's Top Business Leaders Are Revolutionizing Management*. Boston, MA: Harvard Business Review Press, 2010.
21. Effron, Marc, and Miriam Ort. *One Page Talent Management: Eliminating Complexity*. Boston, MA: Harvard Business Review Press, 2018.
22. Ibid.
23. Russi Mody, former chairman and managing director of Tata Steel.
24. Colvin, Geoff. *Talent is Overrated: What Really Separates World-Class Performers from Everybody Else*. New York: Portfolio, 2008.
25. Kokane, Tushar, and Santosh Bagwe. *Chanakya—A Visionary Human Resource Manager*. Chennai: Notion Press, 2019.
26. Schwab, Klaus. The Fourth Industrial Revolution. Presentation at the World Economic Forum.
27. BIMTECH and NHRDN HR Round Table in association with S.V. Nathan, Chief Talent Officer, Deloitte India. Theme: Rewriting the Rules for the Digital Age: Reinventing HR. Subtheme: Finding the Organization of the Future. With support from Deloitte Global Human Capital Trends Report, 2017.
28. Ghosal, Sumantra, Gita Piramal, and Christopher A. Bartlett. *Managing Radical Change: What Indian Companies Must Do to Become World-Class*. New Delhi: Viking, 2000.
29. BIMTECH and NHRDN HR Round Table in association with S.V. Nathan, Chief Talent Officer, Deloitte India. Theme: Rewriting the Rules for the Digital Age: Reinventing HR. Subtheme: Finding the Organization of the Future. With support from Deloitte Global Human Capital Trends Report, 2017.
30. Ibid.
31. Deloitte Global Human Capital Trends Report. Deloitte University Press, 2017.
32. BIMTECH and NHRDN HR Round Table in association with S.V. Nathan, Chief Talent Officer, Deloitte India. Theme: Rewriting the Rules for the Digital

Age: Reinventing HR. Subtheme: Finding the Organization of the Future. With support from Deloitte Global Human Capital Trends Report, 2017.

33. Ibid.
34. Siddharth, P.K. *Sa Me Priyah: Hari Ko Kaun Dularo*. New Delhi: Pragya Prakashan, 2011.
35. Ganguli, Kisari Mohan, trans. *The Mahabharata of Krishna-Dwaipayana Vyasa*. SriPedia. www.ibiblio.org, http://www.ibiblio.org/sripedia/ebooks/mb/m12/
36. Yudhakhand–Uttarakand. *Valmiki Ramayan.*
37. Barrett, Richard. *The New Leadership Paradigm*. Lulu.com, 2011.
38. Athreya, M.B. 'Business Values for the 21st Century.' Presentation at the MRA 50th Anniversary Roundtable. Caux, Switzerland, 23–28 July 1996.
39. Collins, Jim. *Good to Great: Why Some Companies Make the Leap... and Others Don't*. New York: HarperCollins, 1997.
40. Mintzberg, Henry. *Simply Managing: What Managers Do—and Can Do Better*. Financial Times Publishing, 2013.
41. El-Beheary, Ahmed. '25 Lessons from Jack Welch: Management Insight and Leadership Secrets of the Legendary Former CEO of General Electric.' https://www.linkedin.com/pulse/25-lessons-from-jack-welch-ahmed-el-beheary
42. Hewitt Associates Consultants. Best Employers Study.
43. Chanakya. *Chanakyasutrani*. Hindi Sahitya Margadarshan, 2013. http:// www.hindisahityadarpan.in/2013/11/ChanakyaSutrani-chanakya-sutra-inhindi-part1.html
44. Sinha, K.K., Ajay Soni, and Indranil Mitra. *Manthan: Art & Science of Developing Leaders*. New Delhi: Bloomsbury Publishing India Pvt. Ltd, 2017.
45. Ibid.
46. Alleem, Rashid. *The SEWA Way*. Dubai: Motivate Connect, 2017.
47. Linda Chaccour, founder and happiness consultant of Emerge Coaching, Lebanon.
48. Bhutan's Gross National Happiness (GNH) Index. https://ophi.org.uk/policy/gross-national-happiness-index/
49. Deloitte Global Human Capital Trends Report. Deloitte University Press, 2017.
50. BIMTECH and NHRDN HR Round Table in association with S.V. Nathan, Chief Talent Officer, Deloitte India. Theme: Leading the New Way for HR. Subtheme: Culture and Engagement. With support from Deloitte Global Human Capital Trends Report, 2015.
51. Ibid.
52. BIMTECH and NHRDN HR Round Table in association with S.V. Nathan, Chief Talent Officer, Deloitte India. Theme: The Forces of Global Change: Reinventing HR. Subtheme: New Social Contracts: Restructuring Culture and Employee Engagement. With support from Deloitte Global Human Capital Trends Report, 2016.
53. BIMTECH and NHRDN HR Round Table in association with S.V. Nathan, Chief Talent Officer, Deloitte India. Theme: Leading the New Way for HR.

Subtheme: Culture and Engagement. With support from Deloitte Global Human Capital Trends Report, 2015.

54. BIMTECH and NHRDN HR Round Table in association with S.V. Nathan, Chief Talent Officer, Deloitte India. Theme: The Forces of Global Change: Reinventing HR. Subtheme: Demographic Upheavals: Changing Role of HR. With support from Deloitte Global Human Capital Trends Report, 2016.
55. BIMTECH and NHRDN HR Round Table in association with S.V. Nathan, Chief Talent Officer, Deloitte India. Theme: Leading the New Way for HR. Subtheme: Culture and Engagement. With support from Deloitte Global Human Capital Trends Report, 2015.
56. BIMTECH and NHRDN HR Round Table in association with S.V. Nathan, Chief Talent Officer, Deloitte India. Theme: Leading the New Way for HR. Subtheme: Re-imagining Performance Appraisals. With support from Deloitte Global Human Capital Trends Report, 2015.
57. Kokane, Tushar, and Santosh Bagwe. *Chanakya—A Visionary Human Resource Manager*. Chennai: Notion Press, 2019.
58. Sinha, K.K. 'The Changing Face of Work.' Joint paper, Corporate Human Resources, NTPC, 2000.
59. Ulrich, Dave, Michael R. Losey, and Gerry Lake. *Tomorrow's HR Management: 48 Thought Leaders Call for Change.* New York: John Wiley & Sons, 1997.
60. Dave Ulrich at the SHRM Annual Conference, 2005.
61. Rao, T.V., 'In 2018, whom does HR serve?' *People Matters*, December 28, 2017. https://www.peoplematters.in/article/employee-engagement/in-2018-whom-does-hr-serve-17076
62. BIMTECH and NHRDN HR Round Table in association with S.V. Nathan, Chief Talent Officer, Deloitte India. Theme: The Forces of Global Change: Reinventing HR. Subtheme: Demographic Upheavals: Changing Role of HR. With support from Deloitte Global Human Capital Trends Report, 2016.
63. BIMTECH and NHRDN HR Round Table in association with S.V. Nathan, Chief Talent Officer, Deloitte India. Theme: Rewriting the Rules for the Digital Age: Reinventing HR. With support from Deloitte Global Human Capital Trends Report, 2017.
64. BIMTECH and NHRDN HR Round Table in association with S.V. Nathan, Chief Talent Officer, Deloitte India. Theme: Rewriting the Rules for the Digital Age: Reinventing HR. Subtheme: Leadership Disrupted: Pushing the Boundaries. With support from Deloitte Global Human Capital Trends Report, 2017.
65. Ibid.
66. Preparing for the Future. HBR Special Article Collection. Sponsored by NHRDN.
67. Lambert, Andrew. 'The Effective HR Business Partner.' *CRF Research*, November, 2009. https://www.shrm.org/hr-today/news/hr-magazine/documents/crfreseach.pdf
68. 'The HR Function in India in 2030 and the Future of CHRO.' NHRDN.

69. Same as Sl. No. 17 above.
70. Toffler, Alvin. *Future Shock*. New York: Random House, 1970.
71. Toffler, Alvin. *The Third Wave*. New York: William Morrow, 1980.
72. Ghosal, Sumantra, Gita Piramal, and Christopher A. Bartlett. *Managing Radical Change: What Indian Companies Must Do to Become World-Class*. New Delhi: Viking, 2000.
73. Capelli, Peter, Harbir Singh, Jitendra Singh, and Michael Useem. *The India Way: How India's Top Business Leaders Are Revolutionizing Management*. Boston, MA: Harvard Business Review Press, 2010.

PANELLISTS' PROFILES

ANURANJITA KUMAR

Former Chief Human Resource Officer, Citi South Asia

Anuranjita Kumar began her career with Procter & Gamble in 1994 and joined Citibank in 1995. She has worked across various countries, held a variety of roles and is the first South Asian woman to be appointed as head of HR, global banking, EMEA region, in 2007.

An alumnus of XLRI, Anuranjita is the first woman management committee member at Citi India. She is on the board of various organizations and professional bodies and has been recognized as amongst the 'Most Powerful HR Professionals of India' by the World HRD Congress in 2012 and amongst the 'Most Powerful Woman Leaders' by Fortune in 2013. She is an accredited executive coach and a senior trainer for the Senior Leadership Development curriculum at Citibank.

DR. ARVIND N. AGRAWAL

Accredited Executive Coach and Leadership Consultant

Dr. Arvind N. Agrawal is an accredited executive coach and leadership consultant with extensive corporate experience. He has served on the boards of several companies including as a management board member of RPG Group for over 15 years. In this role, he extensively participated in the development of appropriate strategies for the turnaround and growth of the diversified businesses in the Group. Closely working with the chairman, Dr. Agrawal successfully led the top management appointments, succession planning and leadership development initiatives over these years.

Prior to that, he held the positions of chief executive in Escorts JCB and Escorts Construction Equipment; head of HR, TQM, corporate strategy and marketing in Modi Xerox. Since transitioning from his corporate journey, Dr. Agrawal has led the formation of Global HR Lead Partners with a charter to offer executive coaching and consultancy in leadership, organization and human resource management. Dr. Agrawal holds a PhD from IIT Bombay. An alumnus of IIT Kharagpur and IIM Ahmedabad, Dr. Agrawal was awarded the National HRD Award in 1992. He also served as the national president of the National HRD Network during the years 2000–2002.

DR. ASHA BHANDARKER

Distinguished Professor of Organizational Behaviour IMI, New Delhi

Bhandarker is a well-known scholar, consultant and researcher in the field of HR and leadership. Before her current assignment at IMI-Delhi, she was the Raman Munjal Chair Professor of Leadership Studies as well as dean, Research and Consulting at MDI-Gurgaon and dean, International Relations at IMI-Delhi. Currently, she serves as a director on the boards of Punjab National Bank and IMT Ghaziabad.

She consults with boards and top management teams of many organizations like Maruti, DuPont, Bayer, MRPL, Corporation Bank, SAIL on issues of Culture Building, Leadership Development and Organizational Vision Building. She has worked closely with the corporate sector (100 companies) over the last three decades. She has conducted competency assessments in many organizations, the latest being MRPL and Bank of Maharashtra. She is engaged in coaching and mentoring women leaders in different organizations.

Bhandarker is a recognized HR expert and has been invited on many board-level HR committees which include Bank of Baroda, Corporation Bank, Oriental Bank of Commerce, Punjab National Bank, Punjab and Sind Bank and Dena Bank.

She has received many accolades and awards including, the highly coveted Senior Fulbright Fellowship, Leadership Thinker Award, Best Teacher Award, Best Paper Award and Best Case Award.

She is a keen researcher and has published 8 books and 40 research papers in peer-reviewed, national and international journals. Her latest book is *Leadership Odyssey: Darkness to Light*, along with Dr. Pritam Singh. As a scholar, she has presented papers at the Academy of Management annual conference as well as addressed deans and directors of Asia-Pacific Business Schools at the AMBA conference.

Bhandarker is the Visitor's Nominee (President's Nominee) at the H.N.B. University of Garhwal (a central university); member academic council at JK Lakshmipat University; and member committee for formulation of strategic plan and vision document for Indira Gandhi Delhi Technical University for Women.

She has travelled widely across the US, Europe and Asia and has taught as well as consulted and addressed global audiences in the US, Italy, France, Egypt, Mauritius, Afghanistan, China and Sri Lanka. She has studied at leading behavioural science centres like NTL in the US, Tavistock Institute in London and Centre for Transpersonal Psychology in London. She has a PhD from Osmania University, Hyderabad.

DR. ASHOK KUMAR BALYAN

Former Director BD/HR, ONGC; Former MD & CEO, Petronet LNG Ltd; Former CEO (Oil & Gas), Reliance Group

Dr. A.K. Balyan did his MTech from the Indian Institute of Technology, Delhi and PhD from Germany.

He worked as a research officer at Shri Ram Institute of Industrial Research for about three years before joining Oil & Natural Gas Corporation in 1976. He worked in various positions and work centres in ONGC (Keshav Dev Malaviya Institute of Petroleum Exploration, Dehradun; Cambay basin at Ankleshwar, Vadodara; project head at Jorhat, Assam; Corporate office at Delhi; basin manager at Kolkata; before joining the board of ONGC in 2003 as director HR/BD). A few of his major contributions during this period have been the following:

- Preparing the first 25-year Perspective Plan of ONGC, 1990–2015.
- Establishing and demonstrating the production of CBM for the first time in the country.
- Successfully establishing the first 51-MW wind power plant of ONGC. Successfully constructing and commissioning a C2+ extraction plant—unique in the world.
- Leading ONGC in the downstream sector by establishing OPaL—petrochemicals with the biggest cracker.
- Setting up of power plant in Assam utilizing ONGC's own gas.
- Major restructuring transformation exercise in ONGC.

Dr. A.K. Balyan was a director on the board of many companies including ONGC Videsh Ltd, Mangalore Refinery & Petrochemicals, Petronet LNG Ltd, Dahej SEZ Ltd, Mangalore SEZ Ltd, ONGC Tripura Power Company, ONGC Petro-additions Ltd (OPaL) and L&T Hydrocarbons Ltd.

Dr. A.K. Balyan joined as managing director and CEO of Petronet in July 2010 and steered the company to a leadership position in the LNG / Gas business with rapid expansion.

On completion of his tenure at Petronet LNG Ltd, he joined Reliance Group as CEO (Oil & Gas) and worked on challenging projects in Bangladesh on LNG-based power project, CBM and offshore construction projects of converting a drilling rig to MOPU, offshore supply vessels and so on till September 2018.

Dr. A. K. Balyan is presently on the board of few companies and provides advisory services on oil and gas aspects, particularly gas / LNG business.

Dr. A. K. Balyan has held many professional positions and received many recognitions. A few of them are:

- Business Today award of the best CEO in the year 2014
- Inspiration leader
- President of Delhi Management Association
- National president of National Institute of Personnel Management

ASHWANI PRASHARA

CHRO, Reliance Industries

Ashwani Prashara is the chief human resources officer for Reliance Industries. He has over 35 years of global experience across the entire gamut of HR with expertise in driving HR transformational initiatives, change management, HR capability building and industrial relations. He has previously served in various HR leadership positions across companies such as Honeywell, Whirlpool and BILT.

ASIM KUMAR BASU

Former CEO, Hindustan Motors Limited

Mr Basu is a seasoned professional and business leader with over 32 years of rich and diverse work experience in various capacities. His previous assignments include the role of CHRO of very large organizations. He is highly experienced in handling crises and complex organizational issues including production and operations, HR & IR, TQM and business excellence.

He holds postgraduate degrees in HR, Marketing and Finance. He is a certified lead auditor for ISO 9001/14001 and OHSAS 18001, a certified DuPont Safety

Trainer and a Six Sigma Green Belt. He is a certified assessor for Business Excellence and Carbon Footprint with experience in assessing many reputed companies. He taught at ICFAI University as a full-time associate professor for five years and has a few research publications to his credit. Mr Basu was a national scholar student all through his academic career. He is a fellow of the Institution of Engineers (FIE) of India and currently the honorary president of NHRDN, Kolkata Chapter. He is pursuing his PhD in Corporate Ethics and Governance.

A THIRUNAVUKKARASU

Former President, Corporate HR, JK Organization

A. Thirunavukkarasu, popularly known as Thiru, assumed his new role as the president, Corporate HR at JK organization (EZ), in June 2015 and worked there till 31 March 2019. Before that, he was associated with Vedanta Resources Plc, as president, Group HR and member of the executive committee.

His key strength is to provide strategic HR insights and pragmatic solutions to the CEOs of operating companies and their leadership teams. His significant contributions include bringing measurement focus to the HR function, enhancing employee engagement, career development plans, continuous improvements and employer branding initiatives, besides improving diversity at the workplace and aligning HR processes in tandem with the organizational growth. He has also been conferred with several awards.

He is currently associated with a select few management institutes in an advisory role and interacting with students besides being a pro bono coach.

DR. AQUIL BUSRAI

CEO of Aquil Busrai Consulting

Dr. Aquil Busrai is a gold medallist from XLRI and has to his credit a postgraduate degree in Law, an advanced Diploma in Training and Development and a PhD. He is pursuing his second PhD. A university rank holder, he is the recipient of the J.M. Kumarappa and Bharucha gold medals for academic excellence.

Dr. Busrai has had 46 plus years of experience in the industry. He has worked in various HR roles with Unilever in Kenya and India; Motorola in Asia-Pacific countries; Shell in Malaysia and IBM in India. He is currently the CEO of Aquil Busrai Consulting.

Dr. Busrai is a fellow of the All India Management Association and a former national president of the National HRD Network.

Dr. Busrai is a keen student of non-verbal communication and is authoring a book on 'Body Language'. He is an ardent wildlife enthusiast and a serious wildlife photographer.

BALACHANDAR NATARAJAN

Group Head, Human Resources, Coffee Day Enterprises Ltd

N. Balachandar is currently Group director, HR, for the fast-growing and expanding Coffee Day Group, which has an interest in coffee, financial services, resorts and hospitality, infrastructure, logistics and furniture. He is responsible for people strategy and execution for the Group.

Having worked at Asian Paints, Standard Chartered Bank, GE Healthcare, GE Capital and Strides Arcolab, he has a rich experience in multiple industries. He has been teaching at IIM Bangalore and is currently president of National HRD Network, Bangalore Chapter. He is also a member of the Karnataka Knowledge Commission Task Force on Skill Development. Mr Balachandar completed his MS in Industrial Management at IIT Chennai and has a postgraduate degree with a major in PM and IR from Loyola College, Chennai.

BARTTANU KUMAR DAS

Head of HR, Larsen & Toubro (Heavy Civil Infrastructure IC), Chennai

Barttanu Kumar Das is currently heading the Human Resources function in L&T Constructions (Heavy Civil Infrastructure Independent Company), Chennai. Preceding this, he was the Senior Vice President and Head of Human Resources at Blue Dart Express Ltd for 10 years, the leading express and distribution company of India, part of DPDHL Group, Germany.

He has more than 29 years of experience in diverse sectors spanning power, infrastructure and logistics and supply chain with his association with NTPC, Navi Mumbai, SEZ Pvt. Ltd, a Reliance Industries Ltd (RIL) Group Company, and Blue Dart Express Ltd. A strong believer of change and transformation, he has rich experience in HRD, TQM, IR and organization transformation areas.

During his stint in NTPC, Reliance Industries and Blue Dart Express (DHL E-Commerce in India), he worked extensively with leading business and HR consulting organizations such as AT Kearney, Hewitt Associates, Ernst & Young, Mercer and McKinsey in several organizational change and capability development assignments.

Under his HR leadership in Blue Dart Express, the organization has won several recognitions for HR excellence. Some of the coveted ones are: '13th Best Employer Brand Award' by Employer Brand Institute in 2010; 'Best Motivational Work Place Award under services category' by AIMA-IOCL in 2010; 'Innovative HR Practices Award' and 'One of the Top 50/25 Great Places to Work For in India' consecutively for the last nine years and as 'One of Top 11 Best Employers in India' in 2014–2015 and 2015–2016, as recognized by Aon Hewitt Best Employers study.

Barttanu has written articles and presented papers in national and international conferences in the area of talent development, succession planning, vision and values, mentoring and leadership development.

Barttanu was a Board member and regional president (Western Region) of the National HRD Network. Previously, he was involved with the Delhi Management Association from 2002–2005 (Young Manager's Forum). He was also vice-chairman of the HRM committee of Mumbai Chambers of Commerce from 2011 to 2012 and was associated with CII-HRM Committee (Western Region).

He has been invited as a guest speaker/panellist/thought leader by professional bodies such as the National HRD Network, All India Management Association, World HRD Congress and Asia-Pacific HRM Congress in their conferences and seminars; by leading business schools such as IIM, NITIE, TISS, XLRI, etc., and by various magazines and newspapers.

Academically speaking, he is a graduate in Economics and holds a postgraduate degree in Personnel Management and Industrial Relations from Utkal University, Bhubaneswar.

While being a seasoned professional with countless hours amassed under his belt, Barttanu is also certified on Hogan Leadership Assessment Tools from the US. He is a certified MBTI trainer and a certified coach. He is a master facilitator for organizational change and cultural transformation.

BISWAJIT ROY

Director (HR & Business Development), Oil India Ltd

Biswajit Roy has over 36 years of rich experience in the oil industry, spanning across a spectrum of diverse functions. He has been actively associated with the introduction of assessment centres, implementation of an electronic multi-rater performance management system and the formulation of a new vision and its implementation strategy at Oil India Limited. A graduate in Chemical Engineering from the University of Roorkee, he completed his National Management Programme from MDI, Gurgaon. His papers have been presented in international forums and published in national and international journals. He was adjudged the 'Overall Winner' of the prestigious Global HRD Award 2014, presented by the International Federation of Training and Development Organizations.

B. VENKATARAMANA

Group President, Human Resources, Landmark Group India

B. Venkataramana, Group president, HR, of Landmark Group India has over 35 years of experience in Human Resources.

In his tenure of close to a decade with the Landmark Group, he has been instrumental in creating a people-centric organization that has been recognized as one of 'India's Best Companies to Work For in Retail' for six consecutive years by the Great Place to Work Institute.

He was previously the senior vice president, Human Resources, in Reliance Retail Limited, where he played a vital role in building the HR team across the country, as well as formulating its policies. Before this, he headed Human Resources at Reliance BPO, Henkel India and Brigade Solutions.

He is on the CII National Committee on Special Abilities and is the vice president of the Bangalore Chapter for NHRD. He has also served as the former chairman of the HR Panel (Southern Region) for CII and the regional vice president (South) for the Indian Society of Training and Development.

He has won several awards for his service to the HR fraternity from leading publications and industry forums. He is on the advisory committee of several management institutes and enjoys sharing his knowledge gained over the years, in industry forums and especially with the younger generation.

DR. CHRISTINA AUGUSTINE

People Operations & Experience Leader, Sling Sound Inc.

Dr. Christina Augustine is a proficient global HR leader with 18 years of experience in leading HR activities in diverse industries and capacities (IT, Telecom, FMCG and Health Care). Formerly AVP Head, HR, for Ness Technologies, Canada, she currently leads Human Resources, Sling Sound Inc. She has a PhD in Applied Psychology with expertise in leading Digital HR and OD domains. She is honoured to be one of 'Asia's Most Innovative HR Tech Leader (2018)'; '100 Top HR Tech Minds (2018)'; 'Most Talented HR Leader (2017)' and 'Top 25 Most Innovative HR Tech Leader (2016)' in Asia-Pacific HRM and a national award entitled 'Indira Super Achiever (2008)' in HR Excellence. She is internationally recognized as the chair and judge for the Stevies International Business Award and Great Employers platform. She has won several distinguished international HR accolades like the Stevie International, APAC and American Business Award, Asia Best Employer Award, Golden Peacock Award, Britain Top Employer, DQ-CMR IT Best Employer Ranking, etc. She has also been selected by the Canadian government for the Ontario Provincial Nominee Program, 2015. She is an industry expert who is a proud HRPA member in Toronto, Canada, a diversity champion, who leads diversity and inclusion portfolios in all capacities as well as an EAP (Employee Assistance Program) specialist.

She is a CHRL candidate as well as a consultant, HR practitioner and coach certified from NFNLP, USA and NGM@Maxis (Harvard Business School-Maxis Telecom, Malaysia). Chris is trained in Transactional Analysis from ITAA (International Transactional Analysis Association) and the Adlerian approach. She is a career evangelist, Linkedin coach and therapist specialized in counselling and psychotherapy. Additionally, she has participated in several international forums and published several scientific papers.

Christina is an HR evangelist and an international keynote speaker in various television/radio shows, social forums, print and other media. Her buzzing TV shows *Enna Seivadhu?*, *Kelviyum Doctorum* and *Joyful Family* are great family treats. Her other areas of interest include youth reach, community and social work, and evangelism endeavours.

D.D. MISRA

Former Director (HR), ONGC

D.D. Misra is former director (Human Resource) of ONGC, India's leading Maharatna E & P Company of the Union Government. He holds a Master's degree in Public Administration (MPA) from the University of Lucknow. He has undergone Leadership Development Programme at IIM, Bangalore, followed by two overseas programmes at Alberta School of Business, Calgary (Canada) and University of Texas (US) in 2013. Starting his career as Graduate Trainee, he left his imprint in diverse assignments given to him in over three decades with the company.

The Government of India appointed him to the Board of ONGC, as its director (HR) with effect from 1 August 2014, a post which he successfully held till his superannuation on 30 June 2018. During his tenure, he conceptualized and steered numerous sustainable HR initiatives to enthuse the morale and motivation of the 33,000 plus regular employees and about 17,000 secondary workforce. As a unique HR initiative, under his mentorship, he groomed a team of six and nine ONGCians who scaled Mount Everest in May 2017 and Mount Kanchenjunga in May 2018, respectively.

As Chair of Asian-Pacific Resource Centre of United Nations Global Compact (UNGC) Network India (2015–2018), he steered 'Industrial Water Benchmarking Study' for the first time in India which is going to lead to the development of 'Industrial Water Index' to be launched globally very soon.

He was on the governing board of SCOPE (2015–2018) and RGIPT, Raibaraily's Board (2015–2018).

During his career and post-superannuation, he has been regularly sharing his motivational thoughts on national forums.

Despite holding high-pressure assignments during his career in ONGC, he managed to nurture his other interests, particularly his passion for wildlife photography. He has been a regular contributor to magazines about the natural world, like, *Shristi, Swagat, Shubh Yatra, Exotica, G&Y, Times World Travel* and *Outdoor Journal*. In 2014, he published *Karjat Diaries*—the first-ever coffee table book on the biodiversity of the Western Ghats. He is presently working on a book profiling the Rajaji Tiger Reserve of Uttarakhand, which would also be the first-ever coffee table book on this national park. As a wildlife cinematographer, his maiden film is, *Stars in Ranthambore*, on the famous tigress 'Ladli' and her family. He is now working on his second film about the endangered Golden Langurs at the Chakrashila Wildlife Sanctuary, Bodoland.

GANAPATHI SUBRAMANIAN

Head, HR, Sundaram Finance Ltd

A Commerce graduate with a postgraduate degree in Personnel Management and Industrial Relations, Ganapathi wears many hats—an HR professional, motivational speaker and talent developer.

Ganapathi has worked for organizations like TVS, PepsiCo and Britannia. He has a rich experience in setting up HR systems and has been instrumental in setting up innovative HR strategies in recruitment, training and employee engagement. He was recognized by PepsiCo and Britannia for his HR Excellence and awarded by the Madras Management Association for his contribution in the field of HR. He was honoured as one of the 100 Most Talented Global HR Leaders by the World HRD Congress during 2015 in Mumbai.

An avid speaker, he lectures at various forums including B-Schools. His interests include behavioural sciences, writing poems, short stories and reading management books during his free time.

GAUTAM CHAINANI

Group President, HR, JSW Group

Gautam Chainani is a senior human capital executive with experience of around 30 years in leading HR function at both the country and organization level. He has a brilliant track record in leading HR functions across a wide range of industries such as IT / Telecom, FMCG, Financial Service and Manufacturing.

He is currently the Group president, HR of JSW Group, an $11 billion conglomerate, with a presence across India, the US, South America and Africa. The JSW Group is a part of the O.P. Jindal Group with strong footprints across steel, energy, infrastructure, cement, ventures and sports. Gautam Chainani is responsible for the entire gamut of Human Resource function across the JSW Group companies.

Before joining the Group, Gautam Chainani was the chief human resource officer and head, Corporate Communications for UltraTech Cement Limited, Aditya Birla Group.

Gautam Chainani has done his masters in Personnel Management and Industrial Relations. He started his professional career with DCM Data Products Limited and worked in HR Leadership roles in organizations like Hindustan Unilever Ltd, Wipro Consumer Products, Hughes Telecom Limited, WNS Global Services Limited and American Express.

DR. J.K. MITRA

Professor (OB & Strategic Management), FMS, University of Delhi

Dr. J.K. Mitra is the former head and dean (2006–2009) of FMS and had been professor-in-charge of S.P. Jain Centre of Advanced Management Research and director of Centre for Applied Behavioral Science and Action Research, Delhi. He is the first recipient of the Young Scientist Award in Psychology and Educational Sciences from the Indian Science Congress Association. His research interests include Cross Border Post Acquisition Management and Rejuvenation of Old Institutions. Dr. Mitra has conducted numerous organizational diagnosis, strategy planning and team-building workshops for a large number of organizations and is also in the governing body of many national-level institutions.

K.K. SINHA

Dean, Executive Education, BIMTECH

K.K. Sinha is a graduate with honours in Economics and a postgraduate in Personnel Management/LSW (Gold Medalist, University of Patna). He has worked in HR for 42 years and held leadership positions in organizations like Steel Authority of India (SAIL), NTPC, Reliance Energy, Reliance Infocomm and Reliance Industries Limited (RIL) and as the Group director, Human Resources, Jindal Steel & Power.

During his tenure in NTPC, where he was director (HR) for eight years, he transformed the HR processes and the work culture, enabling NTPC to be ranked as the 'Best Employer' and one of the 'Great Places to Work' consecutively for three years.

He has received extensive training in Human Resources from Harvard Business School, Templeton (Oxford), Michigan Business School, Tata Management Centre, IIM (A), IIM (K) and ASCI, Hyderabad.

He has also been invited to deliver talks in academic institutions in India and abroad including Auckland University, Martin Hautus—The Pacific Peoples

Learning Institute and Cornell Institute of Business and Technology, New Zealand.

A keen learner and HR thinker and innovator, he also tailored and executed changes in corporations, working with international level consultants like Mckinsey, Hewitts, Mercer, E&Y, AT Kearny, to name a few.

On his retirement from the active corporate world, currently, he is working as dean, Executive Education, in the leading Business School, Birla Institute of Management Technology (BIMTECH), sharing corporate perspective and experiences as a visiting corporate trainer.

He has also been working as a consultant/advisor in several companies like NTPC, NTPC—SAIL Power Company, UltraTech—Aditya Birla Group, REC, Damodar Valley Corporation, Tata Power, Reliance METL, Adani, NHPC, etc.

He has written three books, including *My Experiments with Unleashing People Power*—which has been featured in *Business Standard's* 'The Strategist Top Five'; *Manthan: Art & Science of Developing Leaders* with two co-authors and *Return of the Surya: The Ever-Rising and Transforming Human Resource*s with a co-author.

K. RAMKUMAR

Former Executive Director, ICICI Bank

Mr K. Ramkumar is the founder of Leadership Centre, an organization dedicated to building world-class thought and practice in the domain of leadership consulting, research and development. Leadership Centre rejects the skill-based approach for developing business leaders. It operates on a personalized leadership development model which believes that leadership is a personal resource. It is by making individuals aware of this resource and harnessing their potential that they can build on their leadership abilities.

Mr K. Ramkumar retired as the executive director on the board of ICICI Bank. He was on the boards of ICICI Prudential Life Insurance and ICICI Ventures. Before his retirement, he was the president of ICICI Foundation and the ICICI Group's CSR arm.

Ram, as he likes to be called, has worked for Hindustan Aeronautics Ltd, Hindustan Unilever Ltd and ICI before his 15-year-long innings at ICICI Bank.

Ram's work over the last 32 years includes HR and business roles where he has remained consistently passionate about leadership development with a special focus on enhancing and strengthening the organizations' leadership capabilities.

Ram has worked with the Manipal Global Education to establish the ICICI Manipal Academy for Banking and Insurance, a project centred on discovering and grooming young leaders from tier-three cities and beyond. This has turned out to be a model today, with a large number of banks adopting it for their leadership roles. During the last 8 years, ICICI Bank has inducted 12,000 young leaders from this programme.

Ram has also envisioned and established the ICICI Academy for Skills, an ICICI CSR initiative for skill development. On the last count, it was present in 23 locations, imparting 15 different skills to 35,000 young people.

Ram has published his first book titled *Leveraging Human Capital: A Practitioner's Perspective* from McGraw Hill Education Pvt. Ltd. He extensively writes on his blog www.theotherview.in and invites you all to come and write.

KRISHNAMURTHY SHANKAR

EVP, Group Head, HRD, Infosys Ltd

Krishnamurthy (Krish) Shankar is executive vice president and the Group head of Human Resource Development at Infosys. In this role, he is responsible for envisioning the roadmap for HR, driving strategy, and implementing operational priorities aligned with the overall organizational mandate.

He has over 30 years of experience and has led several global HR functions in organizations like Bharti Airtel, Hindustan Unilever and Philips. In his wide-ranging experience in these organizations, he has led the transformation of HR into a strategic partner, facilitated organization-wide transformation and capability development and was instrumental in building a strong talent pool through a series of leadership development initiatives.

An alumnus of XLRI Jamshedpur, he holds an executive certificate in Strategy and Organization from the Stanford Graduate School of Business.

DR. KURIAKOSE MAMKOOTTAM

Professor Emeritus, School of Business, Public Policy and Social Entrepreneurship, Ambedkar University

Dr. Kuriakose Mamkoottam is professor emeritus, School of Business, Public Policy and Social Entrepreneurship (SBPPSE) at Ambedkar University, Delhi (AUD). He was the founding dean (director) of SBPPSE at AUD and also dean, Student Services, at Ambedkar University, Delhi.

Earlier, he was professor of Human Resource Management & Industrial Relations at the Faculty of Management Studies (FMS), University of Delhi, from where he retired as the head and dean. He has held several administrative positions in Delhi University and the governing bodies of DU Colleges. He has also served as the chairman and provost of university hostels.

Dr. Mamkoottam has been an independent director on the boards of companies, NGOs and professional journals. He was India-EEC fellow, ESADE, Barcelona (1989–1990. He has undertaken assignments in Mauritius, Nepal, Sri Lanka and Bangladesh. He has done consulting work for the International Labour Organization (ILO), the Planning Commission—GoI, the Fifth Pay Commission—GoI and several MNCs and domestic companies. He has undertaken extensive research in the area of Human Resource Management, Technological Change and Labour issues in India, South Asia and Europe. Dr. Mamkoottam's publications include *Labour & Change: Essays on Globalization, Technological Change, and Labour in India* (Sage Publication, 2004), *Trade Unionism: Myth & Reality: Unionism in the Tata Iron & Steel Company* (Oxford University Press, 1982) and several papers / articles in international and domestic journals. He has presented papers at several national and international conferences.

L. PRABHAKAR

EVP, HR (Agri-Business Division), ITC Ltd

L. Prabhakar is EVP, HR, at the Agri-Business Division of ITC Limited. An alumnus of XLRI, he has been with ITC for 24 years in different capacities across businesses. Earlier, he has worked with TVS Motors and Murugappa Group. He has had vast experience in all facets of HR and ER in his 31 years of professional life.

He has held different positions in National HRD Network at different levels. He has also been associated with Hyderabad Management Association, the CEO Forum on Human Rights under the aegis of Global Compact Network India and CII at Chennai, Kolkata, and Hyderabad. He is currently a committee member of EFSI, Andhra and Telangana.

LAKSHMINARAYANA K.

CEO, Shell MRPL Aviation

Lakshminarayana, CEO in Shell MRPL Aviation Fuels and Services Ltd, is a mechanical engineer with over 36 years of experience in multiple functions across sectors of Petroleum and Petrochemicals Manufacturing and Process Industries. His skill set ranges from developing viable business models, formulating and executing organization-level strategy, owning company-level profit and loss, managing human resources, driving sales and marketing functions, materials planning and project management.

Through some unique initiatives under his leadership, Shell MRPL Aviation has been able to sail through fairly turbulent market conditions. Before this role, he has handled the portfolios of HR, projects, corporate strategy and materials in MRPL-ONGC for over 18 years.

Among other things, one of his most significant contributions has been in the facilitation of building, nurturing and priming an 1,800-strong professional resource pool for leadership.

MIHIR MALLICK

Director & Head, HR & General Affairs, Samsung Electronics India Ltd

Mihir Mallick completed his BSc (Electronics) from Nagpur University and a postgraduate diploma in personnel management and IR from XISS, Ranchi. He has more than 27 years of experience in the fields of HR and IR, in automotive manufacturing, auto components and media. Before joining Samsung, he has worked with Indian Express Newspapers, New Holland Tractors, Goodyear and Honda Cars.

He has worked in a variety of leadership roles in HR and Employee Relations. His expertise lies in performance management, designing and implementation of policies, compensation and benefits, OD interventions and relationship management with all stakeholders. In his current role, he is responsible for building a talent pool for supporting business growth, capability building and establishing a competency framework for the leadership team.

He has been actively handling new investment projects worth more than ₹6,500 crores and front-ending the negotiations with the government on investment approvals, incentive schemes and all the necessary approvals and permissions from various government authorities. He is responsible for establishing the new manufacturing set up, right from the initial stage of land allocation to acquiring the required permissions from the state government.

NARENDRA KOTHARI

Former Chairman-cum-Managing Director, NMDC Limited

Narendra Kothari, former CMD in NMDC Limited, graduated in metallurgical engineering from Rajasthan University and started his career with Steel Authority of India Limited. After an enriching experience in various capacities, he was elevated to the post of CEO of IISCO steel plant, Burnpur.

During his tenure at SAIL, he has brought a lot of accolades to the organization by his able leadership qualities and administrative skills. He has travelled to various countries while carrying out varied responsibilities assigned to him and has been bestowed with the Lifetime Achievement Award from Greentech Foundation for his contribution to the mining and steel industry.

NAVEEN S. PILLAI

Head HR, National Sales and Marketing Division, TAFE

Pillai has about 16 years of experience as an HR Generalist in the automobile, telecommunication and media sectors. His responsibilities include Strategic HR and operational roles in national and regional capacities. He has a master's degree in personnel management and IR and a rich experience of working extensively with business functions as the HR process owner and business partner. In his present role, he is responsible for talent resourcing, management, engagement and capability building across the business function.

P. DWARAKANATH

Chairman, GSK Consumer Healthcare Ltd

Dwarakanath is the Chairman of GSK Consumer Healthcare Ltd and is also associated with Max Group HR. He brings a rich and varied experience of over four decades. Before this, he was director, Human Resources and Administration, India/South Asia, at GlaxoSmithKline (GSK). He was associated with GSK for close to four decades. He was also a member of GSK's International HR team.

Mr Dwarakanath is widely acknowledged as a leader in HR in India. His list of achievements is numerous, but the most important is the culture that he has championed in GSK business. Both internally and externally, GSK is acknowledged as one of the best places to work. His passion for building a progressive and people-centric culture is apparent from the fact that GSK has been judged as one of India's 'Best Employers' for several years. His initiatives to drive the new corporate culture during times of integration, such as through 'Simply Better Way', were benchmarks for then SmithKline Beecham.

He has held several management positions in various professional bodies. To name a few, he was the president of the National Human Resources Development Network (NHRDN), president of the Delhi Management Association (DMA), regional president—Northern Region of All India Management Association (AIMA) and treasurer of AIMA.

Mr Dwarakanath has won several prestigious awards for his valuable contribution in the field of HR, including the 'Pathfinders Award' and 'Lifetime Achievement Award' by the National Human Resource Development Network, the 'Career Achievement Award' by GSK International and 'Chairman's Award' by Max India.

PAVITRA SINGH

Director (HR), PepsiCo

Pavitra Singh is currently the director of Human Resources at PepsiCo. Ms Singh has a rich and diverse experience of 15+ years where she has led large teams and multiple cross-functional groups across geographies. In her current role, she is responsible for strengthening PepsiCo's EVP in a digital era and building a strong pipeline of future leaders. Before this, she was heading the entire gamut of talent management (performance management, leadership and development, culture and change management) and diversity and inclusion for the Indian region.

Before joining PepsiCo, she worked with American Express and Fair Isaac. Very recently, she was recognized in the ET Women Ahead list of 2016 as one of corporate India's fastest rising women leaders.

PRABIR JHA

Founder & CEO of Prabir Jha People Advisory

Prabir Jha, an alumnus of St Stephen's College, Delhi and XLRI, Jamshedpur is the founder and CEO of Prabir Jha People Advisory.

Combining an impeccable academic and professional record in his stint as a civil servant, he handled the entire gamut of HR and IR issues of the Indian Ordnance Factories. On his switch to the corporate world after almost 10 years in the government, his initial HR years were with Thermax and TechMahindra. Thereafter, Prabir served on the executive team as the Global CHRO at two NYSE-listed Indian majors, Dr. Reddy's and Tata Motors, before moving to lead HR at another Fortune 500 giant as the Group CHRO of Reliance Industries Ltd. Before starting his own advisory firm, he was the president and global chief people officer at the pharma major, Cipla.

Prabir has handled all areas in HR, with a special interest in organization transformation, talent management, OD interventions, global HR strategy, employer branding and leadership capability development.

Prabir has, over the last many years, been featured in the 'List of Most Admired HR Professionals in India' and has several awards to his credit, including a consistent Linkedin Power Profile. Among others, he is a recipient of the National Institute of Personnel Management (NIPM) Medal, the Reckitt & Colman Award and the 'Citibank Leaders Award' at XLRI for the 'highest level of academic performance, competence, originality, creativity, communication skills and leadership'. He was also awarded the 'Director's Medal' in the Civil Services Foundation Course. He was given the Asia HRD Award in 2012 for 'outstanding contribution to the field of Human Resource Development' and 'The Distinguished Alumni' Award at XLRI in 2016. He was named the 'Digitalist of the Year' by SAP-Mint in 2018.

Also, Prabir is widely recognized as a transformation guru, an accomplished thought leader/tweeter whose views are closely followed across various platforms. He has been one of the most widely followed CHROs globally with almost 550,000 followers on LinkedIn. He is a sought-after speaker, executive coach and a visiting faculty at various business schools and top management training institutes. He sits on the HR advisory board of the Reserve Bank of India and has been on the board of companies in the Tata/Cipla Group.

PRAMOD MAHATME

VP, Employee Relations, Wipro Consumer Care & Lighting

Pramod Mahatme is vice president, Employee Relations, at Wipro Consumer Care and Lighting. As the Group Employee Relations head, he provides guidance and mentoring to other units of Wipro Corporation on Employee Relations subjects. He has 33 years of work experience in the industry as an HR professional, engaging with talent and labour, facilitating acquisition, engagement, development, compensation and separation.

An alumnus of Symbiosis Institute of Business Management, Pune, he holds a postgraduate degree in personnel management. He started his career in IR in 1981 with the Labour Advisory department at the Bombay Chamber of Commerce and Industry. Before joining Wipro, he worked with Indian Seamless and Hindustan Lever and has been instrumental in shaping the new trends in IR.

PREETI DAS

Executive Vice President (IT Services), Sutherland Global Services

In a career spanning 30 years, Ms Preeti Das has had a rich experience with multiple large organizations globally, holding key leadership positions at Microsoft, Oracle and ICICI. As the CEO of Birlasoft, she led a three-year strategic business transformation through workplace empowerment, operational efficiency and commercial excellence programmes including driving automation and digitization to drive efficiencies.

She has also held board level positions at Birlasoft and Castek and has extensive experience in mergers and acquisition integrations. Her approach to management is notable for transformational expansion, having driven organizations to deliver innovative digital services that respond to customer demands. She is active across the startup ecosystem where she is involved in mentoring digital startups and nurturing entrepreneurship.

A recipient of the '2014 Global CEO' award and a 'Global Women Entrepreneur' award in 2010, her strength lies in leading transformations, shepherding companies beyond their traditional strengths and enabling them to innovate within their organizations.

R.P. SINGH

Director (HR & Legal), IFFCO

R.P. Singh, a veteran HR professional, is presently the director (HR and Legal) at M/s Indian Farmers Fertiliser Cooperative Ltd, New Delhi, the largest manufacturer and marketer of fertilizer in Asia. He is responsible for the HR, administration, legal and corporate affairs of IFFCO and has contributed significantly in formulating corporate policies, statutory compliance, handling arbitrations and litigations, negotiating long-term wage settlements, legal due diligence of prospective acquisitions and collaborations, negotiating mergers and acquisitions, joint venture and so on. Born on 5 January 1953, Mr R.P. Singh graduated in political science (Hons.) from Bhagalpur University and did his postgraduation in labour and social welfare from Patna University.

He started his career with Telco (now Tata Motors) at Jamshedpur, India, in 1975 and worked with British India Corporation, Patna University and Pyrites, Phosphates and Chemicals Ltd before joining IFFCO in May 1996. He is a life member of the National HRD Network (NHRDN), National Institute of Personnel Management (NIPM), Indian Council of Arbitration (ICA), National Employees Federation and PHD Chamber of Commerce and Industry (PHDCCI). He is also a member of the Academic Council of All India Management Association (AIMA).

He has also served as a member on the panel set up by the Minister of Civil Aviation, Government of India, to facilitate the post-merger integration of Air India and Indian Airlines employees. Mr Singh has received several awards and accolades. He has travelled widely and has participated in various national and international seminars, conferences and training programmes.

RACHNA MUKHERJEE

Chief Human Resources Officer, Schneider Electric, India

Rachna Mukherjee, CHRO of Schneider Electric, India, has a rich experience in the areas of talent acquisition, career planning, organization capability, change management, leadership development, employee engagement, compensation and organization design. Earlier when she was VP, HR, at Aircel Ltd, she led the HR operations during the exponential growth phase of doubling the employee base in a short span. She has played strategic HR roles in organizations like Microsoft, IBM, Escotel Mobile Communications and Blue Star—Hewlett Packard. She is a recipient of the 'HR Leadership Award' (2009–2010) at the World HRD Congress, the 'Woman Super Achiever' award and the 'Most powerful HR professionals of India' award at the Asia-Pacific HRD Congress in 2010.

RAJEEV DUBEY

Group President (HR & Corporate Services) & CEO (After-Market Sector); Member of the Group Executive Board, Mahindra & Mahindra Ltd

Rajeev Dubey is the Group president (HR and Corporate Services) and CEO (After-Market Sector), member of the group executive board, Mahindra & Mahindra Ltd. His key focus areas are human capital initiatives of the Group, the after-market businesses whose CEOs report to him, Group communications, government relations, CSR and infrastructure. He is the chairman of Mahindra Insurance Brokers, Mahindra Steel Service Centres and Mahindra First Choice Services and serves on the boards of several group companies including Ssangyong Motors Korea, Mahindra Intertrade and Mahindra First Choice Wheels. He is chairman of the Group CSR council and the Corporate Governance Cell, member of the governing council of the Mahindra Institute of Quality and the advisory board of Bristlecone, USA.

He joined Mahindra & Mahindra Ltd in January 2004 after a career spanning 29 years in the Tata Group, which he joined in 1975 as a member of the TAS—the central managerial cadre of the Tata Group. He spent 21 years with Tata Steel and the next seven years as CEO of Tata Metaliks and then of Rallis India.

He studied economics at St Stephen's College, Delhi University, where he was ranked first in the university, and at the Delhi School of Economics, where he received a national scholarship. He went on to do his MBA from the Yale School of Management as a J.N. Tata scholar and was selected as a distinguished alumnus of the school.

Rajeev is a member of the governing body of the International Labour Organization (ILO), Geneva and serves on the board of the International Organization of Employers (IOE), Geneva, where he is also the chairperson of the Future of Work Policy Group. He is a member of the National Executive Council and the Steering Committee of FICCI (Federation of the Indian Chambers of Commerce and Industry) and is chairman of their HR Committee. He also serves as a core member of the Council of Global Advisors of the Yale School of Management, USA, the advisory board of Konecranes India and is a past President of the National Human Resource Development Network (NHRDN) and the Employers' Federation of India (EFI).

DR. RAJEEV UBEROI

General Counsel and Group Head, Legal and Compliance, IDFC Bank Ltd

Dr. Rajeev Uberoi joined IDFC as general counsel and Group head, Legal and Compliance in 2009. Having worked in the banking and finance space for more than three decades, Dr. Uberoi is looked upon by many institutional heads for his ability to effectively strategize and formulate business. Having worked as an in-house counsel in multifunctional and multijurisdictional organizations with rich experience in banking, he can seamlessly advise on complex matters including cross border regulatory regimes and enforcement practices, local jurisdiction issues, tax implications, capital market regulations, mergers and acquisitions (both domestic and cross border), including the latest demerger of IDFC Limited and IDFC Bank Limited, corporate restructuring, foreign collaborations, divestments and many other incidental issues of legal and regulatory nature.

Before joining IDFC Limited, Dr. Uberoi worked with Standard Chartered Bank where he was regional head, Operational Risk and Assurance, South Asia. Dr. Uberoi is also a profound writer and has a lot of publications to his credit.

He is a recipient of many accolades and awards and his contribution to the legal fraternity has been recognized in the Industry. He is a Canadian Commonwealth scholar with a master's from McMaster University and a PhD in economics.

RAJESH SAHAY

Vice President, HR, Wipro Consumer Care

Rajesh Sahay is the global head of HR for Wipro Consumer Care and Lighting. An alumnus of XISS, Rajesh is a certified black belt in six sigma methodologies and a trained Master Coach. Before joining Wipro, he worked for UBS—a Swiss bank—for three years as head of HR for their off-shore captive centre based in Hyderabad.

Rajesh started his career with NTPC and has also worked with The Arvind Mills Ltd. He had an earlier stint of seven years with Wipro Technologies where he led the talent engagement and development function for about 10,000 employees spread across multiple locations.

RAMKUMAR CHANDRASEKARAN

Director HR, Tata Consultancy Services, UK & Ireland

Ram has been with Tata Consultancy Services (TCS) for 18 years and was appointed as the HR director for UK and Ireland in April 2018. In this role, Ram is responsible for the end-to-end HR function for over 15,000 employees from 50 nationalities.

Ram has been with TCS since 2000 and has global experience handling different HR functions across the US, UK and India. His areas of expertise include driving key initiatives in HR transformation, mergers and acquisitions, leadership development, employee health and safety and deployment of HR practices at scale across the organization.

Before this role, Ram was HR head for TCS Chennai—the largest branch of TCS with more than 60,000 employees.

DR. RITU ANAND

Senior Vice President and Chief Leadership & Diversity Officer, TCS

Dr. Ritu Anand is the senior vice president and chief leadership and diversity officer at Tata Consultancy Services (TCS), a role she was given from 1 April 2019. In this role, she is responsible for the identification and development of senior leaders in TCS. In addition to this, she enhances all aspects of diversity in the workforce, with a focus on creating more women leaders in the leadership pool and a commitment towards building and sustaining a robust pool with diverse representation from all employee segments. Before this role, she led the talent management and total rewards functions in TCS where she implemented progressive policies for women and the Gen Y workforce to enable career growth and close pay gaps. She managed compensation and benefits, workforce policy planning, career, competencies, performance, leadership assessments, employee welfare programmes, including TCS Cares and Counselling.

Ritu began her career in TCS in 1989 with Training and Development and moved on to handle the Performance Management, and Compensation and Benefits for over eight years. She then led the HR for TCS North America from 1998 to 2001. She played a major role in setting up new offices in North America and Canada, forming an HR regional structure to support business growth for years to come. She has travelled extensively across the globe and has developed a framework for the cross-cultural workplace for TCS. In 2008, she launched a diversity platform,

Diversity and Women's Network with the motive of increasing gender diversity in TCS. Today, the Diversity and Inclusion function has moved a step ahead to become a strategic unit within TCS under her guidance.

Under her leadership, TCS has been ranked one of the top 10 companies to work for women in India and the UK by AVTAR and Women in Technology Awards, one of DiversityInc's Top 50 Companies for sustained investments and efforts in diversity and inclusion. She is a renowned speaker at various global forums like Oracle—Inclusive Leadership Summit and 2018 CII WomeNation Summit and academic institutes like IIMs, K.J. Somaiya, Banasthali Vidyapeeth Women's University, to name a few—sharing her visionary views on the future of the workplace, talent and inclusion. Featured on the SAP Game-Changing Women Radio, she has written for Fortune Magazine (Most Powerful Women) on 'Keeping More Women in the Corporate World' and 'Setting Yourself for Success' and attended TCS SAPPHIRE Call2Lead Summit 2017 and 2018.

She serves as an independent director and an advisory board member for many organizations. She is currently appointed as national secretary in the NHRDN national executive board. Recently, she was selected as one of the 20 Top HR Influencers chosen by HR 40under40—a Jombay Initiative—and also recognized as one of the top 'Voices of India' on LinkedIn 2019. An iconic leader, a charismatic speaker in the HR community and a doctorate in psychology, Ritu has been pivotal in bringing diversity, equal opportunity, and advancement of women in corporate leadership along with being a role model to many aspiring young leaders.

S. PARASURAMAN

Former Director, TISS

Professor S. Parasuraman has over 25 years of experience as a teacher, trainer, activist, administrator and development worker. Professor Parasuraman enjoys working in challenging social, political and physical environments. He has always liked to be part of a larger team and has the rare ability to work in a multicultural and multidisciplinary team.

His specific skills lie in establishing and nurturing institutions, facilitating capacity building on a rights-based approach to development, contributing to team building, conflict resolution, professional and personal development of staff at all levels in the organizations served and managing complex programmes spread across large regions.

Professor Parasuraman has held key positions during his career. These are director (vice-chancellor), Tata Institute of Social Sciences; senior advisor to the United Nations Human Rights Commission, UNESCAP, Bangkok, Thailand (responsible for auditing all specialized UN organizations that have been programming development work in rights framework in countries in Asia region); Asia Regional Policy director, ActionAid International, Asia Regional Office, Bangkok, Thailand; team leader of the Secretariat and senior advisor to the Commission, World Commission on Dams; programme director, Oxfam GB, India Programme, New Delhi; professor and head of Unit for Rural Studies, TISS; reader in Social Sciences, TISS; visiting senior fellow, Institute of Social Studies (ISS, The Hague); lecturer, Unit for Child and Youth Research, TISS.

Professor Parasuraman has over 50 publications in the form of articles in international and national journals, books and research reports. He was awarded the Bharat Shreshta Acharya Award in 2012 by MIT, Pune.

S.V. NATHAN
Chief Talent Officer at Deloitte India

Nathan has over 30 years of experience in HR management, across diverse industries including Manufacturing, Services, Telecom, and Information Technology. He is an industry leader, mentor and advocate of ethical leadership, helping develop future leaders through coaching. He has a vast experience in building and leading high-performance teams in both multinational and Indian organizations like ICI, Sterling Holidays, Philips Software, and Reliance, and he is currently the chief talent officer at Deloitte India.

A highly respected voice of the HR profession in India, Nathan speaks regularly at several national and global forums on contemporary HR subjects. He is a behavioral specialist in Sensitivity Training. He is an alumnus of XLRI, a top business school in the country. In 2015, XLRI conferred on him the 'distinguished alumnus' award. Nathan did his bachelor's in mathematics from Vivekananda College, Madras. LinkedIn recognized him as one of the top 25 Voices and an influencer of 2020. He has also been conferred several awards and honours throughout his career.

He serves as the chairman of Sumedhas, a not-for-profit education and research body devoted to self and organization development. Nathan also served on the board of the National HR Development Network (NHRDN) as its national secretary. He worked closely with NASSCOM Hyderabad Chapter and served as its president in the past.

Nathan is an avid reader and writer. He is a regular blogger. He has an active presence on social media and is well known for his '#OfficeTruths' posts on LinkedIn. He is fond of storytelling and recounts them in his #Slice Of Life and #Slice of Work that he posts on social media. He loves shopping for others and cooking for family and friends.

DR. SAAGARIKA GHOSHAL

Director, HR, Metro Cash & Carry

Saagarika Ghoshal, director, HR, for METRO Cash and Carry India, has been listed as one of the '50 Most Influential HR Leaders in Asia' and was covered by *Business Today* as one of the 'Next 30 Most Powerful Women in Indian Business'.

An author and business coach, she drives a people-oriented agenda aligned closely to the business priorities, which focuses on bringing real impact to organizational results by bringing together the best talent practices needed to attract, engage, build, leverage and retain top talent. She is known for leading transformation and innovative practices and her expertise lies in helping organizations foster a culture of diversity and inclusion, leading due diligence for M&As, organizational development and corporate governance for boards.

SAPTARSHI ROY

Former Director (HR), NTPC Ltd

Roy is a graduate in electrical engineering from Visvesvaraya NIT, Nagpur. His career spanning over 36 years involves developing, commissioning and operating power plants and human resource management. He has been instrumental in introducing various pioneering HR initiatives in areas such as talent acquisition, employee welfare, IR, employee engagement, wages and pension. His outstanding contribution has been the takeover and turnaround of low performing power stations in Odisha and UP.

As ED (Corporate Planning and Corporate Communications) and ED to CMD, his responsibilities included business planning, strategy formulation, enterprise risks assessment and apprising the board of directors about the company's risk profile regularly, industry analysis and competitive benchmarking, brand management, providing strategic inputs to the CMD and overseeing NTPC's performance management system. He also led a team of the World Energy Council—India secretariat.

SHIVAKUMAR VENKATESWARAN

CHRO, Indian Institute of Management, Bangalore

Shivakumar Venkateswaran has about 26+ years of corporate experience in diverse sectors like engineering, textiles/apparel/brands and retail, education and consulting. A postgraduate from the Tata Institute of Social Sciences, Mumbai, Shivakumar started his career with Ion Exchange Ltd. During his 26+ plus years of professional experience, Shivakumar has handled contrasting and interesting assignments ranging from international retail and supply chain compliance, geography HR head, strategic/corporate HR at the Group level, HR system, HR and so on.

Shivakumar quickly understands the business and aligns the HR strategy with that of the business. He has lead project management teams and has worked on redesigning HR systems and business processes.

Shivakumar enjoys integrating different parts of the organization under overarching cultural 'pillars' and policies, to create the unifying 'organizational glue'. He has lead and driven innovation, creativity and e-enablement in key HR systems and processes with an aim to 'delight' internal customers. Shivakumar was the honorary joint secretary of National HRD Network, Bangalore Chapter from July 2017–2019. Since April 2012, Shivakumar is the chief human resource officer at the Indian Institute of Management, Bangalore. He provides professional leadership and strategic direction across the spectrum of HR areas which includes leading the review, formulation and implementation of progressive HR policies, practices, initiatives and processes to support the Institute's mission and goals and meet its vision and objectives.

Some of his notable career assignments include:

- General manager, People Office, South Zone of Future Value Retail Ltd, which is part of the Future Group
- Director, Human Resources, Indian School of Business—a globally top-ranked B-School
- Head of Human Resources, lifestyle apparel business of Arvind Ltd
- Regional manager, Ethical Standards for the Global Procurement Division of Walmart Stores Ltd, the largest retailer in the world, across the Indian subcontinent, South Asia, Middle East and Africa
- Vendor compliance officer for Gap International Sourcing Ltd, which is part of Gap Inc., one of the largest apparel retailers
- Senior manager, Human Resources for Ambattur Clothing Limited, a leading apparel exporter
- Senior manager for Mafoi Management Consultants Ltd

SHRIKANT P. GATHOO

Former Director, HR, Bharat Petroleum Corporation Ltd

Shrikant P. Gathoo, director, HR, Bharat Petroleum Corporation Limited, holds a postgraduate degree in management from the University of Pune and is a fellow of the LEAD International Institute. Before joining BPCL in 1986, he had stints at Bharat Heavy Electricals Limited and NTPC Limited. Besides BPCL, he is the chairman of Petronet India Limited and Petronet CCK Limited.

Mr Gathoo has extensive experience in business as well as in information technology. As executive director (HRS), he has led the initiatives in the areas of employee relations, employee development, benefits administration, administrative facilities, services and projects, besides areas like real estate, corporate social responsibility and sports.

SMITA SAHA

Vice President, HR, AstraZeneca

Smita Saha is the vice president, Human Resources and HR Regional Lead, India, for AstraZeneca. She is responsible for the people strategy of the organization. Smita Saha initiated an exciting cultural transformation by making the AstraZeneca values the cornerstone and common language in the organization. Her focus is on driving belief in the organization strategy, talent and building succession pipelines, development and improving the science quotient in the workforce and gender diversity.

Ms Smita, an alumnus of Tata Institute of Social Sciences, Mumbai, has over 20 years of professional experience. Before joining AstraZeneca, Smita held several HR leadership roles in multinational IT companies like Siemens, Oracle, Cisco Systems and IBM. In her previous assignment at Oracle, she was senior director, HR, for the India Development Center. She was a coach to leaders in Asia-Pacific countries, involved in customer presentations and also led many integrations.

SOURAV DASPATNAIK

CEO, Swach Environment Pvt. Ltd, A SREI Group initiative

An engineering and management professional with 30 years of cross-functional experience, Mr Daspatnaik also serves as an independent director in several Indian companies and mentors social enterprises in the area of innovative and clean technologies under the Swachh Bharat Mission of the Ministry of Urban Development. He has been instrumental in nurturing several National Skill Development Corporation (NSDC) initiatives.

With a bachelor's degree in mechanical engineering from BIT Mesra and a master's degree in operations management from the Stevens Institute of Technology, New Jersey, Mr Daspatnaik started his professional career with Tata Motors, and thereafter served in leading companies such as Tata Steel, Ispat Industries Ltd, Mercer HR Consulting and the Apeejay Surendra Group. He possesses a unique mix of managerial talent and leadership skills with deep insights across several functional areas, including engineering, marketing and sales, strategy, human resources, sustainability, project management and infrastructure. He also has a sound understanding of policy advocacy and formulation and social enterprise and has worked extensively in Singapore, Myanmar and Thailand.

SUDHANSHU TRIPATHI

Group Head, HR, Hinduja Group

Sudhanshu Tripathi is a senior HR professional with over 33 years of work experience, of which over 18 years has been at the leadership level (company and Group HR head). He is a strategic HR thinker with a business-focused, hands-on approach. At the leadership level, he has worked in telecom, IT, engineering, steel, power, financial services, media and other diversified domains and brings a strong understanding of business operations to HR. He specializes in large- and group-level entities, having worked entirely in large and diversified multi-location organizations.

Besides shaping Hinduja Group's Human Capital Strategy and its execution, his responsibilities include supporting the group companies' board of directors on Strategic Leadership and Value Creation. Furthermore, he facilitates common governance processes for group companies' boards and their committees and is personally accountable for defining the Nomination Remuneration Committee charter and framework and their implementation for all Hinduja Group companies. He serves as a member of the board of directors for the following companies: Hinduja Ventures Limited, Hinduja Leyland Finance Limited, Hinduja Foundries Limited and Ashley Aviation Limited.

An electrical engineer and an MBA from XLRI, before joining Hinduja Group, Mr Tripathi worked with Essar Group, Reliance Communications, Usha Martin Group and Tata Steel, at various levels.

He has received many awards, the most recent one being the 'Business World Award' for outstanding contribution to the field of HR. He has been a member of the Eastern Regional Council, AIMA and is also associated with FICCI, EFI and Rotary Club. He has taught at XLRI, Indian Institute of Coal Management and other management schools as visiting faculty.

SUDIP BANERJEE
Ex. CEO, L&T InfoTech

Sudip Banerjee is a veteran IT industry leader with more than three decades of experience in the IT industry including 15 years of global experience in creating and leading IT service businesses worldwide. Having started his career with HCL, he worked with Wipro Technologies from 1983 to 2008. During his six years tenure as president of Enterprise Solutions Division, he took over a $160 million business and grew it to $1.4 billion. In 2008, he joined L&T Infotech as CEO and took the company from a $380 million entity to a run rate of $600 million in less than three years. Presently, Mr Banerjee is a member of various governing bodies in the industry as well as academic institutions. He continues to remain an independent director on the board of L&T Infotech in addition to being a former CEO.

SURAJ CHETTRI
Regional Director, HR, Airbus India & South Asia

Suraj completed his bachelor's in sociology from Ranchi University and PGDPM from Xavier Institute of Social Service (XISS), Ranchi where he secured the third rank in the class of 1991–1993.

He started his career with Bata India in 1993 and served in the capacity of assistant manager, Personnel, in their Retail North Zonal Office at New Delhi where he was responsible, amongst other activities, for IR and T&D. During his tenure with Bata, he was certified as a sales trainer and an enquiry officer.

In 1996, he took up a job with Bosch India based out of Bangalore. During his tenure as a manager at Bosch, he headed the recruitment and T&D departments and was deputed to their global headquarters in Stuttgart, Germany, for two years, where he was responsible for international/intercultural sensitization. During his tenure at Bosch, he attained a master practitioner's degree in NLP, team workshop moderator and was qualified as an intercultural trainer. He was also recognized for his contributions by the National Human Resource Development (NHRD) Network, Bangalore Chapter, as an achiever under the Young HR Manager category and was also a part of the team that won the best HR Practices Company Award from NHRD.

In 2003, he left them to join General Motors as general manager, Human Resources, heading the HR function at General Motors Technical Centre, India, which housed the Engineering Services and the India Science Lab at Bangalore and was part of the Project Leadership Team responsible for setting up their operations in India. During his tenure at GM, he was certified as a DDI instructor and recognized by the chairman's appreciation for his contributions in setting up the centre.

In 2006, he joined Textron India in Bangalore, India, as director, Human Resources, and was instrumental in setting up the entire HR infrastructure. In November 2008, he was given the additional responsibility of deputy MD for the Global Technology Centre at Bangalore and inducted as a member of the board.

In 2011, Suraj joined Airbus and is now responsible for India and South Asia as their regional director, HR.

He was also the National Representative for the Airbus Corporate Foundation in 2015 when he was conferred with the 'Gold Karmaveer Chakra' and the 'Rex Karmaveer Global Fellowship' for his contribution towards the Bio-Diversity Program by iCONGO, in association with the UN. He was also recognized as the '100 Most Impactful CSR Leaders' in 2017 and 2018 by the World CSR Day event.

In 2013, Suraj was conferred with the 'HR Leadership Award' in 2015, the 'Top 100 influencing HR leaders in Asia', both by the Asia-Pacific HRM Congress and in 2016 and 2017, with the most influential HR Leaders in India at the World HRD Congress. In 2017, he was also conferred with South India's most talented 'HR Leaders Award' at the APAC HRM Congress, 'Indira Pride of the Profession HR Award' by the Indira Group of Institutes, and the 'University of Engineering and Management Award of Excellence' for his immense contribution to the corporate world. In 2018, he was conferred with the '100 Top HR Minds in

India Award', and in 2019, with the '101 Super HR Achievers (India) Award' by CHRO Asia and the 'Dr Tara Shankar Award of Excellence'.

Under his leadership, Airbus was considered one of the '100 Top Organizations with Innovative HR Practices' in 2018, as well as the 'National Best Employer Brand Award' for 2018 and 2019 by APAC HRM Congress.

Suraj has an overall experience of 26 years in the aerospace, automotive, engineering sales and marketing and manufacturing sectors and is located in Bangalore. He is a life member of NHRD, ISTD, BMA and NIPM and is a regular speaker at all major business schools, seminars and conferences in India.

S.Y. SIDDIQUI

Executive Advisor, Maruti Suzuki India Limited

Positions held at Maruti Suzuki (joined September 2003)

- Executive director, HR
- Chief operating officer (HR/Finance/IT/Legal)
- Chief mentor, executive advisor

He is presently working directly with the managing director on Future Business Strategy and People Challenges 2020 and beyond. He is also heading the Maruti Suzuki Realty Business Vertical.

Board positions:

- Special invitee on the board of Maruti Suzuki since 2006
- Part-time director on the board of Suzuki Motorcycles

A postgraduate in HRM, Mr Siddiqui has a career track of around 40 years in HR and business roles of good Indian corporates as well as MNCs such as:

- Escorts Limited
- DCM Group—DCM Toyota Limited, DCM Daewoo Motors Limited and DCM Benetton India Limited
- New Holland Tractors India (Fiat Group)
- Maruti Suzuki India Ltd

Widely travelled abroad, he has handled global and multicultural HR issues in highly competitive business environments in India and Europe. He has the unique experience of working in diverse cultural settings with people of various nationalities.

He has handled several management and leadership roles from quite an early start of his career. He has been inducted at the company board level at Maruti since 2006.

Passionate about cricket, Mr Siddiqui played cricket at the North Zone Inter-Varsity level from 1974 to 1979 representing Jamia University, New Delhi.

T.K. SRIRANG

Senior General Manager & Head HR, ICICI Bank Ltd

T.K. Srirang, senior general manager and head HR, ICICI Bank Limited, holds an MBA degree in personnel management and IR and an undergraduate degree in industrial engineering.

In his 19 years of work experience at organizations like Coca-Cola India Limited, Ford India Limited, ICI India Limited and ICICI Bank, Mr Srirang has handled IR, mergers, leadership development, performance management and large-scale recruitment and employee engagement processes. Since 2001, at ICICI Bank, he has successfully handled the integration of Sangli Bank and Bank of Rajasthan through an approach based on sensitivity, mutual respect and openness. His current responsibilities include shaping HR policies and culture for the bank and driving these policies and processes across various business groups.

DR. T.V. RAO

Chairman, T.V. Rao Learning Systems Pvt. Ltd

Dr. T.V. Rao, chairman of T.V. Rao Learning Systems, was a professor at IIM, Ahmedabad from 1973 to 1994 and subsequently an adjunct professor and a member on the board of IIMA. He also worked as the L&T chair professor of HRD at XLRI, Jamshedpur. He was the founder and the first president of the National HRD Network and the founder and the first honorary director of the Academy of HRD. He established the first dedicated Department of HRD at L&T along with Dr. Udai Pareek in the mid-1970s, much before HRD was known.

He has authored around 60 books and pioneered the 360-Degree Feedback, Assessment Development Centres and HRD Audit in India. He has won several awards for his outstanding contributions to the field of HRD including the title of 'Ravi Matthai National Fellow' awarded by the Association of Indian Management Schools. He was recently awarded by the Asia-Pacific Federation of HRM as the 'APFHRM Professional' of the year 2019.

DR. TANAYA MISHRA

Former Managing Director, HR, India and APAC, Accenture

Dr. Tanaya Mishra has the unique and diverse experience of having worked across industries ranging from manufacturing, retail, insurance, IT/ITES. She has been the head of HR for ACC Ltd, Shoppers Stop, SBI Life and was the senior vice president, Group HR, for JSW. She has a PhD in manpower planning and a postgraduate degree in Human Resources along with a law degree. She has many articles and publications to her credit. She has held several honorary positions and served as a board member of NHRD Network, CII, subject matter expert with SHRM, executive council member EFI. She has represented India as a member of APERG. She was selected to be part of the prestigious CSC Commonwealth Leaders and invited to Oxford and Buckingham Palace. Dr. Mishra has won many accolades and awards, the recent ones being the 'Women Super Achiever' award 2016 and the 'Most Influential HR Leader' in 2017. She has recently been invited to be an executive council member of the world's most powerful network of women across the globe.

UMA DEVAGUPTAPU

Former Director, HR, Signode Asiapac & MEA Region

Uma Devaguptapu is an alumnus of the Tata Institute of Social Sciences, Mumbai, with undergraduate degrees in Economics and Law. She is also a certified executive coach.

Uma started her career at Blue Star Limited, Mumbai in HR and Employee Relations and later branched out to Marketing and Projects. She joined Signode India in 1991, in corporate communications and after a substantial stint in market development followed by a profit centre management, she took over as chief human resource officer, Signode, India and Middle East and led the development and implementation of Signode India's advancements in talent and career. Under her HR leadership, Signode India has achieved 'SAIL HR Excellence' award in July 2009 and 'NHRD Hyderabad Inspire Award for Innovation' in June 2011.

Her articles have been published by Employer's Federation of India and ICFAI Press. She is also a member of the HR and CSR panels of CII Hyderabad and is currently the convenor of CII Telangana's Human Resources and Industrial Relations Panel 2014–2015.

UMESH DHAL

Chief Relationship Officer, PR, CSR and Corporate Relations, LG Electronics India

Mr Umesh Dhal is an astute HR professional with over 31 years of experience. He has been instrumental in guiding and mentoring the organization towards maintaining and strengthening its position of leadership. Before LG, Mr Dhal worked with leading organizations like Hero Honda Motors Ltd, Sylvania Laxman Ltd and Escorts JCB Ltd.

A keen student of human psychology, he has worked extensively in employee development. A certified analyst in several psychometric tools, he is an expert in the field of Competency Mapping, Coaching and Counselling. He is not only a strategist but also an able administrator in the field of employee relations.

V. KRISHNAN

Executive Director, Human Resources (India + SAARC), Dabur India Limited

V. Krishnan has been a part of the management committee at Dabur, driving transformational excellence through strategic interventions in collaboration with key stakeholders for India and SAARC since 2004. He has demonstrated capabilities in Business Partnering across industries; with Indian transnationals and MNCs, covering human capital management, business processes, quality, knowledge management and technology enablement, with organizations like Dabur (current), Whirlpool, Xerox and Eicher.

Krishnan has extensive exposure to consumer-facing complex businesses with multiple linkages across the value chain from front-end to back-end operations. He has driven initiatives to create an engaging work environment for a multigenerational workforce in the digital age that is fully equipped to respond to the challenges and opportunities of a dynamic industry. Having a keen sense of organizational awareness and deep functional insights has led him to an enriching professional career spanning around 30 years.

V.C. AGRAWAL

President, Corporate HR, RPG

Agrawal brings over 40 years of professional work experience which includes large diversified conglomerates both in the public and private sector. He has the experience of working in line functions as well as in HR.

After joining RPG in 2010, he has taken several initiatives to align the company with high growth in various business ventures. Major highlights include creating a culture of coaching and mentoring, crafting a new vision and core values for the group, redefining a new competency framework aligned with new core values and succession planning for senior leadership positions.

Before this, Mr Agrawal was Director, HR, and Board Member of Indian Oil Corporation Ltd. He is a Fellow Member of the All India Management Association.

DR. VASANTHI SRINIVASAN

Associate Professor (OB & HR), IIM, Bengaluru

Dr. Vasanthi Srinivasan is an associate professor in the area of Organizational Behaviour and HRM and the chairperson, Centre for Corporate Governance and Citizenship at IIM Bangalore. She holds a PG diploma in Personnel Management and Industrial Relations from XLRI Jamshedpur and a fellow in management from IIM Bangalore. Earlier, she worked at Wipro Limited and the P&P Group, a Bangalore-based boutique consulting firm.

Dr. Vasanthi Srinivasan is a member of various professional bodies and also serves on the advisory board of the NHRD Network, Bangalore Chapter. She has been involved in several research, training and consulting projects with various Indian and international companies.

VEENA SWARUP

Former Director (HR), Engineers India Limited

Veena Swarup is a management professional with more than three decades of experience in the public sector. She was director, Human Resources, on the board of Engineers India Limited (EIL), a Navaratna Public Sector under the Ministry of Petroleum and Natural Gas, from October 2012

and superannuated on 30 June 2016. She is now an independent director of a board. An MBA from Lucknow, she worked in Oil & Natural Gas Corporation Limited (ONGC) from 1983 to 2012 in various positions of HR Discipline, including project head for SAP HR implementation. Swarup also had stints in deputation, at the Directorate General of Hydrocarbons (DGH), the upstream Oil and Gas Regulator, and Mangalore Refinery and Petrochemicals Limited (MRPL), a subsidiary of ONGC. Post superannuation, she has also served as chair/member of committees at FICCI, AIMA, DMA, NHRD, in skill development, diversity, HR and CSR and on the board of studies at AIMA, IPE, Hyderabad and academic council of FORE. She has also advised REC, a public sector company in the area of skill development and assisted in the setting up of a centre for underprivileged women.

Swarup is a fellow of All India Management Association (AIMA) and a fellow of the World Academy of Productivity Science (WAPS).

She has been recognized with various awards, which include:

- HR Leadership Award by Asia Oil and Gas Congress
- HR Professional Award by Asia-Pacific HR Congress (APHC)
- IPE HR Leadership Award, World Women Leadership Award by Women Leadership Congress
- Forum for Emotional Intelligence Learning (FEIL) Award for outstanding implementation of Balanced Score Card

She has also been honoured by the Society of Human Resource Management (SHRM) for her outstanding contribution to the field of HR.

VIVEK PARANJPE

Consultant and Executive Coach, Reliance Industries Ltd

Vivek has more than 40 years of work experience both in India and abroad. He is an advisor on matters of strategic HR and business transformation to the chairman of Reliance Industries Limited since 2003. He led the Group HR function of RIL from 2009 to 2013.

Before this, he was with Hewlett Packard for close to 16 years, with the last role as HR director for the Asia-Pacific region, based in Singapore. There, he held several important positions and was part of the team that was responsible for the acquisition and merger of the Compaq Corporation.

He started his career with HUL in 1975. He worked in various companies like Johnson and Johnson and ICIM before joining Hewlett Packard. He is a science graduate with honours from Fergusson College, Pune, and has a postgraduate degree from XLRI Jamshedpur, where he was a gold medalist. He is also a recipient of the 'NHRDN President's Award'. He has also authored two books.

YOGI SRIRAM

Sr Vice President, Corporate HR, Larsen & Toubro Ltd

Yogi Sriram is senior VP, Corporate HR, at Larsen & Toubro Limited. He has 38 years of experience in the HRD function and also leads a world-class institute of project management.

Having pursued his education from SRCC, TISS, FMS and the University of Delhi, Mr Sriram got accredited in psychometric testing techniques, completed a diploma in training and development and a certificate course on 'Appreciative Enquiry' from Case Western Reserve University, Ohio. He had been admitted as the first HR professional in India as a fellow of the AIMA and has received the 'Best HR Professional Award' from the Maharaja Sayajirao University, Vadodara.

His areas of interest are succession planning, career sculpting, team coaching, talent management and change management. He has published in international journals and is on the board of many professional bodies.